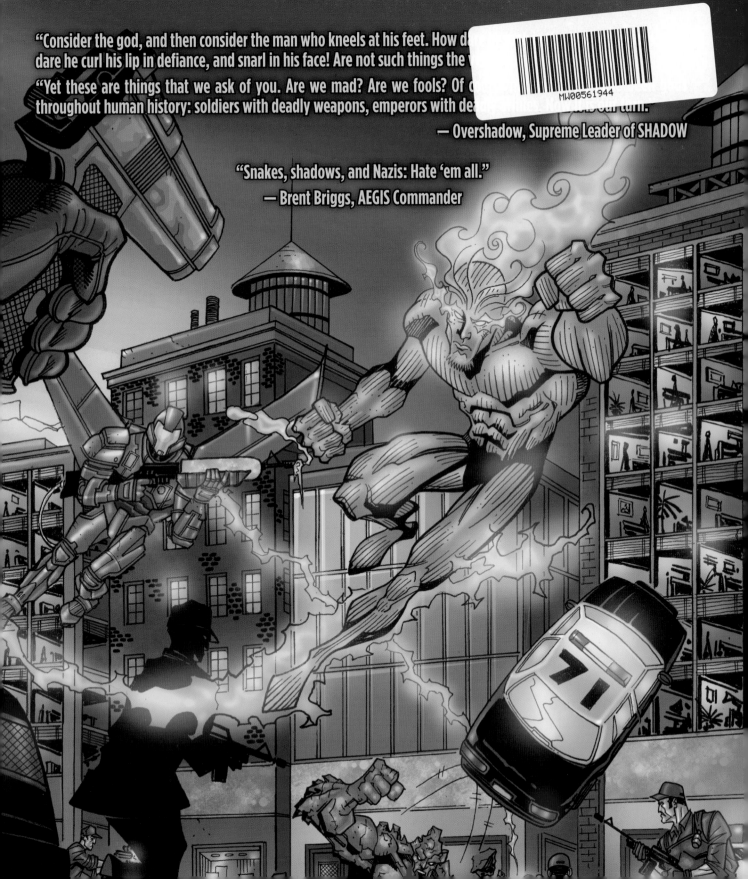

"Consider the god, and then consider the man who kneels at his feet. How da[re] dare he curl his lip in defiance, and snarl in his face! Are not such things the [...]

"Yet these are things that we ask of you. Are we mad? Are we fools? Of c[...] throughout human history: soldiers with deadly weapons, emperors with dea[dly smiles. Now it is our turn.]
— Overshadow, Supreme Leader of SHADOW

"Snakes, shadows, and Nazis: Hate 'em all."
— Brent Briggs, AEGIS Commander

AGENTS OF FREEDOM

A GREEN RONIN PRODUCTION

Design **Scott Bennie**

Development **Steve Kenson**

Graphic Design **Hal Mangold**

Cover Art **Scott James**

Additional Material **Ben Robbins**

Editing **Joanna Hurley**

Art Direction **jim pinto & Hal Mangold**

Executive Producer **Chris Pramas**

Interior Art **Jeff Carlisle, Attila Adorjany, Storn Cook, Anthony Grabski, D'Alexander Gregory, Jonathan Hunt, Scott James, Jake Parker, Tony Parker, and Craig Taillefer**

Organization Logo Designs **Hal Mangold & Steve Kenson**

Playtesters **D.T. Butchino, Bob Huss, Dave Mattingly, Tom Miskey, Shannon Nordmarken, Mike O'Donnell, Wayne Shaw, Steve Sloane, Ben Robbins, Ben Serwa, Aaron Sullivan**

Proofreading **Evan Sass, Bob Russ**

Green Ronin Staff **Chris Pramas, Nicole Lindroos, Hal Mangold, Steve Kenson, Evan Sass, Robert J. " Dr. Evil" Schwalb, Marc Schmalz, Jim Pinto, and Bill Bodden**

First Edition Graphic Design & Art Direction **Sean Glenn**

Author's Dedication To Bob Bell and Monte Cook, for their help with these spooky

Printed in China

Green Ronin Publishing
PO Box 1723
Renton, WA 98057-1723
custserv@greenronin.com
www.greenronin.com
www.mutantsandmasterminds.com

Freedom City was typeset in ITC Quay Sans, designed by David Quay in 1990,
and HTF Gotham Condensed, designed by Tobias Frere-Jones in 2002.

TABLE OF CONTENTS

INTRODUCTION 5
CHAPTER 1: THE AGENT CHARACTER 6
　Agent Creation 7
　　Abilities.. 7
　　Skills.. 8
　　Feats 11
　　Powers 12
　　Agents of Power... 12
　　Drawbacks.. 13
　　Complications 14
　　Hero Points and Extra Effort 14
　　Reputation 14
　Devices and Equipment 15
　Equipment Lists 15
　　Standard Firearms 15
　　Comic Book Firearms 18
　　Chemical Weapons 20
　　Skill Kits 20
　　Vehicles.. 23
　　Headquarters.. 25
　Agent Archetypes.. 26
　Dashing Spy.. 27
　Femme Fatale.. 28
　Field Investigator 29
　Hard-Nosed Commander 30
　Heroic Everyman 31
　Martial Arts Expert 32
　Roughneck Commando 33
　Spymaster 34
　Unwritten Rules, Written 35
CHAPTER 2: STAR SQUAD...................................37
　STAR SQUAD History...37
　STAR SQUAD Structure.. 39
　　Operations... 39
　　Unusual Missions 39
　STAR Squad Resources 40
　　Arsenal.. 40
　　ASTRO Labs Special Weapons 40
　STAR Squad Personnel 41
　Police Show Archetypes.. 42
CHAPTER 3: AEGIS 44
　AEGIS History...44
　AEGIS Structure..47
　AEGIS Resources.. 48
　　Equipment.. 48
　　The AEGIS Arsenal.. 48
　　AEGIS Vehicles... 48
　　Power Armor 49
　　AEGIS Headquarters.. 49
　AEGIS Personnel... 50
　AEGIS in Freedom City 51
　AEGIS Operations 55
CHAPTER 4: UNISON 59
　UNISON HISTORY 59
　UNISON Structure..61

　　Operations.. 62
　UNISON Resources 62
　　Equipment.. 62
　　The UNISON Arsenal 62
　　UNISON Headquarters 63
　UNISON Personnel 64
　　Unison Agent 64
　　Unison Solo 64
　　Chalcedony Johnson 64
　　Mikos West 65
CHAPTER 5: SHADOW 66
　SHADOW History.. 66
　SHADOW Organization..72
　　Overshadow.. 72
　　The Directorate... 73
　　The Penumbra 74
　　The Clones 75
　　SHADOW Worldwide 76
　　Overthrow... 77
　　The Thule Society 78
　　The Corona 81
　　The Eclipse Guard 81
　　The Scions of Sobek 81
　SHADOW Operations...82
　　Mystical Artifacts 82
　　Technological Secrets 82
　　Espionage 82
　　The Midnight Invective 82
　　Project Mimir 83
　　I-Bots.. 83
　　SHADOW Sleeper Agent.. 83
　SHADOW Resources.. 84
　　Equipment.. 84
　　Headquarters.. 85
　SHADOW Personnel.. 88
　　Agents... 88
　　SHADOW Mutates 89
　　Ragnarok...91
　SHADOW in Freedom City... 92
CHAPTER 6: THE AGENT SERIES...........................94
　　Power Level vs. Tone 94
　　The Numbers Game 94
　　Knock 'Em Out 94
　　The Hostage Drama 95
　　How Heroes Can Beat Up Minions 96
　　How Agents Can Take Down Heroes 96
　　Sub-Genres 96
　　Organizing Missions 97
　Supporting Cast: The Archetype Files.......................... 101
　　Supporting Characters 101
　　Callsigns/Codenames.. 111
ADVENTURE: RETURN OF SHADOW 112
INDEX ....
CONTRIBUTORS..
OPEN GAME LICENSE 125

INTRODUCTION

Larger than life soldiers have been a staple of the comics since World War II, when books like *Captain America* placed super-soldiers on the beaches of Normandy, fighting the good fight on behalf of liberty. Over six thrilling decades later, the genre is still with us. Iconic men with machine guns still charge the enemy position, battle cries are heard over the sound of exploding shells, and the bad guys—now terrorists instead of the Axis–still scream and retreat in the face of a determined assault.

Agents of Freedom is about these soldiers, the howling heroic commandos who won the war and kept on charging. It is about bad guys who are genuine threats to democracy, the bizarre things they do, and how an odd bunch of ragtag agents band together to stop them. It is about SHADOW—one of the biggest threats to the World of Freedom–and their plans for conquest. And it is about you, the heroic men and women who will stand directly in the path of their nefarious schemes and stop them dead in their tracks!

HOW TO USE THIS BOOK

Agents of Freedom requires the *Mutants & Masterminds* Second Edition rulebook, the *Freedom City* Second Edition sourcebook, a 20-sided die, and a cadre of enthusiastic players. Some sections of this book recommend options from the *Mastermind's Manual*; however, it is possible to use this book without directly referencing that volume.

Agents of Freedom is divided into three basic sections. **Chapter 1** is an overview of the agent genre and how to organize a game. **Chapter 2** through **Chapter 5** describes some of the most prominent agencies in the world of Freedom City, presenting background details the Gamemaster can incorporate into their campaigns. **Chapter 6** is a Gamemaster resource on agents, followed by an introductory adventure.

CHAPTER 1: THE AGENT CHARACTER

This comprehensive section will get your campaign started, with guidelines on power levels, abilities, skills, feats, and powers, including an equipment list. The unwritten rules of the genre are presented, as well as guidelines for agency sub-genre games. Finally, a list of campaign sub-types is provided.

CHAPTER 2: STAR SQUAD

The elite police officers of Freedom City are the STAR Squad; some bright, some tarnished, these paragons in blue fight a lonely and thankless battle against the forces of evil on the mean streets of the city. Unheralded but not unrewarded, this chapter describes their role in the important struggles of our times, as well as the Squad's background, its key players, its organizational structure, and how they interact with the superheroes. Advice is also provided for running cop games in a superhero world.

CHAPTER 3: AEGIS

AEGIS, the American Elite Government Intervention Service, is on the front lines against terrorism and super-powered violence in the United States. Armed with the finest technology, these defenders of the American Way hold the line against the country's enemies. But, even

the brightest and the best will sometimes be consumed in shadow. This chapter describes the AEGIS organization, its goals, agents, their arsenal of fantastic equipment, their day-to-day operations, and adventuring opportunities for an excited young recruit.

CHAPTER 4: UNISON

UNISON is the United Nations International Superhuman Oversight Network, a group whose task varies from country to country. In most western nations, they are investigators attached to major crime organizations such as Interpol, assisting in tracking superhuman criminals and extra-dimensional and extra-terrestrial threats around the globe. In other nations, they are an aggressive peacekeeping and fighting force, with a mandate to prevent superhumans from using brute force to seize political power. As with the other agencies in this book, this chapter includes information on key players, organizational structure, weapons, and everything UNISON needs to fight evil in your campaign.

CHAPTER 5: SHADOW

Steeped in darkness that dates back to the dawn of time, and led by the mysterious Overshadow, for many years these agents of evil were the archenemy of AEGIS and a threat to heroes everywhere. Fifteen years ago, it seemed as though they were finally defeated, leaving lesser terrorist organizations like Overthrow to take their place. However, from the shadows come hints this dormant agency has only been gathering its forces, and soon it will strike with enough force to threaten the entire globe. This chapter details the resurgent SHADOW, Overshadow, its agents, and the bizarre methods it employs to prepare itself for the ultimate plan of conquest: Operation Inundation!

CHAPTER 6: THE AGENT SERIES

So, you're Gamemastering agents? This chapter assists you in that formidable task by describing some of the pitfalls of the genre, as well as how to organize scenarios, compose briefings and design mission maps, and vary the rules to match different campaign types. Finally, there are lists of supporting cast and supervillain archetypes.

ADVENTURE: RETURN OF SHADOW

An introductory adventure concludes the book. In *Return of SHADOW*, a plot to assassinate a Freedom City councilman presages the reappearance of the ultimate evil: SHADOW!

FREEDOM CITY

Agents of Freedom uses the World of Freedom, detailed in the *Freedom City* campaign sourcebook, as the setting and context for its heroic and villainous agencies and the sample adventure at the end of the book. Even if you don't have access to the *Freedom City* sourcebook, you can still use most of the material in this book: simply transpose appropriate details from your own campaign setting and use the new characters in this book as you see fit. In some cases, *Agents of Freedom* refers to *Freedom City* for additional details on the setting but otherwise this book stands well on its own.

CHAPTER 1: THE AGENT CHARACTER

So, you've decided to play an agent? Congratulations. You've taken your first step into a larger world. David, there's a chap named Goliath who would like to have a word with you. Confident and gifted high school football team, prepare for your next game against... the Denver Broncos!

In short, you have to be *insane* to be an agent in a world of superhumans, which is, of course, much of the genre's charm. Isn't it great that an ordinary person is willing to take a stand to protect society? The spandex crowd may get all the press, but a guy going face-to-face with Talos armed only with a blaster pistol is just as much a hero as Centurion facing down Omega. (Unfortunately for the agent, the ultimate result could well be the same). Courage *is* courage, and it is pretty much a given that agents have it by the boatload.

In the world of Freedom City, people recognize that fact and appreciate it. Centurion himself frequently told cops and AEGIS agents that they were all part of the same team. And, who was going to argue with *him*? So being an agent is a pretty nifty thing—for as long as it lasts, anyway.

WHAT IS AN AGENT?

For our purposes, an "agent" is anyone belonging to an agency or organization who puts on a uniform and straps on a standard complement of weapons to do the job their organization needs done. Agents can work for the good guys and fight alongside superheroes, or they can be bad guys trying to get rich and/or take over the world. Most agents are not superhumans, but superhuman agents do exist: Battle Brutes, the Power Corps, and Omegadrones are all clearly superhuman, but all qualify as agents. Some operatives, such as the Star Knights, have elements of both agents and superheroes.

Agents come in many shapes and sizes. *Powers, Agent of AEGIS* may be the gold standard in the world of Freedom City, but he is by no means the only type. In addition to super-soldiers like Powers, agents can be suave super-spies, hard-boiled policemen, rumpled private detectives, professional ghost hunters/occult investigators, army officers on the run (for a Crime They Didn't Commit), and even a wild gaggle of freelance mercenaries. They don't even need to be proficient in combat: a team composed solely of journalists or doctors is a legitimate concept for an agent game, although most players want guns, and lots of them.

Often agents are pitted against a superior foe, but not always. Agents may face supervillains like Talos or Overshadow, or they might face normals like rank and file SHADOW agents. They may face monsters or street criminals, and let's not even mention government bureaucrats who try to smother them with intrusive regulations or drown them in red tape.

Agents place a high value on skills; most are gifted professionals with years of training that hones their raw talent. They may not have the power to fly or shoot eye beams, but they do get cool toys. Not only do agents have access to more guns than a Wild West show, some of them get nifty devices like fountain pens that shoot darts, wear bow ties fitted with small explosive charges, or ride air-cycles. How cool is that?

Agents work for agencies of all shapes and sizes, from small groups like "Ghosthunters, Inc." to worldwide agencies like UNISON. The agencies may be well known to the general public, or they might be "black-ops" where the agents have to protect their secret at all costs!

So, an agent campaign can include many different settings and roles. In *Agents of Freedom*, we focus on four different types of agent games:

Police Drama is a series where the player characters are cops. This is meant to simulate good crime drama television shows like *Hill Street Blues* or *Homicide*. The sample campaign for this genre is *Precinct 23*, a gritty game where the heroes are ordinary street cops in the Fens neighborhood of Freedom City, widely regarded as the worst example of urban blight in the city.

Top Cops is a series where the heroes are larger than life "super cops" of a sort that doesn't exist in the real world, but which are a staple of over-the-top movies like *Tango and Cash* or TV shows like *CSI: Miami*. The **STAR Squad** chapter describes a Top Cops game in a city where the police have to deal with supervillains on a regular basis.

Agents of Freedom, the primary focus of this book, is a series where the player characters are special agents or commandos of an organization like AEGIS or UNISON, out to thwart sinister organizations like SHADOW or Overthrow and their plans for world domination. The **AEGIS** and **UNISON** chapters of this book describe the heroes for this type of game.

A *Super-Spies* series borders on super-heroic level adventures, with the heroes as suave and skilled secret agents able to thwart the schemes of criminal masterminds on their own. Put a group of them together, and you have a force capable of handling threats even rookie superheroes might find challenging. This is the elite level for a series involving a super-agency like AEGIS or UNISON in the style of espionage action-adventure films (and some comics).

POWER LEVEL IN AN AGENT SERIES

Obviously, an agent, even an elite commando like an AEGIS squad member, is not on par with the average superhero. Even so, a squad of agents, particularly when well coordinated and armed, can be a match for all but the most powerful superhumans (and even then, they'll give it their best try).

STARTING POWER LEVELS AND POWER POINTS

Characters in an *Agents of Freedom* game start at a lower power level than a superhero in a typical *Mutants & Masterminds* game. Well-trained

POWERL LEVELS IN AN AGENT SERIES

	POWER LEVEL	POWER POINTS	MAX ABILITY	MAX SKILL RANK	MAX SAVE DC MODIFIER*
Police Drama	3	45	16	8	6
Top Cops	4	80	18	9	8
Action-Agents	5	100	20	10	10
Super-Spies	6	120	22	11	12

*This is only for devices and equipment; for agent genres where natural powers are allowed, use the normal save modifiers from Mutants & Masterminds, **Chapter 1**.

agents have more experience and *natural* capability than a typical super-hero. Therefore, they may offset the reduced power level by receiving 20 power points per level rather than 15, as shown on the following table.

OPTION: NICHE PROTECTION

Characters in an *Agents of Freedom* series are often extremely good at a defining ability or skill, their "niche" in the game. Gamemasters wanting to emphasize this can allow an agent character to increase the power level limit for *one* ability or skill (and only one) by +1 for an ability bonus or +2 for a skill. No other player character in the game can take that ability or skill as their niche, however.

For instance, "Moose" Moscovitz, Agent of AEGIS, fits the Strong Guy niche. Normally his Strength would be limited to 20 (for a PL 5 game), but because his niche is that he is *really* strong, he can purchase his Strength up to 22 (as if for a PL 6 game) without violating the campaign's power level. None of the other player characters can take Strength as their niche, since that belongs to Moose, the strongest guy in the game.

Note that the modification due to niche is applied *before* any trade-offs in attack/save DC or defense/Toughness. So "Moose" might be able to further increase his Strength limit with an attack trade-off (and the GM's permission).

OPTION: TEAM EQUIPMENT POOL

As a GM option, an agent team can have an allowance of equipment points equal to a starting character's power points, to spend on team equipment. For example, a team in an Action-Agents level series could have a 100-point equipment pool (the same as the starting power points of one character). Team equipment can include spare weapons, team vehicles, and special weapons and vehicles available from the agency, perhaps even a "safe house" or team headquarters. The GM should also decide whether team equipment can be reallocated between adventures, and exactly what equipment is available to the team.

INCREASING CAMPAIGN POWER LEVELS

There is, of course, a downside to the increase in power points, and that is the necessity of keeping agent games on a more human scale. Instead of increasing the power level of the campaign every time the agents earn 15 power points, the power level should be increased every 30 points or so. For every power level increase, the maximum ability and maximum Save DC modifier goes up by 2, and the maximum skill rank goes up by 1. The Gamemaster might also want to consider a final cap on the campaign at PL 9 or 10, unless you really want to take things in a "low-powered superheroes" direction.

AGENT CREATION

This section covers modifications and refinements to the standard *Mutants & Masterminds* character creation rules for designing agent characters. In general, if a particular trait is not detailed here, assume it is acquired in the same manner as described in the *Mutants & Masterminds* rulebook.

ABILITIES

Agents of Freedom is a human level genre, and therefore agents' abilities should remain on a human scale. Agents in these games generally are not superhuman.

STRENGTH

Agents with high strength scores are brick-houses. They are huge men and women who are built like power-lifters, and who spend much of their time hoisting things that "nothing human can possibly lift" (and yet they manage) or breaking down doors.

CONSTITUTION

Agents with high constitution scores are cinematic tough guys worthy of a Hong Kong action film (or Humphrey Bogart). They take an almost comical amount of punishment, yet refuse to die. More than any other ability, high constitution scores are a hallmark of the genre. Agents take a real pounding, but somehow manage to keep going until the bitter end.

DEXTERITY

Agents with high dexterity scores are usually people like circus acrobats or martial artists who employ an acrobatic style (such as cinematic ninja). Other agents may be fast on the trigger finger but not particularly agile (this is usually purchased through feats such as Quick Draw, Improved Initiative, and Seize Initiative).

INTELLIGENCE

Agents with high intelligence scores are typically either lab workers or field investigators. They may not be the most physically adept people in the agency (though field investigators are usually in pretty good shape), but their brains are often essential to a successful mission.

WISDOM

Perhaps this is not a characteristic that shines in most agents, in part because putting your life on the line against people who can easily kill you may not be the wisest career move. Even so, certain aspects of Wisdom—the ability to perceive one's surroundings and the willpower to keep going in the face of impossible odds or against incredible pain—are essential qualities of a good agent.

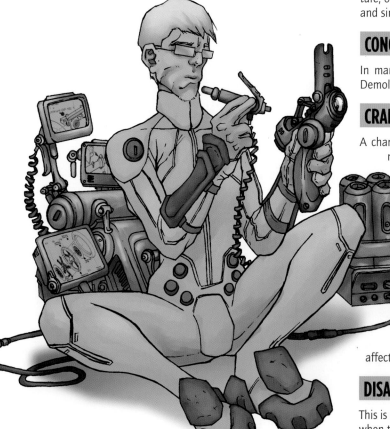

CHARISMA

Agents are usually tall, attractive men and women. They can be extraordinarily persuasive, natural leaders. And in a locked room, you'd probably rather be alone with Talos than an angry Harry Powers.

OPTION: ABILITIES AND HERO POINTS

Heroic level characters are often capable of "spurts" of power that put them into the realm of the superhuman. If the GM chooses to use this option, an agent can spend a hero point to add +5 to an ability or skill bonus for a single check, rather than the usual +2 for extra effort.

SKILLS

The following are some notes on specific skills as they are used in an *Agents of Freedom* series:

ACROBATICS

Agents primarily use this skill for balance checks, or for jumping onto a ledge and making sure that you have grabbed the edges and are able to pull yourself up. The best combat oriented agents have at least 2 ranks in this skill.

BLUFF

Bluff has a number of uses. It can replace Perform (acting) when an agent tries to fake being under the influence of drugs, broken by torture, or mentally dominated. Bluff is a synergy skill for Gamble in poker and similar games (a common spy pursuit).

CONCENTRATION

In many cases in the spy genre, Concentration is a synergy skill for Demolitions or Disable Device.

CRAFT

A character with Craft (chemical) and Demolitions can improvise grenades and chemical weapons (subject to the availability of supplies). Craft (structural) and Demolitions can be combined to destroy bridges, walls, or buildings. Craft (mechanical) is a synergy skill for Repair.

DIPLOMACY

Diplomacy may be used in hostage situations. Treat the starting situation as Hostile; for someone to end a standoff, they must be brought to Friendly. Certain events (pleas from loved ones, responding to minor demands) may modify the check positively, while other actions (pleas from someone who triggered the depressed behavior, someone trying to shoot the person while he is negotiating) affect it negatively.

DISABLE DEVICE

This is a very important skill in the genre. People seem to disarm a bomb when the countdown timer is at less than ten seconds; the Gamemaster should consider awarding a hero point accordingly. Members of a police bomb squad usually have at least 4 ranks in this skill.

DISGUISE

This is another agent genre staple. For agents in the dashing spy sub-genre, this skill is pretty much a necessity, and a Master of Disguise is one of the deadliest opponents one can ever encounter. In a world where characters frequently encounter superhuman shape-shifters, this skill may lose much of its élan; however, it is still a useful talent, especially in conjunction with a good Bluff skill.

DRIVE

A tune-up by a mechanic who makes a DC 15 Craft (mechanical) skill can provide a +2 synergy bonus for the next chase sequence in an adventure. A person in the passenger seat can use Navigation as a synergy skill, though the Gamemaster may require a Notice check to spot the oncoming obstacle or opportunity. Police usually have 2 ranks (or more) in this skill, and Drive is a common skill in the military.

ESCAPE ARTIST

Escape Artist has a secondary use in this genre—knowing where the weak spot is in a security system. It serves as a synergy skill to Demolitions or Craft (structural) checks designed to overcome these systems.

GATHER INFORMATION

This is a critical skill for any detective character, allowing them to pick up information on the background of a character or organization.

Various Knowledge skills can provide a synergy bonus: in the mystical world, Knowledge (arcane lore); in business circles, Knowledge (business); in politics, Knowledge (civics); on the streets, Knowledge (streetwise); in the entertainment field, Knowledge (popular culture); in the high-tech world, Knowledge (technology); and in religious circles, Knowledge (theology and philosophy).

HANDLE ANIMAL

Handle Animal, combined with 5 ranks of Ride, can give someone who is untrained 1 temporary rank with Ride (provided the animal handler escorts them). Consult the following chart for results.

HANDLE ANIMAL DCS

ANIMAL TYPE	HANDLE ANIMAL DC
Tame Animal	5
Feisty domesticated animal	15
Unbroken wild animal	25

INTIMIDATE

An Intimidate contest between team members having a dispute is a part of the genre. In a dispute between a commander and a subordinate over a command decision, an Intimidate contest ends the argument. If the commander wins, the subordinate swallows their objection and carries on with the mission (though if things turn out badly, they'll often throw it back in the commander's face). If the subordinate wins, the decision stands, but the subordinate gets the last word in. (A reconciliation scene is usually required to patch up their differences.) Most army officers and police have at least 2 ranks in Intimidate, and leadership-oriented characters commonly have 5 ranks or more.

MASTERMIND'S MANUAL SKILL OPTIONS

Gamemasters may wish to use the following skills from the *Mastermind's Manual* in an *Agents of Freedom* game: Appraise, Demolitions, Forgery, Gamble, Navigate, Repair, and Research. Skills are more important than powers in agent games, and these skills are all appropriate to agent characters. The sample agent archetypes in **Chapter 6** use these skills in some of the character write-ups.

Sample characters in *Agents of Freedom* do *not* employ the Narrow Skills option from the *Mastermind's Manual*. However, it is appropriate to certain agent-level games, and the Gamemaster is certainly free to use it, as desired.

Suggestions are provided for skill synergies, described in **Chapter 3** of the *Mastermind's Manual*. For those without access to the book, synergies apply when two skills work together. If an agent is using a skill, and has 5 ranks or more in another skill that goes well with the one they're using, they receive a +2 bonus to their check. Synergy allows agents working within the guidelines of a lower power level to still have quite respectable skill bonuses.

For characters performing long-term operations (such as infiltrating a villainous agency) where you don't want to role-play every incident in the operation, you can use the Timed Extended skill check rules from **Chapter 3** of the *Mastermind's Manual*.

Intimidate is the skill used for torture, which is (unfortunately) part of the genre. It requires a day to torture a victim; Knowledge (behavioral sciences) and Medicine are synergy skills. The torturer makes an Intimidate check against a DC equal to the character's Will save result, and consults the **Torture Results** table.

TORTURE RESULTS

WILL SAVE...	EFFECT
Successful	No Effect
Fails	Faltering
Fails by 5 or more	Shaken
Fails by 10 or more	Broken
Fails by 15 or more	Dominated

Faltering means the character is still resisting the torture, but it has taken its toll. They have a –1 cumulative penalty to further Will saves against torture.

Shaken means the character has been badly affected by the torture, but has not been completely broken (yet). They give the enemy information that they believe will not compromise their agency's security or their loved ones.

Broken means the character has succumbed to the torture. They tell the torturer everything. If using options from *Mastermind's Manual*, victims may acquire mental complications as per the Mental Strain rules.

Dominated means the torturer has not only broken the victim, but can implant a command into the target's mind. Whenever the situation is right for the command the torturer implanted (transmit data and forget, pull the trigger on their commander, kill someone who says a code phrase), the victim must make a Will save vs. the Intimidate skill result to resist the mental programming.

You use hero points to resist being tortured. If the enemy ever breaks you, spend a hero point, and the torture result becomes No Effect

OPTION: SPECIAL TRAINING

A Special Training feat is an "enabler," allowing a character to apply an existing skill in a new (usually specialized) way. It reflects the kind of specialized training agents often receive and can help differentiate agents with otherwise similar skills. Gamemasters can allow Special Training feats in place of some specialized narrow skills (see **Mastermind's Manual** Skill Options, previously).

An example of Special Training is parachuting: it's too specialized to create an entirely new skill, but also too specialized to fall under the general use of an existing skill. So the GM decides to make it a Special Training feat, like this:

PARACHUTING

Anyone making a jump with a parachute must make an Acrobatics or Piloting skill check, with the DC based on the conditions.

Condition	DC
Recreational parachuting	10
High-altitude, low-opening (HALO) jump	15
Good weather (no winds, clear visibility)	–5
Bad weather (high winds, poor visibility)	+5
Night jump	+5/+15*

The first modifier is the penalty with night vision goggles, the second without them.

A failed check results in potential injury: falling damage equal to half the normal amount for a fall from the height of the drop. Failing the check by 10 or more results in full falling damage.

Characters lacking Special Training (parachuting) can only make checks for recreational jumps (or must spend a hero point to emulate the Special Training feat for one jump).

instead. Likewise, the GM may award hero points to players whose agents are tortured (usually "off-stage"), particularly if the player role-plays a broken or dominated agent well.

INVESTIGATE

Investigate is a key skill for investigative characters. The skill handles forensic evidence; characters analyzing criminal behavior patterns should pick up Gather Information. If a person has a secret that can be uncovered by finding a clue and subjecting it to scientific examination, then Investigate becomes a synergy skill. Most police officers have at least 1 rank in this skill.

Investigate is also used as a "cleaning" skill to remove evidence from a site. When someone uses Investigate to look for clues at the crime scene, they must check against the cleaner's Investigate check result. If a cleaner wishes to plant false evidence, there is a +5 bonus to the Investigator's check.

KNOWLEDGE

The world of espionage and counterterrorism is its own domain. To know what has happened recently in the espionage world or recognize well-known, currently active agents, use the Knowledge (current events) skill. To know the background of an old, retired agent or an old agency, use Knowledge (history). To identify agency vehicles and weapons, use Knowledge (technology).

Knowledge (tactics) is a common command skill, and even non-command agents often have a couple of ranks in it. Gamemasters may want to use the *Mastermind's Manual* option for substituting a Knowledge (tactics) skill check for the Intelligence check normally used for the Master Plan feat; it fits the genre well.

MEDICINE

Most agents receive basic first aid training. It is reasonable to require law officers to take 1 rank in this skill, military or firefighters to take 2 ranks as part of their training, and lifeguards to take 3 ranks.

NOTICE

Notice is a key skill for any law enforcement or military personnel. Generally, most agency characters should have at least 2 ranks in this skill.

PERFORM

Perform (oratory) can be used as a synergy skill with Diplomacy for the purposes of crowd control.

PILOT

Many agents in higher power level games (Action-Agents, Super-Spies) have at least a passing familiarity with this skill (enough to use it when they need to, since Pilot cannot be used untrained).

SEARCH

This skill is extremely important to characters in the police and agent genres, especially its use in surveillance. If characters spend one minute examining an area before conducting a surveillance to examine the area for entrances, exits, and hiding places, they will receive a +2 bonus to their check.

STEALTH

All agent characters are going want to have at least 2 ranks of this skill. Many commando-type agents have this skill at the maximum rank for the series power level, while ninja-types use the niche guidelines to boost it to superhuman levels.

SLEIGHT OF HAND

As per *Mutants & Masterminds*, **Chapter 7**, this is the skill people use to plant listening and tracking devices, a useful ability in the espionage business.

SURVIVAL

This skill suits agents from non-temperate climates, environment specialists, hunting enthusiasts, or special-forces personnel.

SWIM

This is another handy skill. Most agents have at least 2 ranks in it. Note that even characters without the Swim skill can use it (as it can be used untrained); not being able to swim at all is a drawback, generally worth 1 point.

FEATS

Lacking in powers, feats are vital in an *Agents of Freedom* game, both to give agent characters options and to differentiate agents who may have a number of skills in common.

BENEFIT (RANK)

In an agency game, rank determines one's status within an organization. Characters with higher rank are allowed to give orders to lower-ranked officers, and in agencies with a heavy military influence, must yield in protocol (such as saluting a superior officer). Furthermore, in interaction skill checks involving the agency (requisitions, a dispute over an incident, etc.) one's rank provides a bonus to the check.

Here is a list of benefit ranks with the well-known US Army and Navy ranks given as a reference. The agencies in the later chapters of this book have their own rank structures as well. Generally, the PCs should find it tough to advance beyond rank 4, and nearly impossible to get to rank 6 in most series. The Gamemaster always has the option to veto any promotion a player buys if it is unearned.

There are many other benefits that could apply to agents in an agency campaign: law enforcement perks, security clearance perks, etc. It is probably easiest to fold these into the rank of the agency, so an agency rank subsumes a whole package of benefits. Federal agencies would likely prohibit access to sensitive information from local agents and restrict access to other intelligence agencies by treating their staff as if their rank was halved.

Optionally, characters can purchase a Security Clearance Benefit. For each point of Security Clearance, they receive +3 to their effective rank for access to secured information. This works particularly well in a contemporary spy game where someone's security clearance is not particularly dependent on rank.

CONNECTED

To reflect the different types of connections in the agent genre, Gamemasters may wish to allow other interaction skills to substitute for Diplomacy for this feat, creating a variant for each appropriate interaction skill. So, for example, a character might be more of a con artist who uses Bluff to get favors out of people, or a bully who uses Intimidate to push people around. This reflects a wider range of characters and helps preserve character niches in the game.

LUCK

In an agent series, the heroes are allowed a number of Luck points equal to their power level, not half their power level, as in a standard *Mutants & Masterminds* game. Heroes in an agent series may not be as powerful as superheroes, but they *are* just as lucky.

BENEFIT (RANK) LEVELS

Benefit Rank	US Army	US Navy	Agency Bonus
1	Private/Corporal	Seaman/Petty Officer	+0
2	Sergeant/Master Sergeant	Chief Petty Officer	+1
3	Lieutenant/Captain	Ensign/Lieutenant	+2
4	Major/Lt. Colonel	Lt. Commander/Commander	+3
5	Colonel	Captain	+4
6	General	Admiral	+5

COMMAND FEATS

There are a number of feats any good team commander should have, including Inspire and Leadership. Commanders should also take several ranks of the Benefit (rank) feat to represent their authority and status in the chain of command.

TEAM BUILDING FEATS

Several feats should be in the arsenal of any well-oiled agent team, such as Redirect (good for defending a teammate), Set-Up (good for helping someone set up an attack), and Teamwork (good for enhancing aid actions).

FIGHTING STYLES

Agents like to fight, and spend a lot of their time in training. The fighting styles from *Mutants & Masterminds,* **Chapter 4**, and the *Mastermind's Manual,* **Chapter 4**, come into play frequently in an agent series. If you are looking for a comprehensive martial art for commandos, use Krav Maga (All-out Attack, Chokehold, Dodge Focus, Improved Block, Improved Disarm, Improved Grapple, Improved Trip, Power Attack) as a default fighting style.

POWERS

In a standard *Agents of Freedom* game, characters have no powers. Any "powers" come from gadgets, usually acquired through the Equipment feat. Gamemasters running Super-Spy games might consider giving these agents the option to reallocate their equipment points (see *Mastermind's Manual,* **Chapter 5**) to reflect that genre's tendency to give agents a new set of gadgets for each mission.

Traditionally, agents have access to technology allowing them to compete at superhuman levels; limiting agents' access to equipment based on the power level of most *Agents of Freedom* series is a genre buster. Therefore, *Agents of Freedom* applies a variant that increases the power level limits for devices and equipment *only*.

This makes the agent genre a somewhat deadlier one than a regular *Mutants & Masterminds* game, but that fits the genre too, and it enables agents to compete more effectively against super-human foes.

The spy genre is known for its outlandish technology, not improbably beyond the realm of current technology, but miniaturized and disguised. With "spy-tech," guns are built into fountain pens, people's trench coats turn into short-range aircraft, and rings inject lethal poisons. The **Devices and Equipment** section of this chapter catalogs these devices in detail.

NEW POWER FEAT

The following new power feat is used for many items of equipment in *Agents of Freedom,* particularly spy-gear.

DISGUISED

The device or equipment with this feat is not what it appears to be. This item is disguised as an everyday object, and will not be recognized as unusual unless an observer makes a Notice check (DC 20). Even if the observer believes something is unusual, they will not identify the item's true function unless they make a Knowledge (technology) check at DC 15.

This feat is also used to build objects that can fool detection by normal means; you can disguise a pistol that would normally be detected by a scanner or X-Ray machine with this feat.

Additionally, a disguised item may be miniaturized. There are no specific requirements for the sizes of devices and equipment, but in general, each rank of the feat allows the item to be reduced by one size category.

Disguised also can be used for items hidden in large, innocuous objects (such as lasers built into giant chandeliers). These items may not be "disguised," as such, but it is still hard to spot them amid the object encasing them until they are used.

NEW FLAWS

The following power flaws are applied to the various devices and pieces of equipment in *Agents of Freedom*, and may be suitable for use in other *M&M* games.

ASSEMBLY REQUIRED   −1 MODIFIER PER STEP

This variation on the Action flaw means the effect is not immediately available, but first must be assembled before it can be used. The base assembly time is one minute for a −1 modifier. Every additional step up the Time and Value Progression Table (5 minutes, 20 minutes, etc., *M&M*, page 70) is an additional 1-point drawback. A Craft (electronic or mechanical) check (DC 10) is also required to successfully assemble the item. The user can take 10 on the check, if circumstances allow.

CREW REQUIRED   −1 MODIFIER

This Limited flaw means a single person cannot operate the device or equipment. This could include a power requiring two halves of a ring be joined together, or a vehicle mounted weapon requiring two people working in tandem to function (one to operate and one to load ammo, for example). Both operators must take the normal action required to use the effect. If either is unable to do so, the effect does not work until the missing person is replaced.

AGENTS OF POWER

The regular genre conventions say agents and superpowers don't mix; agents get superhuman abilities from their gear. This grounds agent series at a human level. However, in a genre as broad and as old as comic books, there are going to be exceptions: squads with minor superpowers, or superhumans treated as agents. These are "agents of powers" sub-genres.

The campaign limits on "Agents of Power" games do not need to be modified. For superpowers, just use the normal limits on a power for that power level. Agents of Power series are not meant to compete against full-on superhero games for levels of destruction, though for destructive sub-genres (such as a game based on Stephen King's *Firestarter*, for example), it is appropriate to allow players to use attack/DC trade-offs.

There are three main ways powers are handled in the Agents of Power sub-genre:

ONE POWER

First, there's the *One Power* genre, where agents get one and only one superpower. This harkens back to Silver Age comic books like the *Legion of Super-Heroes* and the original Lee/Kirby *X-Men*, but also subsumes low-powered superhero TV shows like *Misfits of Science* and *Mutant-X*. Typically, no one power can solve every problem and the heroes have to use their powers in concert to achieve a goal.

RELATED POWERS

The second is the *Related Powers* genre. Player characters typically share a background with a common set of powers, such as all being alien half-breeds or exposed to the same weird power source. Sometimes, they will mix up genres so that there is a common set of powers and one unique power per individual, that character's "signature" power. Both genres tend to blur the line between agents and low-level superheroes. Examples include:

Psi-Agents, a game where kids are the products of secret psionic experiments. Perhaps they were exposed to an experimental mutagen when they were infants, or they're the offspring of telepathic supervillains killed fighting the government, who set up a special foster home to raise them. The kids now use their mental powers in service to the government.

Alien Exiles, where the heroes are angsty teenage aliens exiled to earth to avoid an intergalactic war. Blessed with powers beyond Earthlings, they try to blend into the normal high school populace. Of course, they're teenagers, so telling them to show self-control is futile to the point of absurdity. Eventually, a government agent discovered their secret, and made a deal with them. He'd keep their secret, provided he could occasionally call on them to help on his toughest cases. Now the aliens among us are secret defenders of justice; they resent being blackmailed, but are secretly proud of their cause.

AGENCY SUPERSQUAD

The third genre is a full-blown superhero game, the *Agency Supersquad.* In this series, AEGIS or UNISON (or similar organizations, including organized religion or the Army) decides they need their own superhero backup, their own dedicated team. In an Agency Supersquad game, the heroes wear the uniform of the agency and receive the same mission briefings and instructions as other agents, and they are required to show the same loyalty to the agency. But they're as much superheroes as they are agents, and they're there to handle the jobs ordinary agents can't (which is sure to generate some resentment among the rank-and-file).

In Iron Age stories, agency super-teams are often depicted as the vicious puppets of the Evil Government (particularly armed services super-teams, which often seem to embody every negative stereotype about the military), while free-thinking, independent superheroes are the good guys. In such campaigns, looking at things from the agent's perspective, conflict between superheroes and superhuman agents should probably stem from the reckless and irresponsible actions of "cowboy" superheroes, lacking the discipline and training of their agency counterparts.

A variant on the Agency Supersquad is the *Agency Robot* series. Perhaps a lab tech has had too much free time on his hands, or the agency wanted robot bodies to serve as repositories for the memories of dead human agents. In this case, the heroes don't just have to deal with the trials of being superhuman in a human world, they also have to deal with the trauma of dealing with past lives and loves to which they may never be able to return.

Another variation is the *Agency Powered Armor* game. The agency has developed suits of power armor (such as AEGIS' MAX

or Super-MAX suits), but they're dangerous; perhaps wearers run the risk of neural damage or psychosis, or they have a dangerously radioactive or unstable power source or the like. However (for reasons the PCs keep to themselves), these heroes feel they have nothing to lose, so off they go!

The Agency Supersquad shouldn't outstrip super-spies by too much (PL 8 is probably a good starting power level), though a large agency can run at PL 10, and a country's national military team (which often comes into conflict with heroes as well as villains) can be PL 12 or even higher.

DRAWBACKS

Many drawbacks do not apply to agents, since they do not have superhuman powers (or the weaknesses that go with them) and are not likely to be disabled (most agents are *very* physically capable, though occasionally you will see a lab tech in a wheelchair or a Hard-Nosed Commander who lost an eye back in the war). Agents might suffer from "Permanent Nagging Injuries," though, which apply to them throughout the course of their career.

THE NAGGING INJURY

Agents tend to get banged up more than ordinary folk. Injuries in *Mutants & Masterminds* tend to be "heroic"; they may inconvenience someone for a while, but they don't seriously impact most situations. These include:

ALLERGIES

This may be a source of humor to some, but those who have lived under extreme allergy conditions know different. Severe allergies can be handled as minor or moderate Weakness drawbacks for exposure to the allergen (usually resulting in a penalty to checks, attack bonus, and defense bonus). Total value is based on the frequency of the allergen.

BAD GRIP

Conditions like arthritis or carpal tunnel syndrome are common to older or desk-bound characters; their hands are not in the same condition as the rest of their body. They suffer a –2 penalty to any skill requiring manual dexterity (such as Computers, Craft, and Disable Device). This is an uncommon, minor drawback worth 1 point.

BAD BACK

Whenever the character tries to lift more than a light load, they have to make a Fortitude saving throw: DC 10 for a medium load, +5 DC per category above that. A failed save means the character is staggered until they have had 48 hours of rest or sufficient medical attention (Medicine check, DC 15, with appropriate painkillers needed). This is an uncommon, moderate drawback worth 2 points.

CONCUSSION-PRONE

At some point in their life, the character took one too many knocks to the head. Any time a character with this drawback is thrown or suffers knockback into a solid object, make a Will save (DC 10) to remain conscious; even if the save succeeds, the character is automatically at –1 to all Toughness saves for the next 24 hours. This is an uncommon, moderate drawback worth 2 points.

TRICK KNEE

The character was hurt badly playing football in college or in action in the field and has the limp to show for it. While it doesn't hurt under most circumstances, if the character moves all-out on foot, make a Fortitude Save (DC 15) each round. Failure means you lose you move action that round. This is an uncommon, major drawback worth 3 points.

COMPLICATIONS

Perhaps it is comforting to know average agents live no less complicated lives than your typical superhero. Sure, they don't have quite as many problems regarding their costumed identity, but they are afflicted by the same demons as every other member of this race.

ADDICTION

Traditionally, agents are not very seedy. Yes, some may occasionally hit the bottle, and you might run into an agent who has a problem with painkillers they were given while recovering from an injury (or became addicted to drugs when forced to use them on an undercover mission), but by and large, agents are a pretty clean-cut crew. (This is one of the big differences between traditional and Iron Age agencies, where an agent is much more likely to indulge in recreational drug use, pornography, and other vices.)

ENEMY

In an agency game, the player characters have enemies, most of whom show up every session. This complication shouldn't be designated for an enemy agency; instead, it should be reserved for an individual within that agency (an old college football teammate who joined the other side, an evil brother, a former fiancé who turned out to be an enemy plant, or just an enemy special forces commander who won't go away) who doesn't turn up every session, but when they do, things get personal.

FAME

Most agents don't have this complication; they're a rather anonymous group, except within the agent community. However, similar to members of the British Royal Family who go into the military, it is possible that some blue blood, star athlete, boyfriend of a famous pop singer, or other celebrity may tire of their feckless existence and decide to do something positive with their lives. Similarly, an agent may be caught on camera disabling a nuke or doing something else that's incredibly heroic, and the media may want to profile him or follow him around.

HONOR

All characters belonging to a heroic agency have this complication to a certain extent, as they are bound to follow rules of ethics, engagement, war, or police protocols. This complication only suits agents truly obsessive about their honor code (they will meet force with equal force when they clearly possess superior firepower, or agree to a challenge even when it is obvious the other side has no intention of honoring it).

PREJUDICES

Agencies are pretty tolerant, even in the Silver Age (when the Howling Commandos had Germans and people of Italian descent on their team), and minorities are well represented in the armed services. Prejudice is not a huge problem, though individuals from regions associated with terrorist agencies may encounter problems, as may American agents stationed overseas; misogyny and homophobia are still issues in many real world agencies and military organizations, and could also manifest themselves in comic book agencies, as the GM and players choose.

Also, in a superhero world, aliens and extra-dimensional visitors may join earthly agencies and experience xenophobia for a totally different—yet familiar—reason.

SECRET

Characters in an *Agents of Freedom* series usually do not have to worry about their secret identities. However, a defense analyst or a spy probably has to hide their true occupation from their friends, which can certainly cause complications when the friends just happen to be in Hong Kong and encounter the hero looking for a microfilm (when he's supposed be visiting a sick aunt in Sacramento).

HERO POINTS AND EXTRA EFFORT

Hero points have a number of genre-specific uses. You can spend a hero point when you need a clue while investigating a mystery. Similarly, when the enemy has assassinated a witness to a crime or other helpful NPC, you may be able to spend a hero point on a Medicine check to keep them alive, if the GM agrees.

In addition to individual hero points, you can also institute a team "Luck Pool". Characters can designate one hero point per character per session to go into this pool, which may be drawn upon by any team member who is in need, as long as they are working as a team.

OPTION: FINAL EFFORT

This option is an extension of the extraordinary effort and last-ditch effort options from the *Mastermind's Manual,* and is for agents with a real death wish. When the final effort option is invoked, the agent gains five hero points and may spend them as desired. However, at some point in the adventure, the character *will* die and be permanently removed from the game. This feat helps ensure it'll be in a heroic blaze of glory worthy of a super-agent. The GM may wish to waive normal limits on spending hero points when final effort is in play.

REPUTATION

"Agent Powers, I presume?" Reputation can be a significant element of the super-agent genre, one of the things that differentiate between the run-of-the-mill agents and the real standouts. Therefore, the GM may wish to use the optional reputation rules from the *Mastermind's Manual* in an *Agents of Freedom* game, including the option for using reputation to requisition equipment from the agency (*Mastermind's Manual,* page 103). Reputation can be based on power points spent on feats like Fame or Infamy as well as awarded for action taken during play.

REPUTATION CHECK

A Reputation check of d20 + the character's reputation bonus + the observer's Int (or appropriate Knowledge skill) is made against DC 25 whenever the character might be recognized.

A successful check grants an interaction skill bonus equal to half the reputation bonus for Bluff, Diplomacy, Gather Information, and Perform skill checks if the observer is favorably disposed towards the character's reputation. If the observer has a negative view of the character's reputation, the bonus becomes a penalty, but the character gains an equal bonus to Intimidate skill checks.

DEVICES AND EQUIPMENT

Few things are more strongly identified with the agent genre than gear. From "guns, *lots* of guns" to experimental, comically destructive weapons produced by easily disgruntled weapon-smiths, spies and special agents love their toys to death. *Mutants & Masterminds* gives a good description of basic adventuring gear, and that's enough to meet the needs of most campaigns. However, depending on the genre, agents have access to many different kinds of specialty gear.

GETTING EQUIPMENT

Agents acquire gear using the Equipment feat, as usual. Each agency has a list of available equipment; for agents, agency super-tech like blasters or jet packs is considered Equipment, and not Devices. Super-tech items not on the agency list must be purchased as Devices (or, optionally, with the Gadgets power from the *Mastermind's Manual*). The Equipment comprises a personalized complement of agency standard equipment that must be taken on every mission. Agency lists are mutually exclusive: UNISON agents do not have access to AEGIS equipment, even on joint missions.

Those who play in the Super-Spies genre may alter their Equipment from mission to mission without paying extra points (though Dashing Super-Spies in a standard *Agents of Freedom* game play by Agent rules. The rules of the dominant sub-genre take precedence).

An agent can also acquire equipment temporarily as experimental equipment, by attempting an emergency requisition, or by spending a hero point on a gadget flashback.

EXPERIMENTAL EQUIPMENT

The agency (through the auspices of the Gamemaster) may hand out experimental equipment for field-testing from time to time. Since the agents are being used as guinea pigs, the equipment should be given out for free (no cost in equipment or power points). The GM can then use the experimental equipment as a plot-device as they see fit.

Experimental equipment is exempt from campaign power level limits, since it is entirely controlled by the GM, who can choose to have the equipment stop working, malfunction, or do something entirely unexpected, as suits the story. GMs should use caution when handing out powerful experimental equipment, and agents are usually encouraged to reserve such items for when they are absolutely needed (hoping they work as advertised when the time comes).

REQUISITIONING EQUIPMENT

Gamemasters may wish to use the option for requisitioning equipment from the *Mastermind's Manual* in *Agents of Freedom* games, as follows:

Characters can reassign their equipment points between missions. The character makes a Diplomacy check (DC 10 + the equipment's point cost) for each desired piece of equipment. If the check is successful, the agency or patron agrees to assign that equipment. If it fails, the equipment is restricted or otherwise unavailable. Since the character can take 10 on the check, equipment with a point cost equal to or less than the character's Diplomacy bonus is automatically available.

You can mix-and-match options to suit the game. For example, characters may have some equipment they always carry, some equipment points they redistribute from one adventure to another, and some restricted equipment they have to requisition (making a Diplomacy check to access it).

THE GADGET FLASHBACK

Another way to get an item when it is needed is through a gadget flashback. To stage such a flashback, the player spends a hero point, and then describes a flashback scene where the character was assigned an item earlier in the adventure. The item cannot exceed the equipment points available from the character's Equipment feat. The item can, however, be an experimental item that employs super-tech (typically, a Lab Geek explains its use with a darkly comic demonstration involving horrible things happening to a target dummy's head or crotch). This is a variation on the on-hand items guidelines on page 133 of *Mutants & Masterminds*.

Gadget flashbacks are particularly useful for single-use items that only show up at a critical moment in the adventure. As with similar uses of hero points, the GM has the right to veto any gadget flashback that has the potential to short-circuit the entire adventure or make things less fun for all involved. On the other hand, the GM should encourage creative uses of gadget flashbacks that enhance the enjoyment of the game and help further the plot.

EQUIPMENT LISTS

Here are lists and descriptions of common agent equipment and spy-gear. Some, like the exotic firearms and tricked out vehicles, are designed with a comic book universe in mind, while other equipment is thoroughly grounded in the real world. Pick and chose as you wish, as best suits the tone of your campaign.

STANDARD FIREARMS

One thing distinguishing an agency from everyday heroes is the presence of firearms. Agents like guns, the heavier the better. While comic book agencies are more likely to be armed with (non-lethal) blasters, conventional forces such as the police, the military, and common criminals still lug around healthy quantities of conventional firearms.

PISTOLS

- **Holdout pistol:** This is a low-caliber, easily concealed pistol, typically used as a back-up or secondary weapon (especially by villains who accept challenges "unarmed").

- **Light pistol:** A common handgun, light pistols are used by police officers and common criminals.

- **Glock:** A plastic pistol designed to get through metal detectors; it is bought with the Disguised feature. The first cost is for a Glock with the Assembly Required flaw (making it less immediately accessible).

- **Heavy pistol:** A high-caliber handgun, heavy pistols are usually used by those who want a lot of stopping power.

OPTION: BALANCING HEAVY WEAPONS

Although *Agents of Freedom* provides the option for a higher PL limit for devices and equipment, there's also the matter of how to handle "found" weapons and things like heavy combat equipment that doesn't feature in every adventure, but comes up from time to time.

DYNAMIC BALANCE

One option to help balance the occasion when an agent grabs a bazooka (or what have you) and uses it is dynamic trade-offs. That is, for each point the weapon's damage bonus is over the agent's power level limit, reduce the character's effective attack bonus with that weapon by 1; the weapon is simply too powerful (has too much kick, heft, etc.) and the character isn't used to it. So an agent using a weapon that's 2 points over the damage PL limit suffers a –2 on attack rolls with it. This preserves power level balance in a fairly easy-to-use way.

HEAVY WEAPONS

Another option is lighten the power level limit for heavier, less portable weapons. While agents aren't going to have massive-damage sidearms, they might use tank cannons and emplaced machine guns or blaster-cannons to get the job done. As a basic guideline, an emplaced weapon can exceed power level by 2 points, while a weapon with the Crew Required Flaw can exceed it by 4 points. This allows some flexibility in the power of weapons characters can use without really changing their routine equipment.

You can even combine the two options so that *really* heavy weapons get the extra ceiling, then anything over that imposes an attack roll penalty to balance out the difference.

- **Machine pistol:** A small automatic weapon, a machine pistol is usable in one hand. Machine pistols are Autofire weapons.

- **Taser:** This is a compressed-air weapon firing a pair of darts. On impact, they release a powerful electrical charge, requiring a Fortitude save (DC 15) against a Stun effect.

LONGARMS

- **Submachine gun:** Compact automatic weapons that fire pistol ammunition, submachine guns are common military weapons.

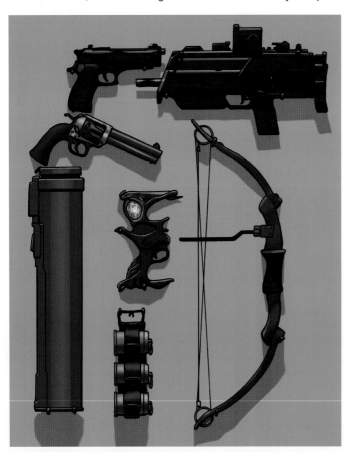

Criminals with access to more serious firepower also use them. Submachine guns are Autofire weapons.

- **Sniper rifle:** These rifles are designed for long-range use, typically in conjunction with a powerful scope or targeting system. They have 2 ranks each of Improved Range and Progression (improved range increment).

- **Assault rifle:** These rifles are designed for military use with both single-fire and Autofire options. This is a weapon of choice for violent street gangs and members of wilder organized crime cartels (such as the Russian Mafia), as well as mercenaries and military heroes.

- **Shotgun:** A shotgun can fire shot, which does +5 damage with a +2 bonus to hit due to the spread, but it does only +3 damage against targets with any increase in their natural Toughness save bonus. It can also load solid slugs, which inflict +6 damage.

MACHINE GUNS

- **Machine gun:** This is an automatic weapon that is typically used as an emplaced weapon. These are likely to be encountered in mercenary situations, as urban gangs prefer more portable technology.

GRENADES AND EXPLOSIVES

- **Flash-bang grenade:** A flash-bang grenade gives off a bright flash and a loud bang that can render targets temporarily blind and deaf (Reflex save, DC 14).

- **Fragmentation grenade:** A "frag" grenade is a common military grenade that sprays shrapnel in all directions.

- **Sleep gas grenade:** This grenade fills a 20-ft. radius with a fatigue-inducing gas (Fortitude save, DC 14).

- **Smoke grenade:** A smoke grenade fills an area with thick smoke (colored as desired), providing total concealment to all visual senses except for X-ray vision.

- **Tear gas grenade:** This type of grenade releases a cloud of gas that irritates the eyes and lungs, causing temporary blindness and nausea (visual Dazzle plus Nauseate, Fortitude save, DC 14).

PISTOLS

WEAPONS	DAMAGE	CRITICAL	RANGE INCREMENT	SIZE	COST
Hold-out Pistol	+2 Ballistic, Concealed	20	20 ft.	Tiny	5
Light pistol	+3 Ballistic	20	30 ft.	Small	6
Glock Pistol	+3 Ballistic	20	30 ft.	Small	4/7*
Machine Pistol	+3 Ballistic	20	30 ft.	Small	9
Heavy pistol	+4 Ballistic	20	40 ft.	Medium	8
Taser	Stun 5	20	5 ft.	Small	12

LONGARMS

WEAPONS	DAMAGE	CRITICAL	RANGE INCREMENT	SIZE	COST
Submachine Gun	+4 Ballistic	20	40 ft.	Medium	12
Sniper rifle	+6 Ballistic	19-20	250 ft.	Large	17
Assault rifle (M16, AK-74, FN)	+5 Ballistic, Autofire	20	50 ft.	Large	15
Pump shotgun	+5/+6** Ballistic	20	40 ft.	Large	11
Hunting Rifle	+6 Ballistic	20	60 ft.	Large	12
Sawed-off shotgun	+6/+7** Ballistic	20	10 ft.	Medium	13
12-gauge shotgun	+6/+7** Ballistic	20	40 ft.	Large	13

MACHINEGUNS

WEAPONS	DAMAGE	CRITICAL	RANGE INCREMENT	SIZE	COST
7.62mm Machine gun (M60)	+6 Ballistic, Autofire	20	50 ft.	Large	18
.50-caliber Machine gun	+7 Ballistic, Autofire	20	70 ft	Large	21

*=See individual descriptions for more information.** = See individual description for more information on the differences between loading up these weapons with shot or slugs

GRENADES AND EXPLOSIVES

WEAPONS	DAMAGE	CRITICAL	RANGE INCREMENT	SIZE	COST
Flash-bang grenade	Dazzle 4 Burst	–	–	Tiny	16
Fragmentation grenade	Blast 5 Explosion	–	–	Tiny	15
Sleep gas grenade	Fatigue 4 Cloud	–	–	Tiny	16
Smoke grenade	Obscure 2 (visual)	–	–	Small	4
Tear gas grenade	Dazzle 4 + Nauseate 4 Explosion	–		Small	28
Dynamite	Blast 5 Explosion	–	–	Tiny	15
Plastic Explosive	Blast 10 Explosion	–	–	Small	30

*=See individual descriptions for more information.

EXOTIC AND HEAVY WEAPONS

WEAPONS	DAMAGE	CRITICAL	RANGE INCREMENT	SIZE	COST
Flame-thrower	Blast 6 Line Area (fire)	–	–	Large	12
Glop gun	Snare 5	–	50 ft.	Medium	10
Grenade launcher	Blast 5 Explosion	-	70 ft.	Large	15*
SAM launcher	Blast 8 Explosion 2	-	2500 ft.	Large	22*
RPG	Blast 8 Explosion 4	-	70 ft.	Large	20
LAW rocket	Blast 10 Explosion 2	_	150 ft.	Large	22

*=See individual descriptions for more information.

- **Dynamite:** This is a common explosive. The damage on the table is for a single stick of dynamite. Each increase of the amount of explosive on the Time and Value Progression Table (*M&M*, page 70) increases damage by +1, and increases cost by 3 equipment points.

- **Plastic explosive:** This is another common explosive, which can be worked into different shapes. The damage listed is for a 1-lb block. Each increase of the amount of explosive on the Time and Value Progression Table increases damage by +1, and increases cost by 3 equipment points.

EXOTIC WEAPONS

- **Flame-thrower:** A flame-thrower shoots a stream of fire 5 feet wide and 25 feet long in front of the attacker as an area attack.

- **Glop gun:** Perhaps inspired by comic book superheroes, this rifle shoots a chemical spray that quickly hardens around its target, a Snare 5 effect. Mostly a novelty weapon, this version assumes the technology has been refined to a point where it is more practical.

HEAVY WEAPONS

- **Grenade launcher:** This is a small cannon that fires grenades. The cost of this device is +1 per additional type of grenade it can fire (making it an array of grenades).

- **SAM launcher:** A surface to air missile is a heavy, portable rocket launcher designed to intercept air-based targets like helicopter gunships (and flying superheroes). It causes a Blast 8 to the main target, with the Explosion modifier applying to 2 ranks of its Blast damage. It has 2 ranks each in Improved Range and Progression (range increment).

- **RPG:** An RPG, or rocket-propelled grenade-launcher, is a mortar that fires rocket-propelled grenades.

- **LAW rocket:** This is a light anti-tank weapon (though some users mistake superheroes for tanks). It has the Explosion modifier on its Blast damage. Most rocket launchers can fire only one or two shots before they must be reloaded as a full-round action.

COMIC BOOK FIREARMS

In a superhero world, firearms come in many shapes and sizes, and the higher tech they are, the better. Compared to conventional weapons, they have fewer ammunition problems, and give less of a kick when fired. In addition, they provide all kinds of interesting effects.

Comic book weapons generally come in three sizes:

- *Pistols* have an effect rank of 5, a range increment of 50 feet, and are medium-sized.

- *Rifles* have an effect rank of 8, a range increment of 80 feet, and are large-sized.

COMIC BOOK FIREARMS

Weapon Type	Effect	Critical	Cost
Autoblaster	Autofire Blast	20	3/rank
Blaster	Blast	20	2/rank
Chaos	Confuse	20	2/rank
Disintegration	Disintegration	20	4/rank
Entropy	Ranged Drain Toughness	20	2/rank
Fear	Ranged Emotion Control, Limited to Fear	20	1/2 ranks
Force Field Projector	Snare, Suffocating	20	5/rank
Freezing	Snare Linked to Ranged Stun	20	5/rank
Gravity	Gravity Control, Continuous, Limited to Increase	20	2/rank
Hypno	Ranged Drain Will, Will Save	20	2/rank
Inertia	Ranged Drain Speed	20	2/rank
Laser	Penetrating Blast	20	3/rank
Leech	Ranged Drain Strength	20	2/rank
Light	Blast Linked to Visual Dazzle	20	4/rank
Net	Snare	20	2/rank
Neuro-Paralyzer	Ranged Paralyze	20	3/rank
Petrification	Transform (stone to flesh)	20	3/rank
Shrink	Ranged Shrinking Attack	20	2/rank
Slick	Environmental Control (Hamper Movement)	20	2/rank
Sonic	Ranged Stun Linked to Auditory Dazzle, Will Save	20	4/rank
Tranquilizer	Ranged Fatigue Poison	20	4/rank
Vertigo	Ranged Nauseate	20	3/rank
Vibration	Blast Explosion, Limited	20	2/rank

- *Heavy weapons* are emplaced or crew-served weapons with an effect rank of 10, a range increment of 100 feet, and are huge-sized.

COMIC BOOK FIREARM TYPES

- An **Autoblaster** is a blaster weapon (see the following) with the Autofire extra.

- **Blaster** is a term for any generic Blast weapon; it fires a highly charged stream of compressed plasma particles that hits with a strong concussive force.

- **Chaos** weapons affect the judgment centers of the target's mind, making them unable to focus on an action while the target is under its effect.

- **Disintegration** guns are evil weapons that dematerialize an object or person. In general, only the bad guys use them.

- **Entropy** guns attack the molecular integrity of an object, causing it to lose cohesion and become more likely to be damaged by an attack.

- The **Fear** gun is an exotic weapon that triggers panic responses by stimulating the fear centers of the brain. Whoever pulls the trigger becomes the target of the fear impulse; at full effect, the target flees in a blind panic.

- **Force Field** weapons are experimental weapons that encase people in force field bonds, with the side effect of suffocating them (until the force field is broken). It uses the Suffocating extra from

Ultimate Power: a target trapped in the snare cannot breathe and must hold their breath (see **Suffocation**, *M&M*, page 168).

- The **Freezing** gun discharges a stream of pressurized water, followed by a stream of liquid nitrogen. The water coats the target, and the liquid nitrogen freezes it, creating instant ice bonds.

- **Gravity** weapons are designed to increase gravitic attraction between an airborne target and the ground, causing them to slow and even tumble from the sky. The Heavy Weapon version of this power is built with Improved Range 1 and Progression (range) 1, giving it a Range of 160 feet and a maximum range of 1600 feet.

- **Hypno** weapons produce a signal to weaken the target's will, making them susceptible to hypnotic commands. They're resisted with a Will saving throw.

- **Inertia** rays increase surface friction, slowing the target's movement. Naturally, it has no effect on airborne targets.

- **Laser** is a term for any generic Blast weapon that produces a concentrated beam that burns through its target.

- **Leech** weapons fire an enervating ray that drains the victim's strength, leaving them weakened and possibly helpless.

- **Light** rays envelop the target in a brilliant swath of energy, burning and blinding them.

- **Net** weapons fire a thick, malleable wire mesh to envelop and entrap their target.

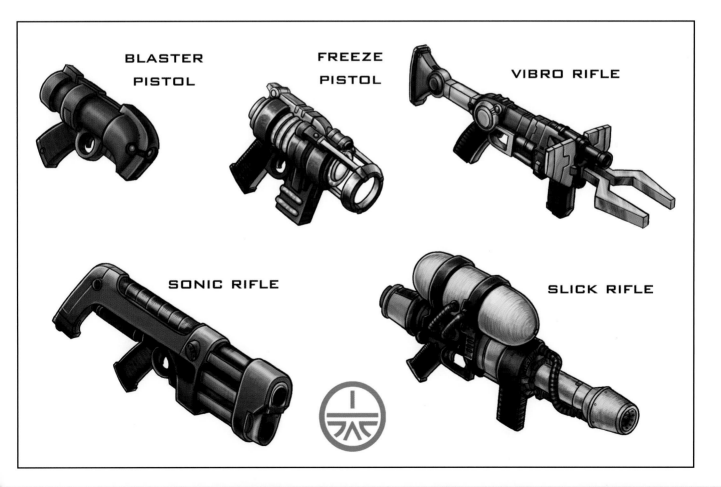

BLASTER PISTOL

FREEZE PISTOL

VIBRO RIFLE

SONIC RIFLE

SLICK RIFLE

- **Neuro-Paralyzer** is a term for any generic weapon that causes involuntary nerve paralysis. It is bought as a Paralyze effect with the Range extra.

- **Petrifaction** guns transform a target from flesh to stone. Only certain chemical formulae, similar molecular transformation powers, or the reverse switch on the gun change them back.

- **Shrink** rays are a classic, though rarely seen, weapon. The target gets a Reflex saving throw to avoid the ray.

- **Slick** guns fire a gooey film that sticks beneath a target's feet, dropping their movement rate by 75%.

- **Sonic** weapons utilize screeching vibrations. They're resisted with a Will saving throw.

- **Tranquilizer** weapons drug their targets, causing fatigue or unconsciousness.

- **Vertigo** weapons attack the balance centers of the brain. This is a great support weapon that can literally put an agent off-balance, setting them up for the kill from another squad member, though some sadistic agents just like the feeling of helplessness it can instill in their enemies.

- **Vibration** weapons set up a vibratory chain reaction in an object, causing it to explode, doing shrapnel damage to the surrounding area. It is bought with a Limited Flaw; if it fails to destroy the object, then it does *no* damage and no explosion occurs.

CHEMICAL WEAPONS

Often as much plot device as attack, these incapacitate more heroes in the spy genre than any other weapon. These can be targeted through a boutonnière, a doll's mouth, pumps in an elevator, or some other innocuous delivery device.

- **Exploding Cufflink:** This is a one-use weapon primarily used as a distraction. The agent removes a cufflink and throws it for the appropriate effect. Sometimes, this produces smoke; that version should be bought as a smoke grenade with the Disguised feature.

- **Laughing Gas:** Although Nauseate may seem like a strange choice, the incapacitation effects match the gas' effect perfectly.

- **Paralyzing Ring:** This is a trick ring, like a joy buzzer, but with a much more powerful effect. When someone shakes the person's hand, they are subjected to paralyzing venom.

- **Poison Lipstick A:** The delight of the femme fatale, this powerful balm weakens agents and other targets with a kiss. The kisser, of course, wears false lips or a protective balm to shield them from their own attack.

- **Poison Lipstick B:** This is identical to the effects of the paralyzing ring, but applied to the lips.

- **Shirt Lining Explosive:** Often used as an explosive for Demolitions, the agent removes the rigid lining of his shirt collar, lines it up, ignites it, and it blows on a 6- to 30-second fuse. It is bought as a one-use Strike with an Area modifier and the Triggered and Disguise power feats.

- **Silence Grenade:** These grenades project a sound cancellation wave over a 50-foot radius that prevents sounds from being heard.

- **Sleep Gas:** This is a chemical mist that creates a Stun effect with the Sleep modifier and may induce unconsciousness.

- **Sleep Gas Pellet:** A concealed weapon for the quick incapacitation of guards and similar foes.

- **Tear Gas Pellet:** The scourge of army recruits, this gas weapon incapacitates people over a wide area. The disguised tear gas dispenser is usually hidden in some innocuous object, though an agent may have a button with a highly concentrated tear gas sample that can be thrown like a grenade.

SKILL KITS

A key element of an agent's arsenal is the kit. All kits allow a trained character to perform a task at a professional level, negating the skill penalty for lack of tools. Kits also supply bonuses to certain skill checks, just like masterwork tools (*M&M,* page 137). In fact, skill kits include masterwork tools and are essentially the same thing.

The general items in a kit are listed in the description, though there may be some variation, as the GM wishes (or if a player chooses to customize). A few of the listed kits have supplies that are useful in combat, or equipment that costs points on its own, such as a re-breather or a cell phone. Where applicable, these are noted and the kit is priced accordingly.

CHEMICAL WEAPONS

Weapons	Damage	Critical	Range	Size	Cost
Laughing Gas	Nauseate 8	20	10 ft. reach	–	17
Paralyzing Ring	Paralyze 7 Poison, Disguised	20	Touch	–	22
Poison Lipstick A	Drain Strength 5 Poison, Disguised	20	Touch	–	11
Poison Lipstick B	Paralyze 7 Poison, Disguised	20	Touch	–	22
Sleep Gas	Stun 5 (Sleep)	20	10 ft. reach	–	11
Grenades and Explosives					
Exploding Cufflink	Blast 2 Explosion, Disguised	20	20 ft.	Diminutive	3
Shirt Lining Explosive	Strike 5 Explosion, Disguised	20	0	Small	7
Silence Grenades	Obscure 4 (auditory)	–	40 ft.	Diminutive	4
Sleep Gas Pellet	Ranged Stun 3 (Sleep) Explosion	20	30 ft.	Diminutive	12
Tear Gas Pellet	Dazzle 4, Nauseate 4 Explosion	–	40 ft.	Small	28

Kits are handy, but there are just some jobs (such as repairing a vehicle that has been totaled) that are too much for a kit; they require a fully stocked workshop. It is up to GMs to determine when a kit can or cannot be used, though a player can always spend a hero point to say, "That wasn't as bad as it looked at first glance," and fix a situation.

- **Arsonist's Kit:** This kit contains small quantities of blasting caps or other explosives, flammable chemicals, timers, gear to handle flammable chemicals, and a re-breather in case the arsonist gets caught in the middle of their handiwork. This kit gives a +2 to the Demolitions check to start a fire; without this kit, an Investigate check may be made on the torch to find trace evidence on their body (which may eventually convict them).

- **Burglar's Kit:** This kit contains the tools of the burglar's trade: a grappling hook attached to a 30-foot line, a glasscutter, aerosol spray (to show laser grids), tongs, a stethoscope (for safecracking), and rubber gloves. This kit gives a +2 to Disable Device checks when it comes to security systems and safes, and +2 to Climb checks when infiltrating a building from a skylight (or similar points of access).

- **Cleaner's Kit:** This kit contains chemicals to cover up fingerprints and make it impossible to find DNA evidence in blood, as well as common tools such as a carpet knife, duct tape, body bags, maps of favorite dump sites (or contact info for super-criminals capable of atomizing evidence), and disposable clothes and gloves (so the cleaner doesn't get the evidence on themselves, etc.). Without this kit, an Investigate check may be made on the cleaner to find trace evidence that connects them to the crime scene (which may eventually convict them).

- **Climber's Kit:** This kit contains a backpack, 200 feet of high-grade rope, an altimeter, a harness, rock shoes (with foot-spikes), pitons, a small hammer, markers, and an ice axe. It allows a person with a Climb skill to scale treacherous surfaces, and provides a +2 to Climb checks.

- **Computer Kit:** Used to extract data from a dead system or repair a crashed system, this kit includes basic mechanical gear to open a system, voltage testers, RAM testers, a laptop with appropriate software to integrate with systems, a portable power supply, and an EPROM burner. This software includes encryption breakers, giving a +2 bonus to Computers checks.

- **Demolitions Kit:** This kit contains tools, timers, wires, waterproof matches, and blasting caps. It is essential for using skills like Craft (or Demolitions from *Mastermind's Manual*) to set explosive charges. The actual explosives are *not* included in the kit's price; the GM decides on their equipment cost (generally three times the base damage of the desired explosion) or the agent can create explosives using Craft (chemical).

- **Disguise Kit:** This is another agent genre staple. The "impossible disguise" kit is a gimmick in some agent shows that reduces preparation time from 10 minutes to 1 minute. The disguise kit also comes with make-up (rouge, eye-liner, etc.), putty, false noses and facial hair, wigs, sponges and other make-up application devices, and theater glue.

- **Electronics' Kit:** This is a key to working with electrical systems that no electrician (or hobbyist) should travel without. This kit

SKILL KITS

Kit	Benefit	Cost
Arsonist's Kit	+2 to Demolitions checks to start fires	2
Burglar's Kit	+2 to some Disable Device and Climb checks	1
Cleaner's Kit	+2 to Investigate checks to clean an area	1
Climber's Kit	+2 to Climb checks	1
Computer Kit	+2 to Computers checks	1
Demolitions Kit	+2 to checks to set explosives	1
Disguise Kit	Reduces time to put on a pre-planned disguise	1
Electronics Kit	+2 to Craft (electronic) checks	1
First Aid Kit	+2 to Medicine checks for first aid	1
Investigator's Kit	+2 to Investigate checks	1
Medical Kit	+2 to Medicine checks	2
Repair Kit	+2 to Craft (mechanics) checks	1
Survival Kit	+2 to Survival checks	1

includes basic equipment to access a system, voltmeters and other measuring devices, splicing cables and wires, soldering irons, spare fuses and transistors, and other parts. This kit provides a +2 bonus to Craft (electronics) checks.

- **First Aid Kit:** This kit provides a +2 bonus on Medicine checks to revive, stabilize, or provide care. A first aid kit contains bandages, gauze, antiseptic, adhesive tape, scissors, latex gloves, antacids, salt tablets, eye-drops, and a splint frame.

- **Investigator's Kit:** This kit contains the tools needed to extract forensic evidence from a crime scene, and provides +2 to Investigate checks. It contains rubber gloves, tweezers, a magnifying glass, fingerprinting tools, sketchpads, plastic bags, markers and labels, duct tape, measuring tape, gunshot and blood residue chemical tests, a handheld vacuum cleaner, markers, and other supplies.

- **Medical Kit:** This kit is similar to a First Aid kit, but also contains surgical supplies (including a defibrillator) and medications. It provides a +2 bonus to Medicine skill checks. Clever characters may use supplies in a medical kit to jury-rig certain inventions or the like with the Gamemaster's permission (and possibly the use of a hero point), an additional benefit that increases the kit's cost by 1 point.

- **Repair Kit:** This contains the necessary items to fix (or at least jury rig) a vehicle that has broken down in the field, and provides +2 to Craft (mechanical) checks. It contains a wrench (also handy for conking one's enemies on the head), a crowbar, lubricant, a hammer, fuses and wires, a voltmeter, safety gloves, a screwdriver kit, oil, antifreeze, a car jack, and an air compressor.

- **Survival Kit:** This contains necessary items to survive for days in a harsh wilderness climate while you wait for help to arrive, providing a +2 to Survival checks. It includes a thermal blanket, a solar battery charger, a small radio distress beacon, a water purification kit, two weeks worth of MREs ("meals ready to eat" or field rations), signal flares, and several canteens.

SPY-GEAR

While **Chapter 7** of *Mutants & Masterminds* gives a pretty good selection of gear, there are a few odds and ends that fit well in a spy campaign. Many spy gadgets can be handled by taking an item from the general equipment list, adding the Disguised feature, and defining an everyday object as valuable equipment (such as bracelets with a magnetic lock that allows them to join together to form a set of handcuffs, a flashlight hidden in a belt buckle, a shoe that doubles as a telephone, or a camera hidden in a pair of glasses). Some other pieces of spy-gear are described here.

- **Boot Jets:** This one shot item allows a person to leap upward 30 feet for one round. Presuming they have a safe place to land, it requires an Acrobatics check (DC 10) to land safely.

- **Broom:** This wand-like device, known as a broom, "sweeps" an area for electronic devices. It allows a Search vs. Sleight of Hand check to find a bug (with no modifiers for size and concealment). Some advanced bugs are invisible to a broom.

- **Camouflage Field:** This sets up a field that blends with its surroundings, a Visual Concealment with the Blending modifier.

- **Flight Suit:** This pressurized suit is designed to relieve stress under high-pressure conditions, and comes with an oxygen supply that gives an additional 15 minutes supply (which can be useful if the cockpit seal is breached). This suit also gives a +2 bonus to Pilot checks in situations where G-forces are an issue (typically in turns).

SPY GEAR

Item	Effect	Cost
Boot Jets	Fly 30 ft. upward once.	1
Broom	Search for bugs electronically	1
Flight Suit	+2 to Pilot checks in sharp turns	2
Footwear Phone	Disguised communications link	2
Geiger Counter	Measures levels of radioactivity	1
HAZMAT Suit	Protection against hostile environments	1
Hologram Cube	Creates an image of a single subject	5
MOLLE Vest	+5 STR for carrying equipment only	1
Parachute	Float to the ground safely from great heights	1
Radio Scrambler	Obscure radio transmissions	3
Signal Flare	Anyone who looks up in the sky, spots the signal	1
Advanced Tech		
Camouflage Field	Blend into surroundings	2
Holo-Disguise	Overlay a hologram on top of you to disguise you.	8
Listening Drone	A disguised listening device, which flies around like an insect	3
Personal Cloak	Have a passive concealment cloak	8
Psi-Detector	Detect whether psionic powers have been used in the area	1
Recall Device	Press a button and go home.	9

- **Footwear Phone:** Concealed in a shoe, sneaker, or moccasin, this footwear has been a staple of spy agencies since the 1960s. Modern versions also have tap dance text messaging (via Morse code). It is also available in a wristwatch phone (without the dance messages).

- **Geiger Counter:** This is a device that measures the quantity of radioactive isotopes in an area and displays it. This device informs the user when localized radiation has reached dangerous levels.

- **HAZMAT Suit:** This suit protects the wearer from the deleterious effects of toxic waste. All hazardous chemicals, toxins, and disease-bearing wastes have no effect on the wearer.

- **Holo-Disguise:** This device is a holographic overlay that provides an instant disguise. The hologram may change skin pigmentation, hair and eye color, create scars, and change the color and/or pattern of existing clothing. It may not change the size or shape of the wearer or significantly change the texture of whatever clothing they are wearing. It is a Morph 4 effect (humanoid forms), providing a +20 bonus on Disguise checks.

- **Hologram Cube:** These cubes project a pre-programmed image in the spot where they are thrown (often that of the agent, or something frightening like a wild animal). A Notice check (DC 15) spots the transmission cube on the floor beneath the illusion. The image stored in the cube can be changed with a minute and a Computers check (DC 10).

- **Listening Drone:** They're called "bugs," and this version takes it literally. Disguised as a fly or a ladybug, a remote control sensor allows a person to fly this device around a room to get into the best location to avoid detection, store its recorded data, and then transmit it as a pulse. Unless it is being operated (or it is in the middle of a pulse transmission), a broom cannot detect this device.

- **MOLLE Vest:** The MOdular Lightweight Load-bearing Equipment (pronounced "Molly") vest, the current generation equipment vest for the army, replaces the Vietnam-era ALICE harness.

- **Parachute:** A parachute allows people to fall to the ground safely like the Slow Fall effect of Super-Movement.

- **Personal Cloak:** This device, worn on one's belt and controlled by one's belt buckle, generates a field that cloaks a person from sight and sound, a Passive Concealment effect (which drops when you make an attack, and may be restored as a free action in the *next* round).

- **Psi-Detector:** This high-tech equipment is appropriate only in campaigns where psionics have been subject to scientific analysis. It allows the user to make a Search check to detect whether psionic powers have been used in an area; every time increment that has passed on the Time and Value Progression Table applies a cumulative –1 penalty to the check.

- **Radio Scrambler:** This device blocks radio signals within a 250-foot radius, an Obscure Radio 6 effect with the flaw Range (touch).

- **Recall Device:** This high-tech device allows the wearer to teleport to one set location anywhere on earth, a Teleport 9 effect with the Long-Range flaw.

- **Signal Flare Gun:** This gun can fire a brightly glowing flare into the air. Anyone within a mile can spot the flare with a DC 10 Notice check.

VEHICLES

Name	Strength	Speed	Defense	Toughness	Size	Cost (EP/PP)
Air Vehicles						
Cloaked Gunship	40	7	6	11	Gargantuan	44/9
Collapsing Attack Helicopter	35	6	6	9	Huge/Medium	34/7
Drone Helicopter	30	5	8	9	Huge	13/3
Flying APC	45	4	8	12	Huge	35/7
Flying Motorcycle	15	5	10	8	Medium	15/3
Flying Platform	20	3	10	8	Medium	11/3
Military Transport Plane	70	7	–2	15	Awesome	21
Stealth Attack Helicopter	35	6	8	9	Huge	41/9
VSTOL Folding Jet	50	9	6	11	Gargantuan	59/12
Ground Vehicles						
Combat Motorcycle	15	5	10	10	Medium	23/5
Combat Van	35	5	8	13	Huge	39/8
Reinforced Van	35	5	8	12	Huge	11/3
Spy Vehicles						
Cloaking Truck	40	5	8	9	Huge	15/3
Disguising Sports Car	25	5	9	8	Large	10/2
Speedy Racing Car	25	5	9	8	Large	15/4
Spy Motorcycle	15	5	10	8	Medium	11/3
Spy Sports Car	25	5	9	8	Large	14/3
Spy Surveillance Van	35	5	8	9	Huge	11/3
Other Vehicles						
Armored Hovercraft	30	4	8	11	Huge	28/6
Combat Speedboat	35	5	8	10	Huge	19/4
Snowmobile	20	4	10	8	Medium	9/2
Spy Jet Ski	15	5	10	8	Medium	15/3

VEHICLES

Vehicles are among an agent's coolest toys. The Vehicles section of *Mutants & Masterminds*, **Chapter 7**, provides quite a few toys for agents to play with, but you can never have too many wonderful toys.

FEATURES

In addition to the normal features of a vehicle, some agents' vehicles also include the following options.

- **Alternate Movement (Flight):** This is a power that is added to a car or a motorcycle. It has a hidden compartment that opens up to reveal wings and small jet engines capable of propelling the vehicle through the air.

- **Alternate Movement (Swimming):** This power is added to a car, motorcycle, or airplane. When engaged, it lowers water seals to prevent it from sinking, and unlocks jet motors to propel it through the water.

- **Collapsing:** A vehicle with this unusual ability can fold up when not in use, so it occupies storage space two size categories smaller than the original vehicle.

- **Computer:** The vehicle has a powerful computer (similar to what would be found at Headquarters) or links to a powerful computer that is elsewhere. Artificial Intelligences should be bought as Constructs (allowing you to have conversations with your car).

- **Communications:** The vehicle has communications gear similar to that found in a headquarters.

- **Costume Changer:** The vehicle includes an incredible costume changer that allows a hero to change into their costume while driving in rush hour traffic.

- **Disguise:** The vehicle has modules that flip into place to disguise it (false fins and ornaments, sections with different paint-jobs, tinted windows, flipped plates), allowing it to appear as a different vehicle. This feature can be purchased multiple times to give it many different appearances.

- **Ejector Seats:** This vehicle is fitted with a seat that automatically ejects a person from the vehicle. The vehicle can be fitted with a small parachute, which allows the person to float to the ground without suffering damage, or they can fall like a stone. Being ejected from a vehicle is treated as if the target had fallen from a distance of 50 feet (see **Falling** in *Mutants & Masterminds,* **Chapter 8**), +1 DC per Speed of the Vehicle.

- **Jumping Jacks:** The vehicle is equipped with pneumatic jacks to jump over obstacles. The driver must make a Drive check, DC 10 +1/10 feet of jumping distance. The driver adds +1 to the check per Speed of the vehicle. Using jacks is a full round action.

- **Nitro Injectors:** The vehicle is equipped with a nitrous oxide boost to the engine, increasing Speed by 1. Every time the injector is used, the driver must make a DC 15 Drive check to keep the vehicle from breaking down.

- **Off Road Movement:** Vehicles tend to assume smooth roads or (in the case of tracked units) reasonably level elevations. This vehicle is also capable of off-road movement with no significant reduction in Speed.

- **Snow Movement:** Many movie chase scenes depict secret agents skiing through beautiful alpine conditions. The vehicle is capable of handling movement across snow with no reduction in speed.

- **Tire Inflators:** If this vehicle is damaged by caltrops, it can re-inflate the tires as a full round action, and continue as if undamaged.

AIR VEHICLES

- **Cloaked Gunship:** This is a military helicopter with cloaking capacity against all visual and auditory detection, as well as radio and radar, except in a round when it fires its weapons (a Conceal effect with the Passive flaw).

- **Collapsing Attack Helicopter:** This is a small military helicopter (or "chopper") with the Collapsing feature for efficient storage (changing it from huge to medium-sized when it is not in use). It

has a machine gun (Autofire Blast 6) mounted on a swiveling forward mount, in addition to its collapsing ability.

- **Drone Helicopter:** This is a normal helicopter with a camera and speaker system and remote control. It is good for villains who want to pick up a hero and fly them to their lair, but who doesn't want to risk exposing a pilot who can be captured and interrogated.

- **Flying APC:** Flying APCs appear to be normal troop carriers, but when they need to reach targets in remote or rugged terrain, they sprout wings and fly over obstacles. They have a forward mounted blaster cannon (Blast 6, Explosion).

- **Flying Motorcycle:** These appear to be normal motorcycles, but can sprout small wings and a jet from the exhaust, allowing them to fly.

- **Flying Platform:** This is a relatively slow-moving two-man anti-gravity vehicle that serves more as a mobile firing platform for agents than a mode of transportation. Agents firing from this platform are treated as if they were under cover.

- **Military Transport Plane:** This is the largest aircraft in the world, transporting armor, heavy equipment, or enough supplies to meet the needs of an army.

- **Stealth Attack Helicopter:** A smaller version of the cloaked gunship, it is invisible to visual, auditory, radio, and radar detection, except in a round when it fires a weapon. It has a machine gun (Autofire Blast 6) mounted as a forward cannon.

- **VSTOL Folding Fighter Jets:** These Vertical/Short Take-Off and Landing fighter jets are designed to land and be stored in a small, urban space. They can take off from any large helipad-sized space, and can fold into the size of a traffic helicopter. Once they become airborne, they function like any other jet aircraft.

GROUND VEHICLES

- **Combat Motorcycle:** This impressive machine (and favorite of gung-ho agents everywhere) is similar to a sports motorcycle, but has special added features: inflatable studded tires and a reinforced suspension that allow it to transform into an all-terrain vehicle and a front-mounted Blast 5 cannon.

- **Combat Van:** This special van has a built-in Disguise (easy to remove paint and plate changer), a concealed mounted autocannon (Blast 8, Autofire), communications equipment, and a parachute.

- **Reinforced Van:** This van is a cheap way to transport a super-powered prisoner. It usually contains heavy shackles and restraints to keep the prisoner in line.

SPY VEHICLES

Spy vehicles are identical to normal vehicles, but have various features to fit the vehicles found in the genre.

- **Cloaking Truck:** This is a transport vehicle with Passive Visual and Auditory Concealment (at a cost of an extra 6 points). Other than this, it is an ordinary small truck that can transport people and goods without being detected.

- **Disguising Car:** This is a normal car bought with the Disguise feature, giving it the ability to turn into a completely different looking vehicle, making it a perfect getaway car. It also comes complete with Hidden Compartments.

- **Speedy Racing Car:** This racecar has many special options, including Hidden Compartments, Communications, Jumping Jacks, Low-Light Vision, Navigation System, Off-Road (a buzz-saw instantly clears trees out of its path), and Alternate Movement (Swimming).

- **Spy Motorcycle:** This is identical to the motorcycle in the Vehicles section of *Mutants & Masterminds* but with two added *Features*: caltrops and a smokescreen.

- **Spy Sports Car:** This sleek sports vehicle includes a number of options you won't find on the factory floor: Alarm, Ejector Seats, Navigation System, Nitro Injector, Oil Slick, and Smoke Screen.

- **Spy Surveillance Van:** These vehicles are used for stakeout missions. They come with their own communications (with visible antennae) and parabolic microphones to overhear conversations, as well as the Disguise feature.

OTHER VEHICLES

Cars, trucks, and planes are not the only vehicles used by spies and agents. Others include:

- **Armored Hovercraft:** This is an amphibious craft designed to function equally well in water or on land (essentially giving it Super-Movement [water walking]). It is otherwise identical to an APC, including its main weapon (which is bought as Blast 6, Explosion). It is also set up so the onboard agents can fire their personal weapons from behind the cover of armor.

- **Combat Speedboat:** This fast speedboat has an armored hull and is augmented with a forward mounted blast cannon (Blast 5).

- **Snowmobile:** Designed to navigate snow-bound landscapes where no other vehicles can travel, snowmobiles are part off-road vehicle, part motorcycle. They cannot run on non-snowy surfaces, but perform admirably in their native conditions.

- **Spy Jet Ski:** This is a motorcycle of the water. This version comes equipped with rear-firing mines (Blast 7, Explosion 2, Limited to Pursuers); without this weapon, the vehicle costs 6 equipment points.

HEADQUARTERS

The headquarters rules in **Chapter 7** of *Mutants & Masterminds* apply as well to agency headquarters as they do to superhero and supervillain bases. Nonetheless, there are a few additional features that can be added to an agency headquarters to better reflect some of the exotic facilities in comic books and spy movies.

ANIMAL PENS

This base contains holding pens for animal companions. These facilities are a source of animal minions, particularly good for steeds (for the good guys) or gladiatorial sport (for the bad guys). Ride checks on mounts from an agent's headquarters are made at +1 bonus, as the agent is presumed to be familiar with the animal and has trained with it (this bonus is only conferred on Trained riders). Similarly, Handle Animal checks on animals from the facility receive a +2 bonus.

COVER FACILITY

Sometimes, it's best to hide in plain sight. In this case, the headquarters contains a large section that is dedicated to another business (which can be as mundane as a corporate bank headquarters or a security firm, or an inconspicuous office of the US Department of Agriculture). This base should be considered Concealed against Gather Information checks. This feature has the added bonus of providing paying employment (*and* health benefits—yes, some insurers do cover laser burns for agents) as well as a place from which to funnel funds to cover the operation.

DEATHTRAP

Villains, they love the death trap. While a good combat simulator can be turned into a decent deathtrap, there's no substitute for the real thing. This may be a room that fills up with water, spiked walls that crush victims, table straps with a descending scythe attached to a pendulum, or a giant Chinese puzzle where pulling the wrong link will electrocute people. Although the GM is welcome to vary the skill or ability that's challenged, as a general rule it requires an Escape Artist check (DC 15) to escape from the deathtrap, and even then, the player characters have to spend time to escape.

Don't be fooled by the name. For Silver Age campaigns, deathtraps actually serve as delaying tactics, *not* killing machines. The base time to escape a death trap is one hour. Every +5 over the required DC improves the escape by one level on the Time and Value Progression Table (M&M, page 70); every –5 that the check fails by increases the escape time by one level, giving the villain that much more time to carry out his scheme!

GLADIATOR ARENA

Send them into the arena of sport! Force our helpless heroes to battle the mind controlled, mutated locals! When your agents get bored of everyday villainy, what better way to pass the day than to force the heroes to take off their shirts, don leather shorts, and fight each other to the death? The Gladiator Arena has no practical function, except to entertain the agents and stroke the local commander's ego, nor any game-meaningful effect, except as a kind of deathtrap.

INTERROGATION CHAMBER

The base contains a team of interrogators and equipment to conduct detailed interviews with captured prisoners or suspected double agents. If an agent brings a prisoner back to a headquarters equipped with an interrogation chamber, the agent receives a +2 bonus to Intimidate checks for interrogation and torture. It requires a day of interrogation to receive this bonus.

PARADE GROUNDS

The parade grounds are a place where agents train and bond together. Parade grounds teach teamwork and camaraderie, and allow agents to look good when they march in front of visiting brass. A headquarters with Parade Grounds produces troops that work well together: the benefits of the Teamwork feat apply to all agents at the HQ when fighting on their home turf.

SELF-DESTRUCT

A villainous headquarters often comes equipped with an autodestruct system. A self-destruct device does double the campaign's power level damage to any unfortunate who is still in the HQ when it explodes. Villains use this feature to stage mysterious disappearances, only to resurface in a later adventure.

THINK-TANK

The base has a team of specialists going over data brought in, discussing it, and developing theories. Working with a headquarters think-tank for a day provides a +2 bonus on Gather Information, Investigate, or Knowledge checks to answer a particular question.

VEHICLES AND HEADQUARTERS

With mobile headquarters, the line between vehicle and headquarters can be a blurry one. A headquarters can be turned into a mobile base using the Power feature to acquire a movement effect. That way, you can have mobile islands, flying zeppelins, mobile asteroids of death, and even more exotic headquarters.

SAMPLE HEADQUARTERS

Gamemasters can use the following sample headquarters as examples of HQs in an *Agents of Freedom* game.

AEGIS FLYING FORTRESS — HEADQUARTERS

Toughness: 15; *Size:* Large; *Speed:* 8 (air); *Features:* Communications, Computer, Defense System, Gym, Hangar, Holding Cell, Infirmary, Isolated, Library, Living Space, Security System, Staff.

Cost: Abilities 12 + Features 20 = 32 equipment points

CULT HQ IN AN ANTIQUE STORE — HEADQUARTERS

Toughness: 5; *Size:* Small; *Features:* Computers, Cover Facility, Library, Living Space

Cost: Abilities 0 + Features 4 = 4 equipment points

OVERTHROW HQ IN A UNIVERSITY — HEADQUARTERS

Toughness: 10; *Size:* Small; *Features:* Computers, Communications, Cover Facility, Defense System, Holding Cell, Library, Living Space, Think-Tank

Cost: Abilities 1 + Features 8 = 9 equipment points

SCIONS OF SOBEK FLYING PYRAMID — HEADQUARTERS

Toughness: 15; *Size:* Huge; *Speed:* 5 (air); *Features:* Animal Pen, Death Trap, Defense System, Hangar (for flying sphinxes), Holding Cell, Invisibility (all visual senses; *Flaw:* Can't be invisible while in Flight), Isolated, Library, Living Space, Security System.

Cost: Abilities 15 + Features 10 = 25 equipment points

AGENT ARCHETYPES

For sheer speed, nothing beats an archetype package to quickly choose a character to play and get into the game. As with other genres, the agent genre has its own niches, presented here. These are appropriate for heroes, heroic NPCs, and some villains; supporting character archetypes and other villain archetypes can be found in **Chapter 6**. Give the hero a gender, a name, a codename, and a quick description, and you're ready to run.

Skills are listed with the number of ranks listed after the skill name, and the total skill bonus listed in parenthesis. For example, Climb 6 (+7) means the character has six ranks of Climb and a total bonus of +7 when making Climb checks.

These characters are all built on power level 5 and 100 power points, the default levels for an *Agents of Freedom* campaign. Adjust their abilities and power point totals accordingly for other levels of play.

THE CHARACTER NICHE

Even more than most genres, the agent genre is dependent on the enforcement of niches to convey its personality and to make players feel like part of the team. With the exception of the leads (the commander or the rebellious second in command), there are few generalists in an *Agents of Freedom* game.

In a baseline *Agents of Freedom* game, heroes can come from all walks of life, blending with little difficulty into a cultural and professional mosaic. They can range from respectable law enforcement roles

like profilers and hostage negotiators, to thinly veiled excuses for eye candy ("This TV series is about fashion models who work as secret agents") or action sequences ("after accidentally killing his teammate, a psychotic ex-college football star now finds himself a secret agent with a *license* to kill!")

The table on page 35 details a list of a few archetypes found in comic books and cartoons suitable as niches.

NICHE BASICS

The basic rules of a specialty niche are simple: there can be only one. A generalist is like Robin Hood; a specialist is like Little John. Robin Hood is a pretty strong human being, but he's not stronger than Little John. No scenario should ever arise where Robin Hood is presented as being a rival for Little John when it comes to strength. Nor should Friar Tuck (who fills the pious man and quarterstaff master niches) ever be presented as John's physical equal. There should be no rivals in the niche, among the player characters or supporting cast.

At the start of the campaign, players should decide whether they are going to play a generalist role like the Roughneck Commando or the Field Investigator, or a more niche role like the ones listed above. In the case of specialists, players should agree to either respect another character's niche, or have the two characters competing as rivals in the same niche, engaging in friendly competition. In this case, both players should agree to share the niche and enjoy the rivalry. If one of the play-

NICHES AND ULTIMATE EFFORT

Niche protection in an *Agents of Freedom* series should also extend to the Ultimate Effort feat (and similar feats related to the character's niche). In particular, only the character in that niche should be able to have Ultimate Effort for it. If he or she does not have it, then *nobody* has it. So, for example, a character in the Strong Guy niche could have Ultimate Effort (Strength checks), but nobody else among the player characters or supporting cast could, even if the Strong Guy chose not to take that feat, just because it belongs to his niche.

Adversaries occupying the same niche *can* take Ultimate Effort for it, but should generally only have it if the player character does, and should not if the hero doesn't.

DASHING SPY

POWER LEVEL 5

STR	DEX	CON	INT	WIS	CHA
+1	+3	+1	+2	+1	+3
12	16	12	14	12	16

TOUGHNESS	FORTITUDE	REFLEX	WILL
+4/+1*	+5	+7	+7

*Flat-footed

"NOBODY DOES IT BETTER..."

Skills: Acrobatics 4 (+7), Bluff 4 (+7), Climb 2 (+3), Computers 3 (+5), Concentration 4 (+5), Craft (electronics) 1 (+3), Craft (mechanical) 1 (+3), Diplomacy 2 (+5), Disable Device 6 (+8), Disguise 1 (+4), Drive 1 (+4), Escape Artist 3 (+6), Gamble 3 (+5), Gather Information 3 (+6), Intimidate 2 (+5), Investigate 4 (+6), Knowledge (art) 1 (+3), Knowledge (current events) 2 (+4), Knowledge (popular culture) 2 (+4), Knowledge (tactics) 4 (+6), Knowledge (technology) 2 (+4), Notice 4 (+5), Pilot 2 (+5), Ride 2 (+5), Search 6 (+8), Sense Motive 5 (+6), Sleight of Hand 2 (+5), Stealth 2 (+5), Survival 4 (+5), Swim 2 (+3)

Feats: Attack Focus (ranged) 1, Attractive, Benefit (rank) 1, Defensive Roll 3, Equipment 4, Evasion, Improved Disarm, Improved Initiative, Luck 2, Quick Draw, Ultimate Save (Reflex), Uncanny Dodge (auditory), Well-Informed

Equipment: Give the Dashing Spy up to 20 equipment points worth of equipment (particularly spy gear).

Combat: Attack +6 (melee), +7 (ranged), Damage +1 (unarmed), Grapple +7, Defense +6 (+3 flat-footed), Knockback –2, Initiative +7

Abilities 22 + Skills 21 (84 ranks) + Feats 18 + Powers 0 + Combat 24 + Saves 14 = 100

You are a glamorous lone wolf who routinely travels the globe in the service of your country. You use your good looks and charm to get into interesting situations, and your skill, combat training, and blind luck to get out of them. You often work alone, or with a good-looking partner of the opposite sex, as you confront a bizarre assortment of menaces.

Usually, your archenemy is a mastermind with plans for world domination and destruction, and you fight assorted goons and thugs along the way - in the most glamorous of backdrops, of course. You're often an old friend of Roughneck Commando agents, but prefer infiltration missions to assaults.

The Infiltrator: A variant on the Dashing Spy is the not-quite-so-dashing Infiltrator. Like the Dashing Spy, you specialize in getting into the enemy camp and extracting information. Trade the Attractive feat and Gamble skill for ranks in Bluff, Disable Device, Disguise, Gather Information, Notice, or Search.

FEMME FATALE

POWER LEVEL 5

STR	DEX	CON	INT	WIS	CHA
+1	+3	+1	+3	+1	+4
12	16	12	16	12	18

TOUGHNESS	FORTITUDE	REFLEX	WILL
+4/+1*	+4	+8	+4

*flat-footed

"I'M NOT A BAD GIRL. I'M A VERY GOOD GIRL... IN A VERY BAD BUSINESS."

Skills: Acrobatics 4 (+7), Bluff 5 (+9), Climb 2 (+3), Computers 2 (+5), Concentration 5 (+6), Diplomacy 5 (+9), Disable Device 5 (+8), Disguise 5 (+9), Drive 2 (+5), Escape Artist 5 (+8), Gather Information 5 (+9), Handle Animal 1 (+5), Intimidate 1 (+5), Investigate 5 (+8), Knowledge (art) 2 (+5), Knowledge (current events) 5 (+8), Knowledge (popular culture) 2 (+5), Knowledge (streetwise) 4 (+7), Knowledge (tactics) 2 (+5), Notice 5 (+6), Perform (dancing or song) 2 (+6), Perform (singing) 2 (+6), Pilot 2 (+5), Search 5 (+8), Sense Motive 3 (+4), Sleight of Hand 5 (+8), Stealth 5 (+8), Survival 2 (+3), Swim 2 (+3)

Feats: Attack Focus (ranged) 2, Attractive, Benefit (rank) 1, Defensive Roll 3, Distract (Bluff), Elusive Target, Equipment 5, Fascinate (Diplomacy), Improved Defense, Taunt, Well-Informed

Equipment: Give the Femme Fatale up to 25 equipment points worth of equipment (particularly spy gear).

Combat: Attack +5 (melee), +7 (ranged), Damage +1 (unarmed), Grapple +6, Defense +5 (+3 flat-footed), Knockback –2, Initiative + 3

Abilities 26 + Skills 25 (100 ranks) + Feats 18 + Powers 0 + Combat 20 + Saves 11 = 100

You are the woman everyone looks up to (whether they want to or not). People may judge you for your appearance, but your skills are almost unrivalled. You're the go-to gal for infiltration and sabotage as well as seduction. Your work requires skill and luck as well as beauty, or you won't survive. Your opposite number is the dashing spy, with whom you frequently hook up as a rival and romantic interest. In an agency, you're rather distant from everyone except the commander; heroic female agents tend to be the Modern Day Amazon variety of the Roughneck Commando. (The two archetypes often view each other with a mix of discomfort and respect.)

The femme fatale comes in three flavors: hero, freelance, and villain. Heroic femme fatales are confident, sexy women who hide an inner pain over the emotional toll the job takes. They are frequently a double—or even triple—agent. The villainous version is often their agency's most competent operative, who hangs with the less competent so she can make sarcastic quips or play games with enemy agents (or because daddy's a criminal mastermind she's desperately trying to please). The freelance version is a ballsy, hard as nails, bad girl mercenary whose only soft spot is for one of the heroes, and even then she'll leave him to flounder if she's in a bad (or playful) mood.

FIELD INVESTIGATOR

POWER LEVEL 5

STR	DEX	CON	INT	WIS	CHA
+1	+1	+1	+4	+2	+3
12	13	13	18	15	16

TOUGHNESS	FORTITUDE	REFLEX	WILL
+5/+3/+1*	+5	+5	+5

*+3 without armor or flat-footed, +1 for both

Skills: Bluff 4 (+7), Computers 6 (+10), Concentration 6 (+8), Diplomacy 4 (+7), Drive 4 (+5), Gather Information 8 (+11), Intimidate 2 (+5), Investigate 8 (+12), Knowledge (behavioral sciences) 4 (+8), Knowledge (current events) 4 (+8), Knowledge (life sciences) 4 (+8), Knowledge (physical sciences) 4 (+8), Knowledge (popular culture) 2 (+6), Knowledge (streetwise) 4 (+8), Medicine 4 (+6), Notice 6 (+8), Profession (investigator) 8 (+10), Search 8 (+12), Sense Motive 6 (+8), Sleight of Hand 4 (+5), Stealth 4 (+5)

Feats: Assessment, Benefit (rank) 2, Connected, Contacts, Defensive Roll 2, Equipment 5, Improvised Tools, Teamwork, Ultimate Effort (Investigate), Well-Informed

Equipment: Light pistol (+3 damage), bulletproof vest (+2 Toughness), handcuffs, commlink, investigator's kit (Investigate +2), plus 9 more points in equipment.

Combat: Attack +5, Damage +1 (unarmed), Grapple +6, Defense +5 (+3 flat-footed), Knockback –2, Initiative +1

Abilities 27 + Skills 25 (100 ranks) + Feats 17 + Powers 0 + Combat 20 + Saves 11 = 100

"I'M FROM THE GOVERNMENT AND I WANT TO FIND OUT THE TRUTH... DON'T LOOK AT ME LIKE THAT."

You are the flip side of the commando. You're the unflappable agent who goes into the field, interviews witnesses, and gathers evidence. As a modern day diviner, you tell macabre jokes about the body parts you find, and then use the clues to track down killers, drug dealers, and other criminal scum. You have a number of useful medical and scientific skills, and can substitute for field medics or lab technicians in a pinch.

In an agency game, you're also a capable combatant—everyone needs to be—though not quite in the same league as the Roughneck Commando.

HARD-NOSED COMMANDER

POWER LEVEL 5

STR	DEX	CON	INT	WIS	CHA
+2	+1	+2	+1	+2	+3
14	12	14	12	14	16

TOUGHNESS	FORTITUDE	REFLEX	WILL
+5/+3/+2*	+7	+5	+7

*Without armor, flat-footed

"IF THERE'S ANYONE HERE WHO WANTS TO LIVE FOREVER... THE LINE FORMS IN ANOTHER STATE!"

Skills: Acrobatics 3 (+4), Bluff 4 (+7), Climb 2 (+4), Computers 4 (+5), Diplomacy 2 (+5), Disable Device 4 (+5), Drive 4 (+5), Gather Information 4 (+7), Intimidate 6 (+9), Investigate 6 (+7), Knowledge (behavioral sciences) 3 (+4), Knowledge (civics) 3 (+4), Knowledge (current event) 2 (+3), Knowledge (streetwise) 2 (+3), Knowledge (tactics) 3 (+4), Notice 4 (+6), Profession (agent) 6 (+8), Search 5 (+6), Sense Motive 3(+5), Sleight of Hand 2 (+3), Stealth 4 (+5), Survival 2 (+4), Swim 2 (+4).

Feats: All-out Attack, Assessment, Benefit (rank) 5, Connected, Contacts, Defensive Roll, Evasion, Equipment 5, Fast Overrun, Fearless, Inspire, Leadership, Move-by Action, Power Attack, Precise Shot, Teamwork

Equipment: Blaster rifle (+8 damage), armored uniform (+2 Toughness), handcuffs, commlink.

Combat: Attack +5, Damage +2 (unarmed), Grapple +7, Defense +5 (+3 flat-footed), Knockback –3, Initiative +1

Abilities 22 + Skills 20 (80 ranks) + Feats 24 + Powers 0 + Combat 20 + Saves 14 = 100

You are the man behind the desk, the hardened father figure who commands the force, administering the local cell, or even the whole damn organization.

You do not live a happy life, spending most of your time arguing with idiotic bureaucrats who don't give you enough support, and screaming at snot-nosed agents who haven't seen one-tenth of what you've seen, yet think they can question your orders (and on occasion, your character). They may call you a "stone-hearted bastard," but you care more than anyone can know about your organization and your agents; they just can't read the concern on your granite-hard face.

Hard-nosed commanders do get involved in the action; they're very "hands on" leaders. They lead by example, and that example often involves leading the charge into an enemy nest with gun in hand. They're also extremely honest. When a hard-nosed commander heads an agency, its integrity is almost always beyond question.

HEROIC EVERYMAN

POWER LEVEL 5

STR	DEX	CON	INT	WIS	CHA
+1	+3	+1	+1	+3	+1
12	16	13	13	17	13

TOUGHNESS	FORTITUDE	REFLEX	WILL
+3/+1*	+4	+9	+6

*Flat-footed

"I DON'T CARE IF I LOOK LIKE THE WORLD'S MOST NOTORIOUS ASSASSIN! GET OUT OF MY LIVING ROOM!"

Skills: Acrobatics 2 (+5), Bluff 6 (+7), Climb 2 (+3), Computers 4 (+5), Concentration 4 (+7), Diplomacy 6 (+7), Disguise 2 (+3), Drive 2 (+5), Gather Information 6 (+7), Intimidate 1 (+2), Knowledge (current events) 8 (+9), Knowledge (history) 2 (+3), Knowledge (popular culture) 8 (+9), Knowledge (technology) 2 (+3), Notice 4 (+7), Perform (oratory) 2 (+3), Profession (choose one) 5 (+8), Search 4 (+5), Sense Motive 6 (+9), Sleight of Hand 5 (+8), Stealth 5 (+8), Swim 2 (+3)

Feats: Beginner's Luck, Benefit (rank) 1, Defensive Roll 2, Distract (Bluff, Intimidate), Dodge Focus 2, Elusive Target, Equipment 4, Evasion 2, Hide in Plain Sight, Improvised Tools, Inspire 2, Luck 5, Taunt, Uncanny Dodge (auditory).

Equipment: Blaster pistol (+5 damage), armored uniform (+2 Toughness), handcuffs, commlink, plus 6 points of additional equipment.

Combat: Attack +4, Damage +1 (unarmed), Grapple +5, Defense +6 (+2 flat-footed), Knockback –1, Initiative +3

Abilities 24 + Skills 22 (88 ranks) + Feats 26 + Powers 0 + Combat 16 + Saves 12 = 100

The Heroic Everyman is a common archetype in the movies; you're the average person who was forced to join the agency by circumstance. You're not a secret agent. You're not a hero. Maybe you're an actor, a reporter, or an everyday guy that somehow stumbled into a larger (and much more dangerous) world. Perhaps your girlfriend was secretly working for SHADOW, and AEGIS hopes you'll remember a critical clue (and SHADOW wants to shut you up for good). Maybe you're the perfect double of a murdered assassin who was going to receive data that could save the free world from disaster, and AEGIS wants you to impersonate the assassin. Maybe you should have kept your mouth shut when you mentioned that your brother's bookie has an uncanny resemblance to one of the five most wanted terrorists in the country.

Fortunately, you have more natural talent than anybody suspected, as well as enough luck to refloat a battleship. As you experience your new life, you'll discover things about yourself you never dreamed, and (despite having little to no training) you'll become a valuable member of a team defending freedom and democracy against the forces of evil, bringing the perspective of the average Joe into the agency. Sometimes, though, your lack of seriousness and your tendency to treat the agency like "the movies" drives the agents around you up the proverbial wall.

MARTIAL ARTS EXPERT

POWER LEVEL 5

STR	DEX	CON	INT	WIS	CHA
+2	+5	+2	+1	+2	+1
14	20	14	12	15	12

TOUGHNESS	FORTITUDE	REFLEX	WILL
+4/+2*	+7	+10	+8

*flat-footed

"MY KUNG FU IS BETTER THAN YOUR... UH.... LACK OF KUNG FU!"

Skills: Acrobatics 8 (+13), Bluff 4 (+5), Climb 6 (+8), Computers 2 (+3), Concentration 6 (+8), Craft (mechanical) 2 (+3), Diplomacy 2 (+3), Disable Device 4 (+5), Disguise 2 (+3), Drive 2 (+7), Escape Artist 6 (+11), Gather Information 2 (+3), Handle Animal 2 (+3), Intimidate 6 (+7), Investigate 2 (+3), Knowledge (current events) 2 (+3), Knowledge (streetwise) 2 (+3), Knowledge (tactics) 4 (+5), Medicine 2 (+4), Notice 6 (+8), Ride 2 (+7), Search 2 (+3), Sense Motive 4 (+6), Sleight of Hand 4 (+9), Stealth 4 (+9), Survival 2 (+4), Swim 2 (+4)

Feats: Benefit (rank) 1, Defensive Attack, Defensive Roll 2, Equipment 2, Improved Block, Improved Critical (unarmed), Improved Disarm, Improved Grapple, Improved Sunder, Instant Up, Power Attack, Takedown Attack

Equipment: Nunchaku (+2 damage bonus), commlink, plus 6 points of other equipment.

Combat: Attack +5, Damage +2 (unarmed), +4 (nunchaku), Grapple +7, Defense +5 (+3 flat-footed), Knockback –2, Initiative +5

Abilities 27 + Skills 23 (92 ranks) + Feats 14 + Powers 0 + Combat 20 + Saves 16 = 100

You are the team's hand-to-hand combat master, a journeyman practitioner of the ancient Chinese fighting art, kung fu. Though your past is clouded in a darkness from which you wish to hide, you still pursue truth, justice, and the light. How you ended up fighting alongside a bunch of paramilitary yahoos is anyone's guess—perhaps you were recruited to infiltrate a SHADOW blood sport ring and everyone liked you.

Needless to say, this archetype is more of a Silver Age (or cartoon) staple than one appropriate for a modern military game. Nonetheless, armies have employed civilian combat instructors, and playing an Asian Zen master (or a modern martial arts student) as a fish out of water can be funny. The Martial Arts Expert is also the subject of a particular style of campaign (see **Sub-Genres** in **Chapter 6**).

The listed version of the archetype uses the Kung-fu Fighting Style from the *Mastermind's Manual*, **Chapter 4**. Other martial art styles are equally applicable; substitute another fighting style package as desired. Quite often, the Martial Arts Expert's niche and style are dictated by the chosen fighting style. Asian unarmed combat styles like kung fu or karate tend to fit the baseline archetype, while variants include the sumo wrestler or pro-wrestling star turned agent (swap the archetype's Str and Dex scores) and the weapon master (exchange Improved Grapple for Attack Focus or Attack Specialization).

ROUGHNECK COMMANDO

POWER LEVEL 5

STR	DEX	CON	INT	WIS	CHA
+3	+2	+3	+1	+1	+0
16	14	16	12	12	10

TOUGHNESS	FORTITUDE	REFLEX	WILL
+5/+4/+3*	+8	+6	+6

*+4 flat-footed or without armor, +3 for both

Skills: Acrobatics 4 (+6), Bluff 2 (+2), Climb 4 (+7), Computers 2 (+3), Craft (mechanical) 4 (+5), Craft (structural) 4 (+5), Diplomacy 2 (+2), Disable Device 2 (+3), Drive 3 (+5), Gather Information 3 (+3), Intimidate 6 (+6), Investigate 6 (+7), Knowledge (behavioral sciences) 3 (+4), Knowledge (civics) 2 (+3), Knowledge (current events) 1 (+2), Knowledge (streetwise) 2 (+3), Knowledge (tactics) 2 (+3), Medicine 2 (+3), Notice 6 (+7), Profession (agent) 6 (+7), Search 4 (+5), Sense Motive 2 (+3), Sleight of Hand 2 (+4), Stealth 4 (+6), Survival 4 (+5), Swim 2 (+5).

Feats: All-out Attack, Assessment, Attack Focus (ranged) 2, Benefit (rank) 1, Defensive Attack, Defensive Roll, Equipment 5, Evasion, Improved Aim, Improved Critical (rifle), Improved Grab, Improved Overrun, Improved Pin, Inspire, Leadership, Move-by Action, Prone Fighting, Set-Up, Sneak Attack, Stunning Attack, Teamwork.

Equipment: Blaster rifle (+8 damage), fragmentation grenades (Blast Explosion 5), armored uniform (+1 Toughness), handcuffs, commlink.

Combat: Attack +5 (melee), +7 (ranged), Damage +3 (unarmed), Grapple +8, Defense +5 (+3 flat-footed), Knockback –2, Initiative +2

Abilities 20 + Skills 21 (84 ranks) + Feats 26 + Powers 0 + Combat 20 + Saves 13 = 100

"CAPTURE TALOS? GOOD AS DONE, SIR."

You are the backbone of all *Agents of Freedom* campaigns. It's you who straps on the suit and carries the big guns into battle. You're young, dedicated to your cause, and a little too cocky for your own good. You treat the Hard-Nosed Commander like your parent, but that doesn't keep you from arguing in their face like a hostile adolescent.

This archetype incorporates many sub-types. The three that are most likely to be the lead character are "the Hot-Headed Lieutenant," "the Modern Day Amazon," and "The Specialist".

The Hot-Headed Lieutenant is the Hard-Nosed Commander in training. You've got a chip on your shoulder that's the size of Montana, you're impulsive to the point of recklessness, but with a little seasoning, you have the potential for greatness.

The Modern Day Amazon is the butt-kicking female. You're the woman who is as capable as any man, and are often the love interest of the Hot-Headed lieutenant and a daughter figure to the Hard-Nosed Commander (metaphorically or even literally).

The Specialist is appropriate to games inspired by agencies in 1980s and '90s animated series where people were agents based on the weapons they carried, the vehicle they drove, or their favored environment (the latter is presented as an archetype in the **Supporting Characters** section in **Chapter 6**). Weapon specialists should trade a combat feat for Attack Specialization in their favored weapon.

SPYMASTER

POWER LEVEL 5

STR	DEX	CON	INT	WIS	CHA
+1	+1	+1	+4	+4	+3
12	12	12	18	18	16

TOUGHNESS	FORTITUDE	REFLEX	WILL
+3/+1*	+4	+6	+8

*flat-footed

"AGENT JONES, YOUR ENERGY WOULD BE BETTER SPENT FIGHTING THE ENEMIES OF YOUR COUNTRY."

Skills: Bluff 8 (+11), Climb 2 (+3), Computers 6 (+10), Concentration 6 (+10), Diplomacy 8 (+11), Disable Device 2 (+6), Disguise 2 (+5), Drive 2 (+3), Escape Artist 2 (+3), Gather Information 8 (+11), Intimidate 8 (+11), Investigate 4 (+8), Knowledge (behavioral sciences) 6 (+10), Knowledge (current events) 2 (+6), Knowledge (tactics) 6 (+10), Notice 6 (+10), Pilot 2 (+3), Ride 2 (+3), Search 6 (+10), Sense Motive 8 (+12), Sleight of Hand 2 (+3), Stealth 2 (+3), Survival 2 (+6), Swim 2 (+3)

Feats: Assessment, Benefit (rank) 4, Contacts, Defensive Roll 2, Equipment 4, Luck, Well-Informed

Equipment: Give the Spymaster 20 points of equipment, particularly spy-gear.

Combat: Attack +5, Damage +1, Grapple +6, Defense +5 (+3 flat-footed), Initiative +1

Abilities 28 + Skills 26 (104 ranks) + Feats 14 + Powers 0 + Combat 20 + Saves 12 = 100

The Spymaster is the flipside of the Hard-Nosed Commander, an enigma who puts the agency's goals well ahead of the agents' well being. They are a manipulative bastard who is not to be trusted; they'll send you into certain death and lie to your face about the mission, playing on your fears and your hopes and your anger like an expert violinist. Their saving grace is they live by the same rules; under the right circumstances, The Spymaster will die for the agency just as quickly as they sends agents to their doom.

Although not the Bad Ass Supreme like the Hard-Nosed Commander, the Spymaster also has surprising combat skills. Of course, it's never explains where or how they were acquired.

Spymasters rarely coexist with Hard-Nosed Commanders, unless they're part of an enigmatic council of superiors overseeing him. Spymasters are usually more appropriate as NPCs than player characters.

CHARACTER NICHES

NICHES	PRIMARY SKILL(S), FEATS(S)	NICHES	PRIMARY SKILL(S), FEATS(S)
Ace Pilot	Pilot	Grizzled Veteran Cop	Investigate, Knowledge (streetwise)
Actor Turned Agent	Bluff	Hostage Negotiator	Diplomacy, Knowledge (behavioral science)
Big, Mean Looking Guy	Intimidate	Lab Geek	Investigate, Knowledge (science)
Chaplain	Knowledge (theology/philosophy)	Master of Disguise	Bluff, Disguise
Circus Acrobat/Gymnast Turned Special Agent	Acrobatics	Model Turned Agent	Perform (acting), Attractive
Combat Engineer	Craft (structure)	Occult Advisor	Knowledge (arcane)
Communications Specialist	Search, Knowledge (technology)	Profiler	Knowledge (behavioral science), Gather Information
Computer Hacker	Computers, Knowledge (technology)	Reformed Cat Burglar	Search, Stealth
Con Artist/Face Man	Bluff, Diplomacy	Reformed Gang Member	Knowledge (streetwise)
Cowboy Turned Special Agent	Ride, Animal Handler	Rock Star Turned Special Agent	Diplomacy, Perform (singing or instrument)
Crusading Journalist	Gather Information, Contacts	Sentry	Notice, Search
Defense Analyst	Gather Information, Well Informed	Sharpshooter	Weapon Specialization
Dog Trainer/K9 Unit	Handle Animal	Stage Magician Turned Special Agent	Knowledge (arcane), Sleight of Hand
Environmental Specialist	Survival	Strongman Agent	Strength
Ex-Football Player	Fast Overrun, Improved Overrun	Survivalist	Survival, Track
Field Medic	Medicine, Concentration, Knowledge (life science)	Wrestler Turned Special Agent	Acrobatics, Intimidate, Wrestling Package
Grease Monkey	Repair, Craft (mechanical)		

ers is not having fun, the Gamemaster should give them the option to play a character filling another niche.

The important thing for the Gamemaster is to encourage players to develop interesting characters and to manipulate the plot so it services that character's niche in ways that make for a more exciting story. Niches exist to be serviced. If a player is running an Arctic Environment Specialist, and the Gamemaster keeps all of the stories set in the deserts of the American southwest, that character's niche isn't being served. Likewise,

every few sessions, the Dog Trainer agent should encounter a wolf, a pack of wild dogs, a dog infected with rabies, or a mean junkyard dog.

It is also possible to run a campaign with every agent belonging to a niche, so the PCs are all members of a squad of secret agents posing as a circus troupe or a traveling promotion of pro wrestlers, for example. It's corny, but it's a way of keeping the players together, and if they all enjoy the role, then it can make for an entertaining campaign.

UNWRITTEN RULES, WRITTEN

The agent genre is a heroic one. Often, it's a gritty one where bad things happen to good people, and some villains have complex motivations for their actions, but when all is said and done, the Good Guys are good guys, and the Bad Guys are pretty bad. Beyond that simplest of pulp dichotomies, there are a number of niceties that need to be observed, the unwritten rules of the genre. This section talks about them and how to apply them, if you wish.

THE BADASS AND HOW TO BE ONE

The protagonists in this genre aren't nice, sensitive guys. The nirvana of this genre's heroism is achieved by the Badass, a primal man with brutal, pure convictions. He kills when he must, without a shred of regret, but rarely kills the wrong man. He tortures when he must, but never an innocent. When he is wronged, he doesn't turn the other cheek, but always gets a grotesque revenge.

There are three things badasses are not. First, they are never bullies and they always try to protect the weak (even though when all hell breaks lose, it is not safe to be around them). Second, badasses are never corrupt; they don't work for greedy, corrupt people and aren't afraid of taking moral stands against the man whom everyone fears. Third, badasses are not psychotic. They kill when it is necessary, but they reserve lethal force for those who deserve it.

NO CODE VS. KILLING, BUT A CODE VS. MURDER

This is a genre where death happens. Agents have no problems using lethal force, and they don't lose sleep when a bad guy dies in a firefight. Often they don't even seem bothered when bystanders die in a chase scene.

However, they are not killers. Do the bad guys have an obnoxiously effective lawyer who keeps getting them off on technicalities? The heroes are not vigilantes; they won't gun him down, not even when no one would notice. Agents don't perform executions. They are the good guys, and professional enough never to take the law into their own hands.

There are, however, two exceptions to the rule. In the Assassin sub-genre, the heroes *will* target people for termination (when the order has been given from above). However, even here there is still a moral division between them and the bad guys: they kill only when it's absolutely necessary to the mission or in self-defense, and they *will* protect hostages. If someone asks them to kill large numbers of innocents, they *will* take a moral stand against it. (Agent heroes do not bomb villages, except in flashback scenes or nightmares depicting events from their past for which they are trying to atone).

The other time they will pull the trigger is during a villain standoff. When a villain calls them on their "softness" and tells them they don't have the guts, they've gone too far and learn their mistake when the blood trickles down between their eyes. Never question a badass' badass-situde.

Torture is another prickly issue. In the agent genre, it is okay to torture the bad guys, falsely imprison them, and do horrible things to them, but they never do it except to anyone who's *obviously* a bad guy.

FRIENDSHIP IS MORE IMPORTANT THAN THE MISSION

There is a tendency when running a game where people are professional agents to place the mission ahead of *everything*, to make the agency an all-consuming beast. This may be appropriate in a hardcore milspec Special Forces game, particularly in campaigns where the heroes are sent on one suicide mission after another. However, all other games are ruled by the pulp code, and that code is simple: *friendship always comes first.* If a friend's life is on the line, or (even more importantly) a commander's life, then the agents must go to any lengths to save him. Would they disobey orders and steal a $50 million aircraft to facilitate the mission? Of course, in a heartbeat! Only the bad guys would let a friend rot for years in some Third World hellhole, or leave a teammate behind.

Furthermore, when agents do disobey orders and steal huge pieces of equipment, they are rarely punished in any serious way. The success of the rescue mission (or the collateral damage done to the enemy during the rescue) inevitably clears the heroes of any charges. Player characters should pay lip service to the prospect of having their pay docked for the rest of their lives, but in the end, they shouldn't sweat too much.

There is one big exception to the rule. Agents take their devotion to king and country very seriously. Agents can defy orders, they can waste the taxpayer's money by the billions, but they *never, ever* sell out their country. Even if a gun is pointed at a friend's head.

COURAGE IS ITS OWN REWARD

The agent genre does not reward caution. The only times when caution is required for a mission are when hostages are at risk or when the commander suspects it's a trap and decides to hold back (much to his subordinates' chagrin).

Beyond those two circumstances, holding back is *not* a virtue in this genre. Agents don't care if the odds are against them. Sneaking around to get the perfect shot never seems to work, so just take out your machine gun, go for the frontal assault, and take down that SHADOW base, old school!

The Gamemaster can help to encourage this style of play by liberally awarding hero points to agents who take the initiative, throw caution to the winds, and take action! Knowing there's a hero point (or two) waiting for them on the other side of an enemy emplacement can often help give players the courage they need to take action.

SILVER AGE VS. IRON AGE AGENTS

The agent genre has always been grittier than the norm, even back in the days when Steranko drew *Nick Fury, Agent of SHIELD*. However, there are a few things separating the genre in the two time periods.

The biggest difference between a Silver Age and an Iron Age game is in their attitude toward the government. In the Silver Age, the government is the Good Guy. Silver Age governmental agencies were well meaning, supportive agencies. Even on those occasions when the agencies had to send men on suicide missions, they agonized over the necessity. When circumstances forced them to abandon an agent in the field or deny responsibility for his actions, they agonized over that, too, and tried to rectify it as quickly as possible (which usually occurred when the agent had finished his mission and *really* needed the cavalry to come in and pull his bacon out of the fire).

There's nothing soft or well meaning about governments in Iron Age books. The only people worse than a national government are the people they're fighting, and even here, the line between them can get blurry. Iron Age agencies are scum. They mutilate and kill innocent people with the same grim abandon as the bad guys, and the only real difference between them is they believe they're trying to do the greatest good for the greatest number, by preserving the social order. Like making laws and sausages, intelligence and security are ugly businesses.

The second change in an Iron Age game is that the lives of innocent people are cheaper. In the Silver Age, our heroes always find a way to protect innocent people (unless they ignored the heroes' advice or orders, which inevitably leads to death via stupidity, for which the heroes aren't responsible. In the Silver Age, writers often spared the characters from the negative consequences of compassion).

The Iron Age, however, is a *lot* messier. Even here, the heroes should try to protect innocent lives. However, if it's a choice between killing an innocent person to maintain your cover, and the failure of a mission and your slow painful death... well, that's why the agency keeps a psychiatrist on-staff. The Iron Age relishes in giving heroes hard moral choices, and then showing off what hard men and women they've become because of them.

The third difference in an Iron Age game concerns issues of torture, murder, and sexuality. Silver Age agents generally don't torture; they may *threaten* torture, but it's all part of a scheme to intimidate the bad guys so they break down. In the Iron Age, however, it is okay for an agent to torture and even execute the bad guys in cold blood. In the Silver Age, when agents encountered an enemy and he didn't die in a firefight, the agents tied him up and put him in a safe place, regardless of the threat the enemy might pose to their mission. In the Iron Age, however, leaving an enemy alive is stupid, and stupid equals dead really fast.

In the Silver Age, men were flirtatious and promiscuous, and they exploited themselves shamelessly, but sex was off-camera, consensual, and (allegedly) all in good fun. In the Iron Age, sex is often degrading and violent. In both eras, sex has kinky, S&M overtones, but the Silver Age expresses it mostly with wry quips and innuendo.

CHAPTER 2: STAR SQUAD

Some people prefer their heroes a little more down to earth, instead of whizzing through the air and tossing cars around. In Freedom City, the most admired of these heroes are the police, the fire department, and the local HAZMAT details, and the most respected of these are the police. The ones that most commonly see action against supervillains are the Freedom City STAR (Superhuman Tactics and Regulation) Squad.

STAR Squad draws its inspiration primarily from sources like Metropolis' Special Crimes Unit in DC Comics' *Superman*, Marvel's *Code: BLUE*, Alan Moore's *Top Ten* for America's Best Comics (although that's a fully superhuman world), and *POWERS*, as well as from television cop shows where the protagonists sometimes seem extra-human, like *Columbo*, *CSI*, or *Due South*, as well as more traditional cop series like *Hill Street Blues* and *NYPD Blue*.

STAR SQUAD HISTORY

Freedom City's history of war on super-powered crime dates back to WWII when Commissioner Bachle's Special Committee Against Sabotage aided the Liberty League against saboteurs and criminals like the original Crime League. This included a small band of cops who called themselves "the Science Brigade," former adventurers of the 1930s who hadn't quite abandoned their old habits (they field-tested a number of special weapons that were developed by Dr. Dingle, one of Freedom City's great eccentric inventors). Both the Committee and the Science Brigade were disbanded at the end of the war (though a few of the inventions, now long forgotten, still sit in the basement of FCPD headquarters).

Over the years, several attempts were made to put together a unique squad of cops to battle super-criminals, from Mad Dog Rae's "Dog Pound Squad" in the 1960s, to the infamous POF-SWAT ("Price of Freedom" Special Weapons and Tactics Team) during the Moore administration. The latter was a bad time for superheroes and the FCPD, as Mayor Moore's corrupt regime took its toll on local law enforcement as it did everything else in the city; from small malignancies do terminal cancers grow, and the POF-SWAT was a tumor, giving the city police a well-deserved reputation for excessive violence. Sadly, as crime rates hit record heights, so did public tolerance of police excesses.

DARKNESS FALLS

The nadir of the FCPD was 1991, when POF-SWAT murdered a defenseless teenaged super-criminal, a street gang member called "Captain Blood." AEGIS had captured him in a raid in Southside when POF-SWAT showed up, took control of the prisoner, and he died, allegedly in an "escape attempt." When secretly shot film footage turned up that showed the Squad torturing and murdering him, the members of POF-SWAT were put on trial. They were eventually cleared of all charges; it is widely believed Police Commissioner Roy Alquist bought their acquittals, as Mayor Franklin Moore often used the team as his personal enforcers. Only an unlikely alliance between AEGIS, local vigilantes, and a few honest cops prevented a major riot in Southside.

Within twelve hours of Moore's electoral defeat, POF-SWAT was officially disbanded, and the officers quietly resigned and slunk away from Freedom City (a common pattern with Moore's stooges). The city still had to deal with a high crime rate and deep public cynicism toward local cops. It required a dramatic event to turn around this malaise, but then came the Terminus Invasion. It was (as one often criticized pundit said), "the wrong tragedy at the right time."

RISING STARS

As the city rebuilt from the disaster, Mayor O'Connor was forced to take a good hard look at the FCPD. He uncovered much graft and corruption, but there were still many fine officers who were doing good work despite public distrust and potential abuse from their corrupt comrades. One of the bravest of these officers was Barbara Kane, a police lieutenant who caught O'Connor's eye when she led a squad of police against a pack of Omegadrones and kept them from panicking despite the nightmarish conditions. Giving Kane a long-deserved promotion to captain, he appointed her as the head of a task force to reform the FCPD. One of Kane's chief recommendations was the establishment of a new organization to directly confront supervillains. O'Connor agreed and immediately began to put together an elite team, but Kane persuaded him the city needed something bigger than just a squad like the old Dog Pound; it needed enough men and women that they could police themselves as well as the city. AEGIS objected to the idea; Director Powers told the mayor AEGIS could perform all of the duties proposed for this new squad, but Mayor O'Connor said he believed in local solutions to local problems. On July 4, 1996, Freedom City's STAR Squad was officially activated.

TRIAL BY FEAR

The STAR Squad faced its first big test soon after its inception, when Fear-Master turned the population of Freedom City against superheroes. Using an experimental device to shield against Fear-Master's technol-

ogy, the STAR Squad managed to rally enough of the citizenry to fight their fears that Fear-Master was forced to retreat.

The official complement of STAR Squad has always been twenty-three officers, including three squads of 6 troopers (use the SWAT Officer archetype from *Mutants & Masterminds*, **Chapter 11**) and five on-call specialists (a HAZMAT expert, a demolitions specialist, a psychologist/profiler, a communications specialist, and Gary, "the magic guy"). The original leader of the squad, Leonard Upton, proved one of Kane's poorer choices (capable administrator, poor field commander), and Upton left the position after two years.

THE BULLDOG

By that time, now-Commissioner Kane realized she needed someone who would provide a shock to the system, and she found it in Bill "Bulldog" Maddicks. Although Maddicks grated on everyone's nerves except for Kane, he was the perfect man to shape STAR Squad into a fighting force that would rival the finest professional teams. He was assisted by ASTRO Labs, which loaned the team amazing pieces of technology like the STAR Squad Decombustion Cannon.

STAR Squad's first big test under Maddicks came when they fought Hades himself. The dark god decided to celebrate the winter solstice by kidnapping Persephone (not the mythological Persephone, but a vapid pop star psychically linked with Hades' beloved). STAR Squad couldn't defeat the villain with force, but used cunning and psychology to hold him at bay long enough for the Freedom League to show up and drive him away.

Mr. Infamy and the Game Master presented the team with its greatest challenge when the two wagered to see whether the STAR Squad could beat AEGIS' finest agents in a fight. The STAR Squad won the contest and, though they later teamed up with AEGIS to turn the tables on Mr. Infamy, they've never let their rivals forget it.

The rivalry between AEGIS and STAR Squad—a polite tension in the case of Director Powers and Commissioner Kane, or unconcealed contempt between Commander Maddicks and Administrator Bonham (who've come to blows in private on three occasions)—is as intense as any rivalry in Freedom City. Maddicks' style is responsible for most of these headaches; he never minces words: the press, the mayor's office (though never the mayor himself), the Freedom League, and AEGIS are all frequent targets of criticism. Kane usually plays "good cop" to smooth over the differences, but quietly approves of Maddicks' tirades and refuses to rein him in.

The battles STAR Squad has waged have not been without their casualties. Five officers have died in the line of duty: Officers Sutherland, Henderson, Daniel, Boielle, and Findley have all laid down their lives to protect the people of Freedom City. Additionally, six other men and women have received permanent injuries while on the job (one, Martin Ferris, still works for the FCPD part time as a computer consultant).

TODAY

Today, STAR Squad is on the front lines against supervillains in Freedom City. While the press sometimes characterizes them as loose cannons, most appreciate the important role they play in that most dangerous of jobs, safeguarding the city, and no one wants to go back to the bad old days of POF-SWAT.

STAR Squad can be hard to deal with. Their official motto is "We bow to the law, not to men or supermen," a saying that concludes every daily briefing. The only authorities they respect are those in their direct chain of command. They are, despite their reputation, humble around the people they serve; it's only when you try to order them around that their now-legendary contrary streak comes out. It has won them grudging respect.

STAR SQUAD STRUCTURE

STAR Squad is an official branch of the Freedom City Police Department, and is based in the 14th Precinct of Freedom City (attached to FCPD headquarters).

There are twenty-three people in STAR Squad, divided into three squads (code-named Ripper, Mad Dog, and Crusher) of six troopers and five full-time support personnel. In addition to this force, five squads from the 12th, 14th, and 18th Precinct have been designated as reserve support to bolster STAR Squad in a major crisis (usually to carry and operate heavy weapons in a support capacity). STAR Squad also employs civilian advisors for technical support, and a few office workers.

As with other members of the FCPD, Star Squad members have ranks. The three squad-leaders are Captains, while Maddicks' official rank is Commander. The highest rank is reserved for Commissioner Kane.

STAR SQUAD RANKS

Benefit Cost	Rank	Agency Bonus
1	Officer	+0
2	Sergeant	+1
3	Lieutenant	+2
4	Captain/Deputy Chief	+3
5	Commander/Chief	+4
6	Commissioner	+5

In addition to the official roster, STAR Squad has a science liaison from ASTRO Labs. There's also supposed to be an AEGIS liaison, but the last one quit after being insulted by Maddicks, and STAR Squad has taken an inordinate amount of time looking for his replacement (one might even conclude that Maddicks doesn't *want* anyone to fill the position). The STAR Squad has an excellent relationship with Fire Chief DuMar and Warden Drummer of Blackstone prison, who gladly lend aid when needed.

OPERATIONS

STAR Squad's official description is "an elite tactical squad of dedicated officers designed to deal with situations outside the purview of normal tactical officers," which is a fancy way of saying they're supposed to fight supervillains.

STAR Squad's primary duty is to fight supervillains when it is within their ability to do so, or contain a supervillain threat until superheroes are available. Their second duty is to assist in the evacuation of innocent bystanders from superhuman combat zones, and their third duty is to assist in the incarceration of supervillains. The latter is what most commonly brings them into conflict with AEGIS, as AEGIS believes supervillain containment is *their* job. Usually cooler heads prevail, and the villain is put in an AEGIS containment unit while STAR Squad escorts the villain to Blackstone or the "Hole" (a temporary lockup in a sub-basement of FCPD headquarters).

Like other police units, the STAR Squad is expected to provide backup during natural disasters and other calamities. Additionally, although it's rarely been used, there's an emergency signal in the STAR Squad precinct house from the Freedom League; when the League needs backup (usually when there are too many opponents for them to handle at one time, but the opposition is relatively low powered), the emergency signal calls for STAR Squad to hit the scene. Perhaps their most unusual duty is for Project Freedom; several times, the program has used the STAR Squad as "bad cops" who visit a reformed supervillain and attempt to provoke him; if the villain responds violently, then the program recognizes that the villain needs further counseling in anger management. It's a dirty, thankless job, but if it helps reform one superhuman, Kane believes it'll be worth it. (Maddicks, who doesn't like putting agents in danger for a psych exam, doesn't agree.)

STAR Squad does not involve itself in vice or undercover operations, or police investigations, although they may provide backup for investigators who go into a place judged to be a high-risk zone. They do not provide bodyguard or escort duties for officials, though in places where supervillains are likely to attack, they are stationed on the perimeter, awaiting trouble. They don't answer calls where supervillains aren't involved, although they'll assist in riot control in major disturbances. They help people when called upon (although they have standing orders to call AEGIS if anyone ever asks them to rescue a cat from a tree).

UNUSUAL MISSIONS

Often an agency can be judged by its most unlikely tasks. Some of the most unusual missions that STAR Squad has undertaken include:

OPTION: PRECINCT 23

The flip side of STAR Squad is Precinct 23, a campaign set in the Fens district of Freedom City. This is the seedy side of Freedom, where people's hopes are abandoned for a cheap fix, and love and respect are replaced by a quickie with an underage prostitute. Keeping watch over this hellhole are the cops of Precinct 23, who have never touched a battlesuit or an experimental weapon from ASTRO Labs.

Precinct 23 is a Gritty Police Drama game, power level 3 with a Team Equipment allowance that only allows for real world weapons and vehicles. Characters investigate murders, vice, gang violence, and other sleaze in the heart of Freedom.

If you want to run a *really* gritty game, require the characters to take at least one complication from the following list: addiction (alcoholism, pornography, gambling), prejudice (racial, teenagers, gender, the elderly), enemy (family member who's involved in gangs or a mob boss who blames you for a tragedy in his life), rivalry (secretly begrudges colleagues who get praise when she doesn't), secret (criminal past, affair), or temper (when quarreling with family members).

If you want to give things a supernatural twist, you can run "Precinct 13" out of the West End or Lantern Hill, where Freedom City cops deal with supernatural crimes like vampire murderers, lycanthropes, ghostly hauntings, and so forth, possibly aided by a local mystic, and with supporting characters like the mysterious Lantern Jack (*Freedom City*, page 141) and Weird Maggie (*Freedom City*, page 63).

INVASION OF THE SKY-SHARKS

In this odd plot by Dr. Simian, sharks were fitted with anti-gravity devices and artificial lungs—and a blood bomb was detonated over downtown Freedom City. The STAR Squad was forced to defend the city from rampaging flying sharks while the Freedom League prevented the Crime League from using the chaos to loot the city.

DOPPLEGANGBANGERS

For 24 hours, everyone in Freedom City was transposed with his or her counterpart from Anti-Earth. One squad of STAR cops was out of town at the time of the transposition, and it was up to them to set things right. Breaking the Courage Foundation (that universe's counterpart of the Crime League) out of Blackstone, the heroes joined forces with Franklin Moore and saved the city.

TOOLING THE TRADE

Maddicks became convinced that small time mobster "Junior" Jurenski was working to bring advanced weapons from some place strange; he didn't realize that he and Baron Broker, the foppish arms trader who sold them, was actually from the Terminus. Maddicks and the Squad managed to bust into their warehouse as they were attempting to kill Captain Thunder, and Jurenski was sent flying through a dimensional warp into the Terminus.

STAR SQUAD RESOURCES

STAR Squad is one of Commissioner Kane's pet projects, and thus receives a lot of public funding. While most of their high-tech gear comes from firms like ASTRO Labs, the cost of vehicles is not a trivial expense (as the press has pointed out on several occasions).

ARSENAL

STAR Squad generally employs real-world personal arms in the fight against evil: pistols, rifles, and automatic rifles. The agency also has access to some big guns from the comic book weapon list, provided by ASTRO Labs. They are only available to STAR Squad in the Heavy weapon size, and must be bought with the Two-Man Crew Required flaw.

TASER CANNON

DECOMBUSTION CANNON

The weapons on STAR Squad's heavy weapons list include: Heavy Blast Cannon, Heavy Cold Cannon, Heavy Inertia Cannon, Heavy Laser Cannon, Heavy Leech Cannon, Heavy Tranquilizer Gun (with a flaw that it's only usable on huge or larger creatures), and the Heavy Vertigo Cannon. There are also several unique weapons that ASTRO Labs has built (see the following).

These weapons are typically brought to the crime scene in a transport van, where they're unloaded by a team of four officers, set up, and operated with a two man crew (while the other officers provide cover fire).

STAR Squad only employs conventional vehicles: police cruisers, motorcycles, armored vans, and helicopters.

ASTRO LABS SPECIAL WEAPONS

Weapons need to be field-tested, and as far as ASTRO Labs is concerned, STAR Squad is a vital component of their R&D division (even if they don't always realize it). The most impressive weapons in STAR Squad's arsenal are the heavy cannons. While many of these cannons are copies of other agencies' technology, ASTRO Labs has provided the Squad with several weapons to help them with their jobs.

TASER CANNON

The Taser Cannon is a special device designed to take out monsters, giant robots, and big supervillains. It looks like a giant harpoon gun. When it hits its target, it covers it in a steel mesh to hold it in place, and then (one round later), the taser effect activates. The taser effect continues until the operators switch off the juice, or the target breaks free of the snare. Some complain the taser effect is too weak, and STAR Squad has petitioned for the development of a Mk. II with a more powerful taser charge.

TASER CANNON, MK. I	DEVICE
Snare 10 (Crew Required) Linked to Stun 3 (Electrical, Ranged, Sustained, Crew Required, Full round delay after Snare to activate charge)	
Cost: 10 (snare) + 9 (Stun) = 19 points (Device 4)	

DECOMBUSTION CANNON

The bane of villains who flee the scene of their crimes in a fancy vehicle, this huge, bizarre looking weapon (which, despite rumors of being captured from the Grue, was actually created by ASTRO labs) fires a beam that affects an engine and causes it to stall. The beam fired has an odd oscillation effect, and the weapon has been nicknamed "the Buck Rogers gun" by STAR Squad personnel.

DECOMBUSTION CANNON — DEVICE

Nullify 10 (all movement effects from an internal combustion, jet, or rocket engine, Sustained, Crew Required)

Cost: 30 points (Device 6)

SLEEP GAS LAUNCHER

Constructed after Fear-Master turned a large portion of Freedom City's populace into a paranoid mob, this lobs containers of sleep gas into the center of a disturbance, distributing it over a wide area in hope of putting targets harmlessly to sleep. This has seen action in several subsequent near-riots, and has been praised as a humane solution to the problems of crowd control.

SLEEP GAS LAUNCHER — DEVICE

Stun 7 (Cloud, Ranged, Sleep, Crew Required, Progression 1 [area])

Cost: 29 points (Device 6)

STAR SQUAD HEADQUARTERS

Sometimes called "the Planetarium" (but more informally known as "the Zoo"), the STAR Squad's headquarters is an adjunct to Freedom City's 14th precinct near Police Headquarters.

STAR SQUAD HEADQUARTERS — HEADQUARTERS

Toughness: 10; *Size:* Large; *Features:* Combat Simulator, Communications, Computers, Fire Prevention System, Garage, Gym, Hangar, Holding Cells, Infirmary, Living Space, Power System, Security System, Workshop.

Agent Complement: 1 Commander (SWAT Leader), 3 Squads (15 STAR Squad members and 3 SWAT Leaders), 5 Technical Staff, and 6 Support Staff

Vehicles: 2 Superhuman Containment Trucks (Reinforced Vans with the Holding Cell feature), 12 Motorcycles, 12 Police Cruisers, 1 Helicopter, 12 Vans, 3 Reinforced Vans, 1 Surveillance/Communications Van

Cost: Abilities 3 + Features 13 = 16 equipment points

STAR SQUAD PERSONNEL

STAR Squad is at the lower-end of the super-agents spectrum. It is recommended that characters in a STAR Squad game start as Top Cops (power level 4), workaday Joes who get together to defend the city, or Action-Agents (power level 5). Characters should be members of one of the regular squads (Crusher squad is available for this function), or members of a newly created 4th squad (which the PCs get to name). In this campaign, a team has access to an 80 point team equipment pool, which can be spent on vehicles and heavy weapons.

STAR SQUAD TEAMS

There are three main teams in the STAR Squad, Team Ripper, Team Mad Dog, and Team Crusher.

STAR SQUAD OFFICER — POWER LEVEL 4

Str 15	Dex 14	Con 14	Int 12	Wis 12	Cha 12

Skills: Acrobatics 3 (+5), Bluff 3 (+4), Climb 3 (+5), Diplomacy 2 (+3), Disable Device 2 (+3), Drive 2 (+4), Escape Artist 2 (+4), Gather Info 2 (+3), Intimidate 6 (+7), Investigate 3 (+4), Knowledge (civics) 1 (+2), Knowledge (current events) 2 (+3), Knowledge (streetwise) 2 (+3), Knowledge (tactics) 3 (+4), Medicine 2 (+3), Notice 6 (+7), Profession (cop) 4 (+5), Search 4 (+5), Sense Motive 2 (+3), Stealth 4 (+6), Swim 2 (+4)

Feats: Benefit (rank) 1, Equipment 8, Improved Disarm, Improved Grab, Improved Trip, Precise Shot, Prone Fighting, Set-Up, Stunning Attack, Teamwork

Equipment: Sub-machine gun (+4 damage, Autofire), riot armor (+4 Toughness), tear gas, climbing harness, gas mask, flash goggles, camo-clothing, handcuffs, police radio

Combat: Attack +4, Damage +2 (unarmed), Grapple +6, Defense +4 (+2 flat-footed), Knockback –3, Initiative +2

Saving Throws: Toughness +6 (+2 without armor), Fortitude +6, Reflex +6, Will +6

Abilities 19 + Skills 15 (60 ranks) + Feats 18 + Powers 0 + Combat 16 + Saves 13 = 80

TEAM RIPPER

Team Ripper (the "A-Team") is led by Hank Warren, an old, tougher-than-shoe leather vet who still walks with a limp, courtesy of a beating he received from dirty cops during the Moore administration. He was formerly with internal affairs, however he has put that role behind him. He's even more hardcore military than Maddicks, but he prefers to cut a man down not with words, but with a graveyard stare.

TEAM MAD DOG

Team Mad Dog (the "B-Team") is led by Hector Molina, a former Olympic middleweight boxer who took up the call to become a cop when Mayor O'Connor called for honest citizens to take back their city. He's a Southside native and doesn't tolerate disrespect toward minorities or women. His men respect him for his bravery and toughness, but bemoan his lack of a sense of humor.

TEAM CRUSHER

Team Crusher is in disarray following the death of their captain, Britt Daniel, who sacrificed his life to buy time for the evacuation of a building filled with innocent people during a Talos attack. The team expects to be reorganized under a new captain in the near future. Team Crusher can be taken over by PCs, or a fourth team can be formed to fill the void.

OTHER PERSONNEL

In addition to the STAR Squad's three teams of officers, the division also has a small support staff of technicians and office personnel.

The squad's technical staff is top-notch and a plum assignment for anyone in the FCPD's Technical Services Division, even if it does mean working with "the Bulldog." STAR Squad techies get to play with all the best toys, including experimental equipment from ASTRO Labs and items impounded from super-criminals. Naturally, instances of on-the-job injuries, fatalities, and mysterious transformations are fairly high.

STAR Squad's small office staff is kept busy handling paperwork, filing reports, doing research and, most often, fielding calls from the Commissioner, the Mayor, city officials, and concerned citizens. The staff does its best to insulate Commander Maddicks from these sorts of things, since they're only likely to set him off.

IRONJAW, STAR SQUAD MASCOT

A mutant German Shepherd rescued from a dog fight ring by STAR Squad officer Orlando Baker, Ironjaw was successfully rehabilitated and is now a STAR Squad fixture, often running alongside their cars or vans on their way to stop a crime. As intelligent as any human, Ironjaw does a better job of following verbal instructions than many human members of the squad.

Recently, Ironjaw fell in love with expensive show dog Wilhelmina, a German Shepherd, and the champion of last year's North Bay Kennel Club dog show (in the working dog category). Despite being from the "wrong side of the tracks" (the non-purebred side), Ironjaw has managed to become part of her life, and she is now expecting a litter of puppies. Whether they will inherit their sire's abilities is yet to be seen.

IRONJAW — POWER LEVEL 5

Str 18	Dex 14	Con 14	Int 10	Wis 14	Cha 12

Skills: Acrobatics 2 (+4), Climb 4 (+8), Concentration 4 (+6), Handle Animal 2 (+3), Intimidate 6 (+7), Investigate 2 (+2), Notice 5 (+7), Profession (police officer) 3 (+5), Search 4 (+4), Sense Motive 6 (+8), Stealth 2 (+4).

Feats: Animal Empathy, Instant Up, Improved Grab, Improved Overrun, Improved Trip, Prone Fighting, Set-Up

Powers: Protection 2, Speed 4, Super-Senses 3 (scent, track, ultra-hearing)

Combat: Attack +6, Damage +4 (unarmed), Grapple +10, Defense +6 (+3 flat-footed), Knockback –2, Initiative +2

Saving Throws: Toughness +4, Fortitude +5, Reflex +4, Will +5

Drawbacks: Disabilities (cannot speak, no hands, –8 points)

Abilities 22 + Skills 10 (40 ranks) + Feats 7 + Powers 9 + Combat 24 + Saves 8 – Drawbacks 8 = 72

POLICE SHOW ARCHETYPES

For players in a campaign based on police television shows, there are certain archetypes that come into play. Players who play a cop can look over the archetypes and choose a suitable role. Cops often come in pairs, so when one player is playing a "By the Book Cop," encourage someone else to play a "Cowboy Who Throws Out the Rulebook" to provide contrast. Characters should have a partner, another PC who is always paired up with them.

This list covers urban cop shows only; kickboxing Texas rangers, Satanic sheriffs and their hapless deputies, or seemingly redneck white sheriffs and their black lieutenants belong to a separate sub-genre, the rural cops show.

THE LACONIC BEAT COP

This individual is a capable cop or detective, but sometimes needs to watch his mouth. The very personification of "unflappable," nothing seems to faze this cop or prevent him from making a darkly humorous (and often inappropriate) quip.

THE COCKY POLICEWOMAN HIDING SECRET DOUBTS

In genre fiction, two stereotypes are often attached to female characters; they're extremely competent and self-assured—tougher than the toughest tough guy—but they also usually have some secret that comes out and shows their sensitive side.

BY THE BOOK COP

This cop is best noted because he is married to the rulebook. He's memorized it, and goes into a state of shock when someone suggests violating procedure.

THE COWBOY

The opposite of the By The Book Cop, this cop loves to break down doors, pull out his gun, and perform crazy stunts. He usually doesn't go *too* far (the player should be amenable to GM advice on when he's going too far over the top).

THE DIRTY COP

Not a PC archetype, this guy is on the take. In particularly corrupt squad rooms, it's an open secret, and anyone who decides to go boy scout on him regrets it real fast.

THE FATHERLY CAPTAIN

Everyone in the squad room reveres the Fatherly Captain. He takes everyone's problems on his broad shoulders. Grizzled veterans treat him like a respected older brother, and everyone (particularly the policewomen) look up to him like a father.

THE ANGRY OFFICER IN CHARGE

For situations where you're running the police squad not as a family, but as "rebel cops against the system," the fatherly captain goes out the window, replaced by this hotheaded comic foil. Some really want to bust the PCs' chops, while others secretly like the PCs and fight to save their careers (even if they never admit it).

THE AMBITIOUS SECOND-IN-COMMAND

Some people are more interested in "the career" than "the job." This guy is looking to move up through the ranks, networks with the big brass, and doesn't associate very often with lower tier officers. Few people like him, but it is dangerous (politically) to be his enemy.

THE AMATEUR PSYCHOLOGIST DETECTIVE

This guy is a profiler or a detective obsessed with criminal behavior. He finds himself inevitably drawn into complicated games with his quarry, and whether or not he wants to play is irrelevant.

THE FISH OUT OF WATER

This cop doesn't belong in the big city. Maybe he's a small town Southern sheriff or an overly uptight police officer from another country. (Periodically, you should run a scenario based in the guy's native environment for appropriate comic role-reversals).

THE STREETWISE URBAN COP

Often a foil to the Fish Out of Water, this guy grew up in the poor section of the city and still maintains his family connections. (And while any archetype can have a family member working for the bad guys, this one tends to have it more often than most).

THE CRAZY UNDERCOVER GUY

This guy works under cover, usually in an outrageous disguise (often in drag, working for the vice squad) that allows him to act half-insane, and he's the only one who doesn't see a problem with it. Even so, there's something oddly endearing about him.

THE ROOKIE

This kid has two things in abundance: cockiness and ideals. Maybe he's the latest son in a long line of top-cops, or maybe he's a handsome jock who's never had a serious setback in his life. The kid is capable but arrogant, and he's due for a nasty reality check.

The *Psychotic Rookie* is a subset of cop; this is a guy who seems like a sweet kid, but when the pressure gets on him, he reacts with excessive, tragic force. (Usually this variation has a nervous breakdown, is forced to spend time with a shrink, and comes back to fight his demons, or else he dies tragically.)

THE GRIZZLED VETERAN

One of the most common archetypes, and one encompassing numerous variations, from Shaft to Sipowicz. What these characters have in common is they have seen it all, and the world has worn them down. Some have become practical, capable adjusters to the tragedy around them, others have become bitter shells of their former self who don't give a damn about their cases or the people they protect (though often with just enough of their ideals left that a rookie can reignite some of their passion).

Related to the Grizzled Veteran is the *Psychotic Veteran*. Somehow, he has forgotten everything he was taught in his police procedures class, and is actually surprised when his collars are set free by the courts— when they survive to make it to the courtroom.

A version of this character common in the movies is the *Officer About to Retire*. Which is another way of saying this character will die a messy death so his partner and colleagues can avenge him.

THE OUTSIDER

For reasons known only to the player and the GM, nobody one likes this guy. Maybe it's because he did something to disgrace the force, or brought shame (or death) to one of the squad's favorite officers, or maybe he's a conspiracy theorist everyone thinks is nuts. If he's lucky, he has one person in the squad room who'll actually talk to him.

THE TYRANNICAL DISTRICT ATTORNEY

This person is a foil for the police, an obstacle who can turn a case upside down, or put pressure on the PCs to find more evidence. Often cop shows end at the arrest; in campaigns with Tyrannical D.A.s, cases actually have to go to trial, and sometimes the D.A demands the PCs find more evidence to ensure a conviction (or more annoyingly, cuts a deal that puts a criminal back on the street). This is usually an NPC role.

THE UNDERCOVER COP

This guy doesn't socialize with the main force, because he's undercover with the bad guys. Perhaps he's living a glamorous lifestyle as part of a Vice unit, or perhaps he's dealing with the scum of the earth (or, in Freedom City, working as a supervillain's henchman). He relies on the PCs to protect his secret, but sometimes has to be as dirty as the crooks he's trying to take down.

THE UNLIKELY SUPERCOP

This guy is the last person who should be a cop. Maybe he's openly gay in a macho world, maybe he's a quiet and studious guy who's more knowledgeable than your average college professor, maybe he's a scruffy, incredibly persistent detective, or a neurotic phobic detective. What they have in common is they're quirky and shockingly competent, enough to earn the respect of their colleagues.

STAR SQUAD AND SUPERHEROES

STAR Squad has a somewhat uneasy relationship with Freedom City's costumed defenders. On the one hand, the Freedom City Police Department officially cooperates with superheroes, particularly groups in good standing like the Freedom League. The administration knows full well that ordinary cops can't be expected to take on the likes of the Crime League or the Factor Four on a regular basis, so they need super-powered help.

On the other hand, Commander Maddicks *hates* having to accept help from "amateurs" and "civilians," even if they do have super-powers and an orbital satellite headquarters. More than a few cops share Maddicks' view that "the capes" are just glory hounds who happen to be lucky enough to have powers. Sure, they're helpful, but they also grab all the glory and credit for the collar, and they willfully ignore police procedure when they do. Naturally, at least part of the jealousy on the part of the cops comes from wishing they could do the same.

Still, although Maddicks and STAR Squad don't like calling upon super-powered aid, they're not stupid, and they'll get on the horn to Freedom Hall or the Nucleus when things get rough, doing their best to contain the threat until help arrives, and then cleaning up the mess that gets left behind afterwards. After all, it's the job that comes first, because that's the real meaning of being a cop and a member of the FCPD's top squad.

CHAPTER 3: AEGIS

AEGIS, Defenders of Liberty, the Shield of Freedom; that's not what people called them when they first began operations,, but sometimes you *can* earn respect.

AEGIS is a curious beast: a mix of highly trained investigators and the most heavily armed military Special Forces personnel in the world. Their mission: counterterrorism. Within America's borders, AEGIS is the government's response to superhuman crime and violence. When a superhuman threat emerges to threaten lives and freedom, AEGIS is the first—and often the best—line of defense.

Though sometimes a cynical world has trouble believing it, AEGIS agents *are* the good guys. For the most part, they are true patriots, ready at a moment's notice to risk their lives to protect America and its citizens. They are far from perfect, but then again, even the superheroes aren't *that* good.

AEGIS HISTORY

The history of AEGIS is the history of struggle in the 20th and early 21st centuries. The organization has faced challenges from the moment of its inception, and not always from America's enemies. Still, AEGIS has always overcome any obstacles in its path when it comes to keeping the nation safe.

MY NAME IS JACK, AND I'M A PATRIOT...

For many servicemen, World War II was a crucible, which they entered as immature boys, and emerged from as the living standard of courage. One of the men who spent the longest time in the crucible was Jack Simmons, America's Icon of Liberty, the Patriot. He fought numerous battles in the war, against Nazi troops and Nazi supervillains like Nacht-Krieger, Totenkopf, and the infamous Wilhelm Kantor.

After the war, Simmons wanted to pursue Kantor into his South American bolt hole to finish the job— he remembered how Nacht-Krieger had massacred the Allies of Freedom to cover Kantor's escape—but the army refused to believe the slippery Kantor was worth the effort. Jack was loaned out to the OSS, where he worked as a secret agent for several years. He still did the superhero gig on the side, though Freedom City was quiet in the post-War years.

In 1950, Simmons signed up for the bloody stalemate of Korea. He hoped for a quick victory; however, the Patriot found the fighting even more bitter and intense than it had been in the Second World War. He recruited a new team of superhumans and trained them as a fighting force in the spirit of the superheroes of the Second World War. Christened the Atomic Brigade (because Simmons hoped they would be an alternative to the use of nuclear weapons), the team is one of the great forgotten superhero groups of history. After several initial successes, four team members were killed in a futile defense of the Chosin Reservoir in December of 1950. Despite Simmons' best efforts, the team was never reformed to full strength. Korea turned into a quagmire in which superheroes made little difference.

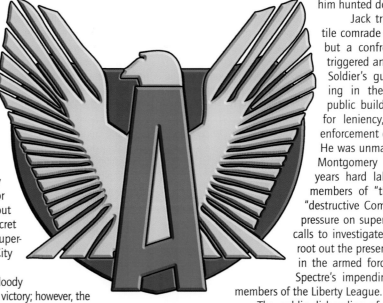

After the cease-fire, the Patriot returned to the United States, where he was recruited into the CIA. Unfortunately, other events would overtake Jack's life. While he had been fighting communists in Asia, a different type of enemy threatened America. It was the time of the HUAC hearings, and superheroes were not impervious to the committee's scrutiny. One of the people called to the hearings was the Silver Soldier, a former member of the Atomic Brigade with decidedly leftist leanings. When the Soldier left the hearings and snapped at the press that he was "running away to become a supervillain, since this country doesn't appreciate its heroes anymore," the committee ordered him hunted down.

Jack tried to intercept his volatile comrade before tragedy occurred, but a confrontation with the press triggered an ugly incident. The Silver Soldier's gun started a fire, resulting in the destruction of several public buildings. Despite Jack's call for leniency, HUAC and local law enforcement came down hard on him. He was unmasked as playwright Todd Montgomery and sentenced to ten years hard labor. The revelation that members of "the Patriot's team" were "destructive Communists" intensified the pressure on superheroes. There were even calls to investigate the Patriot himself and root out the presence of "elite communists" in the armed forces. It led to the Scarlet Spectre's impending testimony about the members of the Liberty League.

The public disbanding of the Liberty League took attention away from Jack's role in the proceedings, but the Patriot was left with a decidedly bitter taste in his mouth. When it came to superhumans, the system didn't handle them very well. America needed a security force that specialized in dealing with superhumans, but one that could be kept at arm's length from what Jack called "enemies blatant and pernicious." Simmons envisioned an umbrella organization that would draw in the best talent from the military and security organizations, which would work with established, respectable superheroes to defend the country. Employing the same strategic skills he'd

> *"THERE IS NO 'I' IN USA. THERE IS, HOWEVER, AN 'US'."*
> —JACK SIMMONS, THE PATRIOT

used to fight the Nazis, Simmons put together a plan to build a new, better system of superhuman law enforcement.

He started using his army connections to cherry pick the best from each branch of the service (and from security agencies), looking for those who displayed the qualities of initiative and competence. "A soldier with brains and a little swagger beats an obedient drone every time," Simmons said. Little did he know how ironic those words would prove to be.

By 1958, Simmons' project began to bear fruit. He had received permission from the Eisenhower administration to put together a task force of forty agents to serve as a special mission force. Many people laughed at the idea; the brass said Simmons had scoured every brig to recruit each service's most insubordinate soldiers. Simmons was choosing men (and more than a few women) who were not afraid to speak their minds and were willing to stand up to bad command decisions. Once his team was assembled, two years of intense training followed.

On June 24, 1960, Simmons' task force was placed (for reasons that only made sense to bureaucrats) under the authority of the IRS, designated as the "American Elite Government Intervention Service," and given office space in the Treasury building. Simmons' critics mocked the name, and predicted his "washout brigade" wouldn't last six months.

LAUNCH-POINT

Behind the scenes, however, Simmons had made several moves that would prove critical to AEGIS' success. First, he tapped his CIA and FBI contacts to recruit good law enforcement personnel to supplement his soldiers. Whenever possible, AEGIS would have the best intelligence available before they acted.

Second, he used his friendships in the superhero community to make contact with the latest generation of superheroes, proposing covert partnerships. Now, Jack promised, someone in government circles would fight for superhero rights in the event of another HUAC witch-hunt. Centurion agreed enthusiastically and, following his lead, many heroes agreed to collaborate. This included a new Freedom City superhero named the Scarab who would prove an invaluable asset.

The acid test came in 1961, when SHADOW launched the first Operation Inundation, an ambitious scheme to seize simultaneous control of every major institution in the western world. The Scarab's psychic talents warned him of imminent danger, but no one in government listened to his warnings except Jack Simmons. Simmons mobilized AEGIS forces to protect key American installations when zero hour struck. More importantly, he contacted friends in the armed services across the world, and put his reputation on the line to get their forces placed on high alert. SHADOW's attack was even more intense than the Scarab feared, but in the end, it was AEGIS that saved the day.

AEGIS investigators tracked SHADOW to the Virginia estate of Dr. Jonathan Darke, where the man believed to be SHADOW's Supreme Commander was killed in the ensuing firefight. The world celebrated, and critics' voices were muted. The "Contraterror Cowboys" (as AEGIS had been derisively called) had won the day.

AEGIS was lauded, but not respected in all quarters. To further silence their critics, Simmons insisted AEGIS take on the toughest cases that could be found (many involving supervillains or the paranormal). For decades, AEGIS fought a plethora of organizations with bizarre motifs: the Counter-Clock Culture, Apocalypse Today!, the Secret Society of Firebrands, the Green Liberation Front (a secret society of green-skinned mutants who felt their pigmentation made them a superior "race"), and Invisible, Inc. They opposed superhuman criminals like the serial killer Gemini, the catastrophic Exploding Man, and the mysterious Mr. Infamy. They worked alongside heroes like Centurion, the Scarab, the Freedom League, and the Atom Family.

By 1970, AEGIS had expanded to over a thousand personnel, including a young Georgetown graduate named Harry Powers, whose investigative skills, combined with his daring, quickly made him one of the agency's most valuable assets. AEGIS also established ties with Canada and the United Kingdom through the RCMP and Scotland Yard to coordinate their efforts with the British Commonwealth and safeguard America's allies. Their adventures made headlines all over the world, and a few agents, like AEGIS spokesman Luke Bonham, achieved celebrity status. In 1983, Harry Powers' Gemini investigation was adapted into the film *Gemini and Scorpio,* and *The AEGIS Files* ran on television for nearly a decade. Many called it the agency's golden age. Jack Simmons called the media spotlight "an enormous pain in the neck," and focused on his duties.

SHADOW was always a constant menace during those years. Led by a mysterious figure named Overshadow, the terrorist organization constantly reared its head with one labyrinthine scheme after another. From building weather control machines to summoning elite zombie armies from military graveyards, SHADOW constantly prodded the defenses of the western world. They seemed like just another bizarre menace, but Simmons thought he detected a more malevolent, even familiar, hand behind their actions. While Wilhelm Kantor was presumed to have gone insane and died in the 1950s, Simmons could almost feel his old foe's presence.

In 1979, Overshadow launched a second Operation Inundation, this time using a clone army. Fortunately, AEGIS was ready for them, and they cleaned up the clone army after the Scarab managed to turn the clones against each other. Unfortunately, they were unable to track down Overshadow, nor were they prepared for his counterattack—the assault by the Scions of Sobek on Freedom City.

DIVIDED WE FALL

When word reached AEGIS of the Scions' attack, the Freedom City Operations Chief dispatched two squads of troopers to Pyramid Plaza. All twelve troopers died in the onslaught. They failed to prevent the deaths of the Scarab and Brainstorm, and when a television exposé revealed Freedom City Operations Chief Luke Bonham had withheld two-thirds of his available forces from the battle, the Freedom League went ballistic.

Bonham defended his decision, saying it had taken less than thirty seconds for the possessed League to kill two fully equipped AEGIS squads, and throwing more agents into the situation would have been a suicide mission. Director Simmons backed Bonham's decision (though many AEGIS agents privately disagreed). Simmons' show of support caused a rift between the Freedom League and AEGIS, one that was soon to reverberate throughout the entire superhero community.

The Scarab's death was only the beginning of the dark times. Throughout the 1980s, anti-superhero organizations sprang up like brushfires, and a concerted effort was made to tarnish the reputation of many of the world's superheroes. Politicians like Franklin Moore were elected in many of America's major cities. Many cities, including Freedom City, enacted draconian anti-superhero laws, and the media played into fiery anti-supers rhetoric. AEGIS was exempt from the legislation, but was under intense pressure to hunt down anyone who violated the Moore Act.

For Jack Simmons, the situation was almost more than he could bear. He had not forgotten his own superhero career, nor the superheroes he'd known who had lost their lives; nor had he forgotten the promise he'd made to protect superheroes from another witch hunt. Behind the scenes he worked to protect the best heroes, the ones who hadn't succumbed to vigilantism, and to put pressure on people like Moore and mob bosses like August Roman, who were behind much of the trouble. Most of his lobbying was covert, and some young superheroes began referring to Simmons as a traitor, and AEGIS as "the enemy." The brutal

THE GEMINI CASE

In the 1980s, one of the most famous AEGIS cases occurred when the telepathic serial killer Gemini terrorized people from Washington to Freedom City. Forty-six people were murdered in the killing spree. Gemini's victims were telepathically commanded to wear airtight masks that suffocated them (the slow suffocation produced a fear reaction on which Gemini fed); when his victims' bodies were found, they were wearing faceless masks that bore the astrological sign of the twin. His earliest victims were twins; he forced one to watch helplessly as the other died.

The only time that the police caught up to Gemini, he proved impervious to their weapons. The authorities feared he was unstoppable.

Gemini's path of carnage attracted law enforcement experts from around the world, including AEGIS, who sent young agent Horatio (Harry) Powers to solve the case. Powers managed to identify Gemini as carnival mind reader Stefano Vezini. When Vezini's powers emerged, he accidentally killed his twin brother Lorenzo, driving him insane. Vezini believed his brother's ghost possessed him when he performed the killings. Vezini's mother was a bitter, manipulative gypsy mystic with her own sanity issues. Powers tracked down the mother first; she poisoned him and tried to stab him, but the hardy Powers shot her. Seeing his dead mother, Gemini went berserk and threatened to kill three hostages, but Powers goaded him into using his telepathic powers on him.

This was Harry Powers' plan all along. Thanks to experimental anti-psionic technology, Vezini burned out his powers trying to get Harry to put on the mask, lowering his force field defenses to a level where AEGIS could kill him. Four hostages were saved, and Harry's guts and determination were universally proclaimed. Harry went on to become the director of AEGIS, and while he modestly says that the incident was blown out of proportion, privately he admits the sensation of Gemini crawling around in his head still gives him nightmares.

Freedom City describes some options and plot twists for Gemini. His ultimate fate and game statistics are left for the Gamemaster to develop as desired.

actions of many of these vigilantes, which forced AEGIS to take a stand against them, did nothing to help the situation.

In 1990, the overstressed Director Simmons suffered a heart attack that forced him to retire from AEGIS. Harry Powers was appointed as his successor with Simmons' blessing. As a final insult to his old enemy, Overshadow used the Tapestry of Fate to magically seize control of AEGIS HQ and command Simmons' closest friends in AEGIS to hunt him down like a dog. Simmons, with the help of blind seamstress Roz King, took control of the Tapestry and, in a breathtaking hand-to-hand struggle, threw his archenemy from the gondola of Overshadow's flying battle fortress. During the battle, Overshadow claimed to be Simmons' old enemy, Wilhelm Kantor, but subsequent investigation concluded he was actually Kantor's insane son Heinrich, following a protocol set for him by his dead father.

If SHADOW continued to exist in the years following Heinrich Kantor's demise, they didn't show themselves openly. With their greatest enemy seemingly defeated for good, Jack Simmons finally retired in peace, leaving Harry Powers to continue his work. Powers' biggest task was repairing the damage between the agency and the superhero community. Rapprochement between the two would soon come, though in a way nobody suspected (or wanted). It was called "the Terminus Invasion."

Alien troops swarmed through Freedom City. AEGIS quickly realized the scope of Omega's incursion into our dimension. Director Powers unleashed the arsenal of high tech weapons he had been holding in reserve for the next major invasion, and an aging Luke Bonham led the first generation of MAX armor units against the invading force. Stung by years of accusations of cowardice, Bonham refused to retreat from the fight, and died facing Omega himself, just before Centurion arrived for the climactic battle. In this, Agent Bonham atoned for what small part he played in the death of the Scarab. Even in what followed, it did not go unnoticed.

Centurion fought Omega and broke his power, driving him back to his dimension at the cost of his own life. The sacrifices of Bonham and Centurion helped bring the public (and many of the angry vigilante heroes who had railed at AEGIS) back to their senses. Powers (and Jack Simmons, who refused to be left out of action even when he was confined to a wheelchair) was determined to take advantage of the opportunity.

At Centurion's funeral, ten years of frustration boiled over, and Simmons delivered a blazing eulogy where he railed against "garbage like the Moore Act" and the people who had enacted it, whom he called "the worst examples of political corruption." He called upon America to reject any politician who stood against the defenders of the public good, and

declared that Freedom City should welcome the Freedom League back with open arms. He called for heroes to rally beside AEGIS, whom, he insisted, had always supported those who stood for the public good and had never stood against any hero of conscience. It was, arguably, the finest hour of a man who had more fine hours than any other person alive.

At the dedication of the Sentry Statue, the surviving members of the Freedom League shook hands with Stewart Bonham (Luke Bonham's son, himself a novice AEGIS agent), symbolically bridging the gap between AEGIS and the superhero community. Since then, AEGIS and the world's superheroes have enjoyed (for the most part) a positive, mutually supportive relationship.

AEGIS TODAY

With the nightmare of the Terminus Invasion behind it, AEGIS used its reservoir of public goodwill and federal funding to rebuild itself into a position of strength. The 1990s were good to AEGIS and Powers, who while not respected in some circles, made a surprisingly positive impact as Senior Director.

Unfortunately, the good times were not to last, and today AEGIS faces many new challenges. Foremost among them is the "Midnight Invective," the codename for a mysterious wave of assassinations targeting AEGIS agents; over the last three years, an as yet unidentified culprit has murdered nearly fifty agents. Not only is the loss of life appalling, it is a direct challenge to the organization's ability to defend itself. It is also forcing AEGIS to recruit new agents more quickly than they would like.

SHADOW's inactivity poses a second, unexpected problem. SHADOW always justified a reasonable share of the federal budget for the AEGIS organization, but with their archenemy gone for so long, it is becoming harder to finance the agency at the levels it needs to remain effective as America's watchman. There have been signs of SHADOW's reemergence with Nacht-Krieger as the new Overshadow, and AEGIS' Think-Tank continues to warn of a major attack, but they are largely a voice in the wilderness, and some accuse the agency of inventing a new SHADOW threat so it can increase its budget.

AEGIS' independent attitude has never made it popular in government circles. There have been rumblings of folding AEGIS into other government agencies to regulate it more heavily or replacing it entirely with a new organization called Project: America, directly answerable to the top brass at the Pentagon. Whether anything will develop out of this proposal remains to be seen.

So far as Director Powers is concerned, administrations and congresses come and go, but threats to America remain constant, and therefore so will AEGIS' vigilance. As far as he is concerned, he spends far too much time wrangling with pencil-pushing bureaucrats and not enough time doing his job (and he's increasingly coming to the disturbing realization that dealing with the bureaucrats is his job).

Presently, AEGIS enjoys good relations with the general public and with the superhero community at large. Harry Powers worked with a number of the most prominent superheroes and hero groups, and continues to do so. While some AEGIS agents bristle at the idea of being relegated to a "support" function, they mostly toe the agency line on the matter. Even relations with UNISON have improved, although AEGIS still jealously guards its jurisdiction over superhuman matters in the United States.

Although AEGIS is probably the only government organization that believes SHADOW is still a threat, even they are not fully aware of the extent of that threat, at least, not yet, anyway. (See **Chapter 5** for details.)

AEGIS STRUCTURE

AEGIS is a division of the Department of the Treasury (like the Secret Service), though it effectively has complete autonomy. Officially based out of the Treasury Building in Washington DC, AEGIS' real center of operations is the Sword Building in Baltimore, Maryland, in a large, fortified sub-basement.

Currently, there are over 8,500 personnel serving in the organization, including 6,200 field agents. Agents are drawn from law enforcement, military Special Forces, and the intelligence communities. AEGIS' American Shield program provides an exception to the rule: every year, forty of the finest high school students in the nation compete at a grueling boot camp for the attention of AEGIS recruiters. Those who succeed in meeting AEGIS' physical and mental standards receive AEGIS scholarships at top American universities in exchange for an eventual career as a "Contraterror Cowboy."

Occasionally, a recruit is so impressive they join the agency straight out of high school; these agents are often quite rough around the edges, but with a little experience and mentoring, they can become some of AEGIS' finest. AEGIS does not have its own academy, but maintains formal associations in several American universities and military academies. Unfortunately, some of the best and brightest members of these student associations have been targeted recently (by SHADOW, of course; Overshadow refers to these attacks as "an ounce of prevention") forcing AEGIS to rethink the program. Being AEGIS cadets in every sense, some association members are banding together to fight the threat and prove they are worthy of the Shield of Freedom.

Some grade schools have the "Junior AEGIS" program, which trains children in civic responsibility. This program focuses on raising money to help young victims of superhuman violence, children who have lost their homes during extradimensional invasions, and other tragedies.

The AEGIS agency is divided into three divisions: Agent division (the military/defense arm), the Command division (the intelligence and local administrative arm), and the Directorate (the overseeing bureaucracy for the whole organization). Higher ranked members of a division can give orders to lower ranked members of the same division. Agent division members cannot give orders to anyone in other divisions; higher or equal ranked members of the Directorate may give orders to members of the Command division, and higher or equal ranked members of the Command Division may give orders to the Agent division. Most AEGIS player characters will belong to the Agent Division.

The Senior Director is the leader for the whole organization; the current Senior Director is Harry Powers. A Special Director is the organization's official liaison to Congress and the National Security Council.

AEGIS also has a Technologies Section to conduct research into new vehicles and weapons like the Super-MAX armor, as well as a Special Projects Section, which is the agency's euphemism for supernatural investigations. The Technologies Section, headed by Dr. Doris Volk, is based out of Concord, NH, though much of their work has been subcontracted to ASTRO Labs. The Special Projects Section, headed by Damantha DeMaurier, also has ties to Freedom City, as ten years ago AEGIS quietly bought the old Gerber House on Lantern Hill to use as a base of operations; the manor lies on a nexus of mystic power, and AEGIS serves as a guardian of the forces that could be unleashed if it fell into the wrong hands.

RELATIONSHIPS

AEGIS maintains good relations with most other American security agencies, especially the FBI and the Secret Service. The Pentagon, on the other hand, considers them cowboys and resents that they don't control (or have much influence over) the agency. Most actual field commanders, appreciative of the military backgrounds of many AEGIS agents, are more respectful and cooperative. However, the two bureaucracies do not mesh well. A similar situation exists between AEGIS and the CIA.

AEGIS is on very good terms with UNISON, largely because of the respect and friendship between their two commanders. Many of the agents, on the other hand, view each other with suspicion and distrust, and an intense rivalry sometimes flares when agents are forced to work together.

AEGIS DIVISIONS

BENEFIT RANK	AGENT DIVISION	COMMAND DIVISION	DIRECTORATE	AGENCY BONUS
1	Junior Agent	Junior Analyst	Intern	+0
2	Agent	Analyst	Aide	+1
3	Special Agent	Junior Administrator	Senior Aide	+2
4	Senior Agent/Tactical Officer	Administrator	Deputy Director	+3
5	Captain	Chief Administrator	Director	+4
6	(none)	(none)	Senior Director	+5

AEGIS RESOURCES

AEGIS is a resource-heavy organization (in fact, there are a few people in Congress who say it's *too* resource heavy and would like to cut it back), and these resources can mean the difference between life and death.

In addition to the equipment listed in this book, AEGIS also has access to the devices listed in **Chapter 3** of *Freedom City*.

EQUIPMENT

A typical AEGIS agent has an Equipment allowance, which can be spent in numerous ways. Here are some packages for each of the major archetypes:

AEGIS AGENT (EQUIPMENT 3, 15 POINTS)

Blaster pistol (10 points), body armor (Toughness +2, 2 points), hand-cuffs (1 point), commlink (1 point), multi-tool (1 point)

AEGIS FIELD INVESTIGATOR (EQUIPMENT 4, 20 POINTS)

Blaster pistol (10 points), body armor (Toughness +2, 2 points), hand-cuffs (1 point), commlink (1 point), multi-tool (1 point), investigator's kit (2 points), broom (1 point), camera (1 point), PDA (1 point)

AEGIS COMMANDO (EQUIPMENT 5, 25 POINTS)

Blast rifle (16 points), body armor (Toughness +2, 2 points), handcuffs (1 point), commlink (1 point), binoculars (1 point); flash goggles (1 point), gas mask (1 point), multi-tool (1 point), night-vision goggles (1 point)

THE AEGIS ARSENAL

AEGIS agents may not possess great superhuman powers, but the strength of the weapons in their arsenal makes them a match for many villains. The arsenal of freedom contains a large number of weapons and vehicles that can be taken (or requisitioned) by enterprising agents who want to complete their mission.

Weapon availability is subject to the size of the local base. Experimental weapons and heavy military vehicles are probably only going to be stored at installations with a large agent base. Availability is at the Gamemaster's discretion - though if someone spends a hero point, well... you might be surprised what some other agent managed to drag back from the field earlier in the day.

Note that using captured weapons as trophies is against AEGIS regulations, punishable by 30 days of lock-up and a reprimand. Many agents do it anyway. Some Operations Centers mount (disabled) captured weapons in a lounge or a trophy area, along with pictures of prominent enemies they've captured or killed.

AEGIS WEAPONS

All conventional modern military weapons are available in AEGIS' arsenal. In addition, these comic book weapons can be taken or requisitioned by agents looking for something a little different.

EXPERIMENTAL WEAPONS

The following weapons are experimental. They are allowed at the GM's discretion, but are subject to malfunctions and failures. Agents who take out experimental weapons without their commander's permission are just asking for trouble.

All other weapons are not in AEGIS' regular arsenal, though a character who spends a hero point could have access to another agency's technology, provided the Gamemaster allows it into the campaign.

STANDARD AEGIS WEAPONS

CLASSIFICATION	WEAPON TYPE
Eagle	Blaster Pistol
Golden Eagle	Blaster Rifle
Thunderbird	Blaster Heavy Cannon
Hoplite	Autoblast Rifle
Serpent	Net Rifle
Louis	Tranquilizer Pistol
Dempsey	Tranquilizer Rifle
Screech Owl	Sonic Pistol
Horned Owl	Sonic Rifle
Paladin	Laser Pistol
Chevalier	Laser Rifle
Lantern	Light Rifle
MAX	Battlesuit

EXPERIMENTAL AEGIS WEAPONS

CLASSIFICATION	WEAPON TYPE
Curse	Leech Rifle
Cyclops	Inertia Rifle
Basilisk	Paralysis Rifle
Charybdis	Vertigo Rifle
Smother	Gravity Rifle

AEGIS VEHICLES

CLASSIFICATION	VEHICLE TYPE
Gator	Combat Hovercraft (ports only)
Bloodkite	Combat Motorcycle
Draconis	Combat Helicopter
Gyrfalcon	Flying Cycle
Kingfisher	Combat Speedboat (ports only)
Raptor	Flying APC
Sparrow Hawk	Collapsible Helicopter
Razorhawk	VSTOL Folding Fighter Jet
King Condor	Fighter Jet

AEGIS VEHICLES

While AEGIS' greatest weapon is the strength of its personnel, having a hangar full of APCs and gunships doesn't hurt either. Personal vehicles such as a compact car, mid-size car, large car, motorcycle, pickup truck, or SUV are considered part of an agent's everyday gear; PCs do not need to pay points for them. Also, AEGIS always allows an agent to take out a reinforced van if there's a report of a supervillain who needs to be picked up, and a surveillance van is standard issue on stakeouts.

Other common vehicles (sports cars, limousines, busses, jet-skis, snowmobiles, and semis) are usually not stocked by AEGIS, but in situations where there is a clear need for a cover vehicle, AEGIS finds a way to quickly provide one for their agents. For some reason, agents want to form a task force to investigate supervillain activity in street racing and the high performance sports car industry. Beyond that, agents need to requisition or pay points for the vehicles listed on the previous page.

Sometimes a major mission requires AEGIS to bring out the big guns. Though certain bureaucrats hate it, a Condition: Red (or worse) situation authorizes AEGIS to empty the armories so agents are free to defend the city.

POWER ARMOR

By far, the most impressive and distinctive pieces of AEGIS technology are the MAX and Super-MAX armors. All AEGIS agents are trained to use MAX armor, while Super-MAX is reserved for AEGIS vets. Both are designed and constructed by an in-house AEGIS technologies group led by Dr. Doris Volk. Parts for the MAX suits are manufactured overseas, but the final construction is overseen at an AEGIS facility in Maryland, with a back-up facility located in the AEGIS base in Freedom City.

MAX ARMOR	DEVICE
Device 11 (hard to lose): **Blast 7** (*Alternate Powers:* **Dazzle 7** (visual), **Snare 7**), **Communication 4** (radio), **Enhanced Strength 10**, **Immunity 9** (life-support), **Protection 7** (Impervious), **Super-Senses 1** (low-light vision)	
Cost: 44 power points	

SUPER-MAX ARMOR	DEVICE
Device 14 (hard to lose): **Blast 9** (*Alternate Powers:* **Dazzle 9** (visual), **Snare 9**), **Communication 4** (radio), **Enhanced Strength 10**, **Immunity 9** (life-support), **Protection 9** (Impervious), **Super-Senses 1** (low-light vision), **Super-Strength 4**	
Cost: 56 power points	

AEGIS HEADQUARTERS

No organization can survive long without strongholds, and AEGIS' foes mandate equally tough defenses.

AEGIS headquarters (officially referred to as "Operations Centers" or "OCs") can be found in most American cities, in every state of the union. Even mid-sized and remote American cities have small bases, while large fortified buildings can be found in most major metropolises. Connected via a network of nearly unassailable computers, these bases work in conjunction with each other to form the true shield of AEGIS, fortresses for the defenders of American liberty.

AEGIS SATELLITE HQ

Even cities without an AEGIS base rent an office for a few staff members, often operating in conjunction with local police, government, or (if desperate) at a government office like an army recruiting center. These offices, known as satellite headquarters, serve as a base of operations for a small group of investigators and field agents. Their job is to gather local information for AEGIS and to be on hand to serve AEGIS agents who visit the city. In the absence of superheroes and a dedicated anti-superhuman squad, these agents are occasionally asked to put their lives on the line against a supervillain.

AEGIS SATELLITE HQ	HEADQUARTERS
Toughness: 5; *Size:* Tiny; *Features:* Communications, Computers, Fire Prevention System, Garage, Security System.	
Agent Complement: 1 Commander (Roughneck Commando), 1 Squad (5 AEGIS Agents), 2 Investigators.	
Vehicles: Superhuman Containment Truck, 2 Combat Motorcycles., 1 MAX armor.	
Cost: Abilities –1 + Features 5 = 4	

SMALL AEGIS BASE

Small AEGIS bases are located in most major American cities. Unlike satellites, agents are permanently stationed at a base and there is one agent team available for duty at all times (on an eight hour rotating shift). Agents probably live in a home or apartment somewhere in the campaign city, but there is space within the base for the agents to sleep when they are off-shift and stationed on extended duty shifts.

SMALL AEGIS BASE	HEADQUARTERS
Toughness: 5; *Size:* Small; *Features:* Communications, Computers, Fire Prevention System, Garage, Hangar, Infirmary, Living Space, Security System, Workshop.	
Agent Complement: 1 Commander (Roughneck Commando), 3 Squads (15 AEGIS Agents and 3 Roughneck Commandos), 4-6 Field Investigators, 1 Lab Tech, 4-6 Support.	
Vehicles: Superhuman Containment Truck, 4 Combat Motorcycle, 2 Flying Motorcycles, 1 Collapsing Helicopter, 2 MAX armor, 1 Super-MAX armor.	
Cost: Abilities 0 + Features 9 = 9	

LARGE AEGIS BASE

In major metropolitan areas, AEGIS either occupies large sections of a big government building or has a small building of their own (which is usually a requirement because of their Holding Cells). AEGIS defines a major base as one able to field at least two six-man combat squads at a time, and have six two-man investigation squads busy at the same time. Half of the combat teams are required to live on base in their spare time.

LARGE AEGIS BASE	HEADQUARTERS
Toughness: 10; *Size:* Large; *Features:* Combat Simulator, Communications, Computers, Fire Prevention System, Garage, Gym, Hangar, Holding Cells, Infirmary, Laboratory, Library, Living Space, Power System, Security System, Workshop.	
Agent Complement: 1 Commander (Hard-Nosed Commander), 7 Squads (35 AEGIS Agents and 7 Roughneck Commandos), 12-15 Field Investigators, 1 Combat Trainer (Martial Artist), 2-3 Defense Analysts, 4-6 Lab Techs, 2-3 Motor Pool Workers (Grease Monkeys), 1 Combat Engineer, 15-25 Support Staff.	
Vehicles: 2 Superhuman Containment Trucks, 6 Combat Motorcycles, 6 Flying Motorcycles, 3 Collapsing Helicopters, 2 Combat Speedboats (in port cities), 1 Flying APC, 1 VTOL Folding Fighter Jet, 6 MAX armor, 3 Super-MAX armor.	
Cost: Abilities 3 + Features 15 = 18	

AEGIS MILITARY BASE

AEGIS cannot stockpile large quantities of heavy military equipment in urban centers, so large cities are often adjacent to a military base, primarily designed to field equipment and provide rapid deployment reinforcements to AEGIS bases in the surrounding cities in the event of an emergency. Commando teams, not investigators, are their focus. These aren't large military bases like the USMC base at Camp Pendleton; instead, they're laid out on a 100-200 acre spread that includes an airstrip. There are six AEGIS military bases in the United States (including one 30 miles southwest of Freedom City).

AEGIS MILITARY BASE	HEADQUARTERS
Toughness: 10; *Size:* Colossal; *Features:* Combat Simulator, Communications, Computers, Defense System, Fire Prevention System, Garage, Gym, Hangar, Holding Cells, Infirmary, Isolated, Laboratory, Library, Living Space, Parade Grounds, Power System, Security System, Workshop.	
Agent Complement: 1 Commander (Hard-Nosed Commander), 7 Squads (35 AEGIS Agents and 7 Roughneck Commandos), 6-8 Field Investigators, 1 Combat Trainer (Martial Artist), 2-3 Motor Pool Workers (Grease Monkeys), 1 Combat Engineer, 15-25 Support Staff.	
Vehicles: 1 Superhuman Containment Trucks, 5 APCs, 5 Tanks, 5 Military Helicopters, 5 Fighter Jets, 2 Flying APCs, 6 MAX armor, 3 Super-MAX armor.	
Cost: Abilities 6 + Features 18 = 24	

SECRET AEGIS BASE

While AEGIS is not an especially secretive organization, there is a virtue in having a few bases hidden from the sight of their enemies. While these bases are not particularly combat heavy, they can be used as safe houses for undercover AEGIS investigators or a fallback position if a nearby public AEGIS base gets overrun.

SECRET AEGIS BASE	HEADQUARTERS
Toughness: 5; *Size:* Small; *Features:* Communications, Computers, Cover Identity, Fire Prevention System, Garage, Hangar, Infirmary, Living Space, Security System, Workshop.	
Agent Complement: 1 Commander (Spymaster), 1 Squad (5 AEGIS Agents and 1 Roughneck Commandos, posing as security guards), 4-6 Field Investigators, 1 Lab Tech, 4-6 Support.	
Cost: Abilities 0 + Features 10 = 10	

AEGIS PERSONNEL

AEGIS is the archetypal Action-Agents *Agents of Freedom* campaign. It is recommended that characters start at a standard Action-Agents level (power level 5). Characters may use their team equipment to purchase suits of MAX armor, however Super-MAX armor should not be available at the start of the campaign. (Let the heroes work up to that.)

Characters are idealistic rookies and battle-hardened patriots who come from all walks of life and all parts of the country, united by one common purpose: to defend their nation from superhuman enemies who intend to destroy America and everything it stands for. Intelligent, capable, resourceful, and sometimes a little ruthless, a typical AEGIS agent on the front lines of America has the statslisted on the following page.

This agent has come through an intelligence service and received basic combat training. They're not the best fighter (use the Roughneck Commando from **Chapter 1** for that) or the best investigator (use the Field Investigator archetype for that), but they have received a fair amount of training. This agent is a competent, well-rounded patriot who loves their country and is willing to put their life on the line at a moment's notice to protect it.

Allocate the basic agent's equipment points (from the Equipment feat) as best suits the series and the agent's standard field equipment. Players may wish to allocate more points to the Equipment feat, depending on the style of the game, and Gamemasters should provide a guideline for how many Equipment ranks are expected and required.

ELITE AGENTS

The basic AEGIS agent archetype is only the beginning of AEGIS (as a power level 4 character, four points remain unspent and are available for customization if using 15 points/PL, or 24 points if using 20 points/PL). All agents should have the listed abilities, feats, and skills unless there is a good reason for the difference (for example, an agent who gets crippled in the field is not going to get kicked out because he has a low Dexterity, and a Heroic Everyman is pretty much an exception to all the rules.)

Archetypes from the **Supporting Cast** section can represent particular specialists within the agency, particularly the Ace Pilot, Combat Engineer, Field Medic, Grease Monkey, Master of Disguise, Sharpshooter, and the Strong Guy.

Advanced agents use the archetypes from **Chapter 1**. A base commander is probably a Hard-Nosed Commander or a Spymaster, while other elite agents may employ the archetypes from **Chapter 6** (these probably require a little customization to fit the agency's specs).

BASIC AEGIS AGENT					POWER LEVEL 4
Str 10	Dex 12	Con 13	Int 15	Wis 14	Cha 10

Skills: Acrobatics 2 (+3), Bluff 2 (+2), Climb 2 (+2), Computers 2 (+4), Diplomacy 3 (+3), Drive 4 (+5), Gather Information 4 (+4), Intimidate 4 (+4), Investigate 6 (+8), Knowledge (behavioral sciences) 3 (+5), Knowledge (civics) 2 (+4), Knowledge (current events) 2 (+4), Knowledge (streetwise) 2 (+4), Knowledge (tactics) 2 (+4), Notice 4 (+6), Profession (agent) 3 (+5), Search 4 (+6), Stealth 2 (+3), Survival 1 (+3), Swim 2 (+2).

Feats: Attack Focus (ranged), Benefit 1 (rank), Defensive Roll 1, Equipment 3, Teamwork

Combat: Attack +3 (melee), +4 (ranged), Damage +0 (unarmed), Grapple +3, Defense +4 (+2 flat-footed), Knockback -2, Initiative +1

Saving Throws: Toughness +4 (+3 flat-footed, +1 without armor), Fortitude +4, Reflex +1, Will +6

Abilities 14 + **Skills** 14 (56 ranks) + **Feats** 7 + **Powers** 0 + **Combat** 14 + **Saves** 7 = 56

AEGIS IN FREEDOM CITY

Since its founding, AEGIS has had a strong presence in Freedom City, to such an extent that many people think Freedom City is the *real* headquarters for the organization—and they'd be right. Jack Simmons, never a Washington man, viewed Freedom City as the front line in the war against his country's enemies, and was determined that his organization would have a strong presence in the city of capes and cowls for as long as it was needed, working side-by-side with local superheroes for as long the country needed them.

More than forty years later, the wisdom of Simmons' decision has been proven time and again. Freedom City has always seemed to bring out the best in those who wear the AEGIS uniform.

A legacy of mistrust still persists in some areas of Freedom. AEGIS agents have pulled rank on local law enforcement officers too many times not to be resented, and some STAR Squad officers take a sadistic delight in misdirecting AEGIS so they stay out of their way. The relationship between the Freedom League and AEGIS is similarly complicated. They frequently collaborate, but both organizations are also suspicious of each other and constantly on their guard.

STEWART BONHAM

Stewart "Rock Star" Bonham recently took over as Chief Administrator of the Freedom City Operations Center, commanding AEGIS forces in the region. Bonham is well known as the son of legendary AEGIS agent Luke "The Duke" Bonham, second only to Director Powers in deeds of daring-do. Raised since childhood to be the perfect AEGIS agent, Stewart joined the organization and found himself standing in his father's very large shadow; however (as he once put it), "For AEGIS, shadows are a piece of cake."

Bonham is young, impetuous, too good looking and athletic for his own good, and the callsign, "Rock Star," doesn't stray too far from his public persona. He loves the spotlight, and sometimes appears on *A.M. Freedom* to talk about security issues in Freedom City. He's played on his image and even appeared onstage with prominent rock bands to perform on the guitar (although not always for self-aggrandizement; one time he leapt into a mosh pit to beat up a terrorist who planned to blow up the concert). The tabloids have linked him romantically to numerous eligible superhumans, including everyone from Siren to Johnny Rocket. (He's dated a few, but never answers such personal questions.)

Nobody thinks he's boring. People either hate Stewart's guts, or they'd follow him into Hell (which, on one occasion, was more than a figure of speech). It's a mistake to interpret his style as a lack of respect for AEGIS, even if his excesses frequently raise Harry Powers' blood pressure. The one thing that really annoys him is when an agent doesn't take a mission seriously.

Stewart is a handsome man in his early 30s with light brown hair, sparkling blue eyes, and an athletic frame. Off-duty, he often wears Freedom Blades memorabilia, usually the now-retired #19 jersey of former team captain Brent Ironwood (a boyhood chum who made it to NHL stardom only to die in a car accident eight years ago).

STEWART "ROCK STAR" BONHAM					POWER LEVEL 6
Str 16	Dex 16	Con 18	Int 15	Wis 13	Cha 18

Skills: Acrobatics 4 (+7), Bluff 7 (+11), Climb 4 (+7), Computers 6 (+8), Diplomacy 6 (+10), Disable Device 4 (+6), Drive 2 (+5), Escape Artist 2 (+5), Gather Information 6 (+10), Intimidate 6 (+10), Investigate 5 (+7), Knowledge (behavioral Sciences) 6 (+8), Knowledge (current events) 5 (+7), Knowledge (streetwise) 2 (+4), Knowledge (tactics) 5 (+7), Medicine 2 (+3), Notice 6 (+7), Perform (singing) 4 (+8), Perform (string instruments) 6 (+10), Pilot 2 (+5), Ride 2 (+5), Search 7 (+9), Sense Motive 7 (+8), Sleight of Hand 4 (+7), Stealth 6 (+9), Survival 5 (+6), Swim 3 (+6)

Feats: All-out Attack, Assessment, Attractive, Benefit (Rank, Captain) 5, Connected, Contacts, Defensive Roll 2, Equipment 5, Evasion 2, Fast Overrun, Fearless, Grappling Finesse, Improved Aim, Improved Block 1, Improved Critical (pistol), Improved Disarm, Improved Grapple, Improved Trip, Inspire 3, Leadership, Move-by Action, Precise Shot 1, Prone Fighting, Quick Draw 2, Takedown Attack, Teamwork 2.

Combat: Attack +5, Damage +3 (unarmed), Grapple +8, Defense +5 (+3 flat-footed), Initiative +3

Saving Throws: Toughness +6 (+4 flat-footed), Fortitude +9, Reflex +10, Will +8

Abilities 36 + **Skills** 31 (124 ranks) + **Feats** 40 + **Powers** 0 + **Combat** 20 + **Saves** 19 = 146

OTHER AGENTS

Other top agents in the Freedom City AEGIS base include Bonham's second-in-command, Michael Hughes, a straight arrow who stands in stark contrast to his boss. They make a strong team, but there's an underlying resentment between them. Several years ago, Hughes inadvertently allowed his then-girlfriend, who was really an Overthrow agent named Hilda Reinholdt, to steal AEGIS secrets; Hughes was demoted, and when the time came to select a new AEGIS director, Bonham was chosen over him. In Hughes' eyes, Bonham stole his job.

Keeping a watchful eye on Hughes are two close friends and confidantes: one is Rita "Dynamite" Reznor, a she-devil commando who is one of the most celebrated female agents—from any agency–in the world. The other is Alex Vezini, nephew of the notorious Gemini. Like his uncle, Alex is a (low-grade) telepath, but he hasn't fallen prey to the mental illness that seems rooted in his family tree (not yet, anyway).

DR. DORIS VOLK				POWER LEVEL 4	
Str 10	Dex 12	Con 15	Int 22	Wis 15	Cha 12

Skills: Bluff 4 (+5), Computers 9 (+15), Concentration 6 (+8), Craft (chemical) 6 (+12), Craft (electronics) 8 (+14), Craft (mechanical) 8 (+14), Diplomacy 7 (+8), Disable Device 6 (+12), Gather Information 9 (+10), Intimidate 9 (+10), Investigate 2 (+8), Knowledge (earth sciences) 6 (+12), Knowledge (life sciences) 4 (+10), Knowledge (physical sciences) 9 (+15), Knowledge (popular culture) 6 (+12), Knowledge (technology) 9 (+15), Medicine 6 (+8), Notice 6 (+8), Research 8 (+14), Search 2 (+8), Sense Motive 4 (+6), Sleight of Hand 6 (+7).

Feats: Benefit (rank) 6, Connected, Contacts, Eidetic Memory, Equipment 5, Fearless, Improvised Tools, Inventor, Well-Informed

Combat: Attack +3, Damage +0 (unarmed), Grapple +4, Defense +6 (+3 flat-footed), Knockback –1, Initiative +1

Saving Throws: Toughness +2, Fortitude +8, Reflex +2, Will +8

Drawbacks: Disability (overweight, –1 point)

Abilities 26 + **Skills** 35 (140 ranks) + **Feats** 18 + **Powers** 0 + **Combat** 18 + **Saves** 13 – **Drawbacks** –1 = **109**

"DAME" DAMANTHA DEMAURIER				POWER LEVEL 6	
Str 10	Dex 12	Con 12	Int 17	Wis 16	Cha 16

Skills: Bluff 7 (+10), Computers 1 (+4), Concentration 5 (+8), Diplomacy 7 (+10), Disable Device 2 (+5), Gather Information 6 (+9), Intimidate 6 (+9), Investigate 4 (+7), Knowledge (arcane lore) 7 (+10), Knowledge (art) 4 (+7), Knowledge (behavioral sciences) 6 (+9), Knowledge (civics) 6 (+9), Knowledge (tactics) 2 (+5), Notice 6 (+9), Search 4 (+7), Sense Motive 7 (+10), Sleight of Hand 6 (+7), Stealth 2 (+3)

Feats: Assessment, Beginner's Luck, Benefit (AEGIS rank) 6, Inspire (Diplomacy), Luck, Equipment 3, Ritualist, Well-Informed, Ultimate Effort (Knowledge—arcane lore checks)

Powers: Magic 6 (*Power Feats:* **Air Control 6, Dazzle (visual) 6, Illusion (visual) 6, Mental Blast 3, Obscure (visual) 6, Snare 6, Water Control 6**; choose six other suitable spells as power feats)

Combat: Attack +4, Damage +0 (unarmed) or by power, Grapple +4, Defense +5 (+3 flat-footed), Knockback –0, Initiative +1

Saving Throws: Toughness +1, Fortitude +3, Reflex +5, Will +10

Abilities 23 + **Skills** 22 (88 ranks) + **Feats** 16 + **Powers** 23 + **Combat** 18 + **Saves** 13 = **115**

The unofficial chief of detectives, head of the investigative wing of AEGIS in Freedom City, is Connor Wayne, a brilliant but eccentric ex-Scotland Yard inspector. Unfortunately, he is recovering from head injuries suffered in a failed assassination attempt by SHADOW agents; in his absence, he has been replaced by perky coroner-turned-detective, Sierra Howell.

Powers, Bonham, Hughes, Reznor, Vezini, Wayne, and Howell would be an impressive crew on their own. However, in addition to dozens of top-flight agents, Freedom City has two special individuals who provide valuable (and sometimes dangerous) technical support.

DR. DORIS VOLK

The head of AEGIS' Technologies Section, Doris Volk is a brilliant engineer and one of the few people ever taken under the wing of Daedalus to work as his protégé. Volk left Daedalus in 1997 to pursue her own projects, but Daedalus asked AEGIS to bring her onboard. The two have remained close, and some fear she's actually Daedalus' eyes and ears within AEGIS, but Harry Powers seems unconcerned. A workaholic, Volk was behind the development of the Super-MAX armor, and is spearheading the development of the next generation of battlesuit, which some are calling "The Super-Duper-MAX" against her wishes. Volk has said not to expect a prototype anytime soon.

The product of a Midwestern farm family who fled Germany before the Second World War, Doris was raised with a decidedly Calvinist work ethic. She is perhaps the most demanding taskmaster at AEGIS, and while the results are worth it, her methods take a toll on her research team. Dr. Volk's staff has an alarmingly high turnover rate, and some of her best designers have quit—only to find work at the Foundry.

Doris is a plain looking woman in her late 30s, with short auburn hair and carrying some extra weight. She is always dressed in a lab coat, even at AEGIS staff meetings.

DAMANTHA "DAME" DEMAURIER

No one is quite sure where Damantha DeMaurier comes from, but clearly, she's not from around here. She has described her home as an ethereal dimension where nigh immortal witches float on the clouds and bend reality with a blink (or a twitch of the ears or nose). Dame (as she's commonly called) came from that world to marry a mortal, giving up much of her supernatural power in the process.

Dame's husband turned out to be an abusive lout who constantly belittled her heritage. Dame sacrificed nearly all of her power to please him, but it was still not enough—he turned his vitriol on her family. After his hectoring drove one of Dame's kindly aunts to dissipate her essence into the ether (the witchly equivalent of suicide), she abandoned the marriage. AEGIS had known of her magical ability for years, thanks to a neighbor's reports of assorted supernatural mishaps. They contacted her and asked her to join the agency.

As Special Director Damantha DeMaurier, Dame uses her knowledge of magic along with her cleverness and charm to help identify magical threats to the United States. She and Adrian Eldrich have a cordial friendship. Dame is a tall, attractive blond woman. She lives in Gerber House on Lantern Hill, which is the center of her Section's operations (though she also maintains office space at AEGIS HQ in downtown Freedom City).

PROJECT EYESPY

Project Eyespy is AEGIS' psionic research section. The project's major goal is to identify young psychics with potential and train them to be socially responsible with their powers (which, of course, includes the option of using them for the good of their country by coming to work for AEGIS).

AEGIS PSI-AGENT				POWER LEVEL 3	
Str 10	**Dex 12**	**Con 13**	**Int 15**	**Wis 14**	**Cha 10**

Skills: Acrobatics 1 (+2), Bluff 4 (+4), Computers 2 (+4), Concentration 4 (+6), Diplomacy 5 (+5), Disguise 2 (+2), Drive 4 (+5), Gather Information 4 (+4), Handle Animal 2 (+2), Intimidate 6 (+6), Investigate 6 (+8), Knowledge (behavioral sciences) 3 (+5), Knowledge (civics) 6 (+8), Knowledge (current events) 2 (+4), Knowledge (streetwise) 2 (+4), Notice 4 (+6), Profession (choose one) 3 (+5), Search 4 (+6), Sense Motive 6 (+8), Stealth 2 (+3).

Feats: Defensive Roll 1, Equipment 3

Equipment: armored uniform (+2 Toughness), plus 13 points in other equipment.

Powers: Telepathy 5

Combat: Attack +3, Damage +0 (unarmed), Grapple +3, Defense +4 (+2 flat-footed), Knockback –2, Initiative +1

Saving Throws: Toughness +4 (+3 flat-footed, +1 without armor), Fortitude +4, Reflex +1, Will +9

Abilities 14 + Skills 18 (72 ranks) + Feats 4 + Powers 10 + Combat 14 + Saves 10 = 70

Project Eyespy believes telepaths, especially those young and confused about their powers, relate best to their own kind, so telepathic agents often lead the search for new psis. Some finds end up at the Claremont Academy, while others undergo study and training with the agency.

AEGIS does have a handful of telepaths in its service. It occasionally employs mind readers on major intelligence gathering operations, though to keep public debate to a minimum, they only use them on missions related to national security (or *really* important local cases). AEGIS hasn't always been so cautious, which has led to serious vulnerabilities in the past, such as when agency telepaths were taken over by the Cosmic Mind. These days, AEGIS is far more judicious in its use of telepaths.

PROJECT GORGON

The most controversial of AEGIS' operations (at least internally) is Project Gorgon, a deep cover operation involving reformed supervillains who pose as active criminals to infiltrate the supervillain community, with undercover AEGIS agents acting as their "minions." This is attached to Project Freedom, though Harriet Wainwright is not particularly fond of it. Still, even she concedes this might be a good way for supervillains with a thrill-seeking motivation to get their "fix" while operating in a more socially controlled environment.

The Gorgons hit pre-arranged targets in order to set up their cover identity, or attack criminals (while pretending to be rival mobsters out to get their share of the goods). The Gorgons are looking to expand their membership, which makes it a good excuse to run a "reformed villain" campaign (employ standard *Mutants & Masterminds* rules at power level 10 for the campaign). Likewise, a group of PC agents pretending to be the minions of a single supervillain who is half-heartedly trying to make good is a good basis for a comedy campaign.

THE PATRIOT AND PROJECT IRONMONGER

Evil never dies, so why should the guardians of liberty? That was the reasoning that led to the top-secret "Project Ironmonger," which transferred the memories and consciousness of former AEGIS Director Jack Simmons into an android body (as detailed in **Chapter 3** of *Freedom City*). Now, years after his official, biological death, the Patriot still stands guard against the forces that would threaten his nation.

The Patriot's cover identity is AEGIS Special Agent Faraday Irons, who is on "detached duty," reporting to Deputy Director Bonham and Director Powers, both aware of his true identity. There was a real Faraday Irons, killed in the line of duty not long before Simmons underwent the transfer process. He has no living relatives and AEGIS higher-ups felt he was a suitable cover. A few AEGIS agents wonder about "Agent Irons," but are well disciplined enough not to ask awkward questions.

Thus far, AEGIS is quite pleased with the effectiveness of the neural transfer: all the Patriot's knowledge and experience along with a superhumanly capable, ageless, tireless physical form. Director Powers is considering a proposal to arrange an "origin" for Agent Irons and have a "new" Patriot join the Freedom League as a way of keeping an eye on them. The only details to work out are just how much to reveal about the new Patriot's physical status; concealing his android nature from the League members could be problematic, but hiding that he's really Jack Simmons shouldn't be all that difficult. An alternate possibility is for the Patriot to become leader of a new team of AEGIS super-agents. The GM can choose whatever direction suits the series.

For his part, Simmons has acclimated to his new existence and continues to serve his country and the agency he founded. He occasionally runs into trouble with his old "take charge" reflexes, realizes he's *not* in charge any more, and allows Harry Powers to do his job (since Jack considers him "a good kid").

AEGIS' Tech Section continues to study the Ironmonger technology, advancing android design and construction as well as the neural transfer process. Ideally, AEGIS will be able to offer dying or critically injured agents the option of transfer into android bodies. For now, progress is cautious while a team of experts keeps tabs on the Patriot's condition. If the GM wishes, Ironmonger could have enough of a breakthrough to outfit an entire team of android agents for AEGIS, a good setup for a super-agents style game at power level 8 or higher.

Game information on the new Patriot can be found in **Chapter 3** of the *Freedom City* sourcebook.

FREEDOM CITY OPERATIONS: THE ICEBERG

AEGIS headquarters is officially in Washington DC, but its *real* operations center can be found in downtown Freedom City, in the city's Federal Building. AEGIS' office occupies the 23rd floor, but their true headquarters (nicknamed "the Iceberg") is deep below the building, where AEGIS conducts operations and coordinates much of its national strategy.

THE ICEBERG	HEADQUARTERS

Toughness: 15; *Size:* Gargantuan; *Features:* Combat Simulator, Communications, Computer, Concealed, Defense System, Fire Prevention System, Garage, Gym, Hangar, Holding Cells, Infirmary, Laboratory, Library, Living Space, Power System, Security System, Workshop.

Cost: Cost: Abilities 6 + Features 17 = 23

THE 23RD FLOOR

These are the official offices of AEGIS in Freedom City. This is where AEGIS personnel meet with local law enforcement and bureaucrats. Stewart Bonham has an office here (a corner office, of course) with an army of secretaries who work with the official budget. There is also a media center that AEGIS uses when giving office tours to grade school students. (They had a much more extensive tour, but they were forced to discontinue them several years ago after Toy Boy used it as an opportunity to smuggle his action figures into the building.)

In Bonham's office (and a permanently "Out of Order" stall of the restroom) there are hidden elevators to the roof and the sub-basement. There

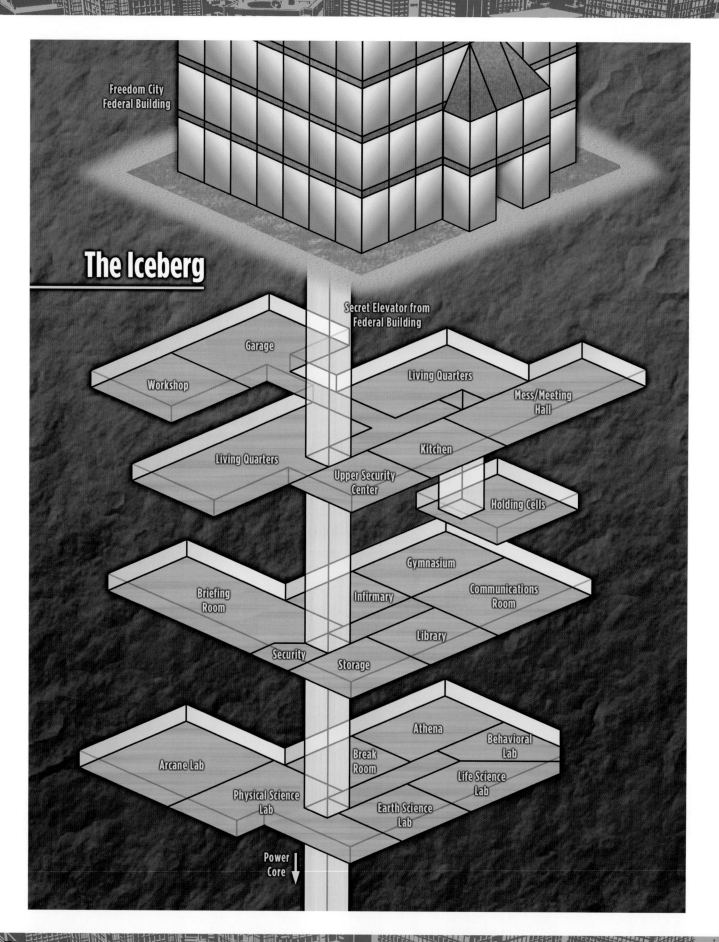

Freedom City
Federal Building

The Iceberg

Secret Elevator from
Federal Building

Garage

Workshop

Living Quarters

Mess/Meeting
Hall

Kitchen

Living Quarters

Upper Security
Center

Holding Cells

Gymnasium

Briefing
Room

Infirmary

Communications
Room

Library

Security

Storage

Athena

Break
Room

Behavioral
Lab

Arcane Lab

Life Science
Lab

Physical Science
Lab

Earth Science
Lab

Power
Core ↓

is a third entrance accessible by a special "overflow parking lot" in the lowest level of the Federal Building underground employee parking lot.

ROOF LEVEL

Although AEGIS doesn't officially keep office space in the penthouse, there are six small laser turrets (Penetrating Blast 8) on the roof with four emplaced heavy blasters (Blast 10) and two heavy gravity weapons (Gravity Control 10) that can be manned if the building comes under attack. See **Comic Book Firearms** in **Chapter 1** for details. There is also a small hangar where five AEGIS collapsing helicopters and two VSTOL folding fighter jets are kept (see **Air Vehicles** in **Chapter 1**).

SUB-BASEMENT-E

This section contains a concealed ramp connecting the bottom parking level to a special agent parking lot (with an attached garage and workshop).

A short staircase leads to the real base. Sub-Basement E (nicknamed "The Gallows") contains living quarters for agents: a bunkroom that can hold up to 20 visiting agents on short notice, 30 small barracks housing two agents apiece, and six full suites for officers and their families. There is also a common mess with a very modern kitchen—Raymond Bell, a master chef, is the head of the kitchen and the agents eat *well*.

SUB-BASEMENT-F

This small, isolated sub-level houses cells to temporarily contain superhuman prisoners until they can be shipped elsewhere, usually to Blackstone Island off the coast.

SUB-BASEMENT-G

This is where the agents live, work, and train when they are not in the field or in an office on the 23rd floor. This level includes a well-stocked library, a communications room, and the ever-popular House of Sweat (a gymnasium with a large weight room and training facilities for gymnastics, boxing, wrestling, and shooting). Not coincidentally, the base's infirmary is located next door. There is also a security office on this floor, which includes the base's arsenal.

SUB-BASEMENT-H

"Section H" (a homonym with Section 8, the military's discharge due to mental incompetence, though sometimes also called "Section Hell") is the Iceberg's lab complex. Powered by a small nuclear reactor (itself encased in an extremely tough Impervium shell), this is where alien artifacts and supervillain gadgets are taken for analysis.

The lab section is divided into five wings: one each for arcane/magic, behavioral science, earth sciences, life sciences, and physical sciences. The physical sciences lab includes a section dedicated to battlesuit research, and a repair and maintenance facility for AEGIS Super-MAX suits.

Also housed in Sub-Basement H is "Athena," an advanced computer system storing the memories of key AEGIS agents, tracking criminal activity worldwide, and coordinating the agency's considerable information resources. At the GM's discretion, Athena *may* be a full-fledged artificial intelligence working for the agency; otherwise "she" is simply a highly sophisticated expert system.

AEGIS OPERATIONS

AEGIS conducts operations wherever superhuman activity is known or suspected. Their primary role iof the organization is information gathering; they send teams to monitor incidents while they are in progress, interview witnesses, and dispatch forensic teams to comb crime scenes for evidence.

Their second (and most prominent) role is threat engagement. The organization's official policy is to avoid direct confrontations with superhumans, unless there is no other possibility of assistance and there is an imminent threat to the well being of the public. Whenever possible, AEGIS is supposed to defer to recognized local superheroes in handling supervillains. Of course, AEGIS agents didn't get their reputation for cowboy law enforcement by sitting on the sidelines. Therein lie the seeds of glory (and the occasional tragedy).

AEGIS' third role is cleaning up the mess. Superheroes have the pesky habit of beating up their opponent and walking away, leaving a supervillain body on the pavement. Sometimes, when no one picks them up, these bodies get off the pavement and start hurting people again. To prevent this, local law enforcement agencies often call in AEGIS assistance in getting them to prison. Of course, AEGIS uses their role in this task to try to impose their strictures on local law enforcement, which rankles more than a few locals (especially, of course, STAR Squad).

SPECIAL FORCES

In addition to their everyday work, AEGIS also has a number of special teams and task forces to organize information on special threats to America. There is a small SHADOW Task Force based in Freedom City that is going to get a lot bigger when SHADOW publicly reemerges.

Other AEGIS task forces are dedicated to a number of interesting topics: Superhuman Serial Killers, Apocalyptic Cults, Dimensional Rifts, Telepathic Political Tampering, Superhuman Commodities Fraud, Machine Empathy Crime, Superhuman Death Match Fighting, and the Great Alien Survey (an attempt to catalogue every known extraterrestrial and extradimensional species).

Characters, of course, might have separate affiliations with different task forces; a task force can brief the character of a situation (and introduce plot information into the game), and they also serve as a place to send an agent when their player is running late or absent from a game.

THE DANGERS OF SUPER SCIENCE

Arguably, AEGIS' most dangerous function is to examine supervillain weapons and alien artifacts to determine their properties. This is the job of the lab boys, and it's a testament to the dangers of the task that AEGIS' labs are often the most heavily secured section of their base. Some villains have left behind "Trojan horse" artifacts, which come to life and wreak havoc in a base, blow up in spectacular ways (one major city's headquarters was blown up by a bomb set by the Crime League in 2003), or mutate unfortunate scientists. (As is typical of an agent's gallows humor, a large sign hangs in each AEGIS laboratory that reads, "X days since last accidental monster creation.")

AEGIS does not involve itself in local affairs. They don't investigate local crime bosses unless they have connections to crime on a national scale. They don't perform bodyguard or escort missions unless they're related to a larger case. They will go undercover, but only when the ultimate target is a big one.

UNUSUAL MISSIONS

On the main bulletin board at AEGIS HQ is the so-called "Hall of Havoc," clippings of the most unusual missions AEGIS ever undertook.

THE CAPE OF GOOD HOPE

Centurion's cape was blown off his body during his fight with Omega, and lofted around the world, carried on the winds. The cape was seized by Toy-Boy, who tried to use it to make clothing for his action figures—and planned to sell the remainder to an assassin to turn into garrotes. AEGIS busted Toy-Boy and the assassin and tried to return the cape to the appropriate memorial, only to have to battle the cape itself when Quirk temporarily brought it to life.

AGONE OF DEFEAT

An AEGIS squad found itself transported back in time by the goddess Athena, who wished to defeat Hades' plan to use the powers of the titan Chronos to send the stolen arsenal of Olympus to his future self. The agents were forced to compete in the ancient Olympic games to win a laurel wreath (winning the Olympic wreath allegedly gave the athlete godhood, and only gods could enter the arsenal). And yes, one of the agents did have a camera and took some potentially embarrassing pictures.

TRIAL

A powerful alien captured a squad of AEGIS agents and put America, Earth's preeminent nation, on trial for its alleged "crimes." AEGIS was forced to defend their country in an alien court of law, and won interstellar respect for the organization and its deeds.

AEGIS AND SUPERHEROES

Using AEGIS in a supers game brings up the perennial problem with combat-capable NPCs: how to keep the PCs from becoming too reliant on them, and to keep them from upstaging the PCs, while still making them a useful and interesting addition to your *Mutants & Masterminds* game.

CAVALRY

Agents upstage PCs when they serve as cavalry to haul the PCs from a bad situation after they have failed. This is *not* how cavalry is effectively used in any genre. When the PCs have sacrificed themselves to win a victory and are now resigned to certain death, *that's* when you send in the cavalry. The cavalry rewards a hero's willingness to sacrifice themselves; they don't correct failure.

AEGIS GO-FERS

Superheroes may decide AEGIS agents make good go-fers, jumping to their side every time they call. At some point, have AEGIS request some very ugly or unappealing favors in exchange, have them be too busy to help out, or have them agree to come and then get distracted by another catastrophe.

There are, of course, good ways to use AEGIS in a campaign. Friendly AEGIS agents will help take supervillains into custody when the heroes have done their job and make sure they know who is responsible, they'll offer clues to their cases when a superhero's leads have run dry, they'll defend them to the press when someone's doing a hatchet job, and they'll even take them out for a stiff drink now and again.

COMPLICATING AEGIS

If you want to involve AEGIS in the series in interesting ways, encourage your heroes to link them to one of their complications. Examples include:

ENEMY

A fellow AEGIS agent is a traitor. You know it, he knows it, but you can't prove it, and you don't want to tip your hand (or you've tried, and no one believed you because everyone believed him when he showed evidence he was framed). You're trying to find ways to prove his disloyalty. He's trying to find ways to turn AEGIS against you and kill you before you can expose his secret.

HATRED

A supervillain killed someone you loved... and an AEGIS agent on the scene launched the attack that triggered the tragedy. Then, adding insult to injury, the AEGIS Commander of that squad was promoted to a top position in the agency and fawned over by the press. Everyone's forgotten about the death he caused, except you.

OBSESSION

You're a conspiracy theorist. Of *course* AEGIS is at the root of a secret plot to take over the world! And, you're going to prove it! But, then there's always the possibility that you're right....

REPUTATION

You encounter AEGIS agents when you need help, but, given your reputation, they don't help and may even try to arrest you.

RIVAL

There are a number of ways that this complication can play out. An AEGIS agent can be an old high school rival who married the girl you loved and throws it in your face every chance he gets. The local AEGIS commander may have a habit of showing up after you've all-but-beaten the bad guy, fire the final shot, and then take credit for the capture in the press.

SECRET IDENTITY

Perhaps your roommate's an AEGIS agent curious about some of your unexplained absences. Perhaps AEGIS suspects your costumed identity of doubling as a supervillain, and the only way they can be sure you're innocent is to find out who you really are. Perhaps the government is secretly putting together a database on the secret identities of superheroes and you're next on the list. In any event, your secret's in danger, and AEGIS is at the heart of things.

TEMPER

At some point in the past, you were brainwashed into having a psychotic episode whenever you saw an AEGIS emblem. The brainwashing hasn't entirely faded, and it takes an act of will to keep from going berserk when you see an AEGIS uniform.

TEMPORARY POWER LOSS

An AEGIS agent became involved in an accident with strange alien technology, and now he's sharing your powers. Whenever one of you gets overstressed, you lose control of the superhuman abilities and they get shifted to the other guy. You need to learn how to work together to keep each other alive while you figure out how to reverse the process, assuming the agent is willing.

EVERYDAY LIFE IN AEGIS

The everyday life of an AEGIS Agent is much like any military man or law enforcement officer: long stretches of boredom, cases that turn out to be false alarms or confrontation with society's dregs at their most pathetic, occasionally broken by moments of heart-pounding terror when a powerful supervillain raises a supercharged fist in your direction.

Young AEGIS agents are expected to serve the agency 24 hours a day, 7 days a week, with no time allotted for things like second jobs, raising a family, or taking a leave of absence to pursue a degree. Young AEGIS agents are either assigned to a satellite (where there's more freedom, but much less action) or live full-time at a major base. AEGIS tries to create a sense of bonding and camaraderie between junior agents. More experienced agents are allowed to live off base, raise a family, and take (approved) leaves of absence.

Between missions, agent life is taken up with training, intelligence briefings, and social gatherings with comrades (and sometimes plans to sneak off base without being caught). AEGIS is not quite as strict as the military, but a number of incidents involving off-duty AEGIS agents have hit the press lately, and AEGIS is a little sensitive about its image (particularly during Congressional budget hearings).

Of course, AEGIS agents have their hobbies. Agents from a military background are fitness buffs, and wrestling, boxing, and martial arts are very popular activities. AEGIS hosts biannual games where agents compete in boxing, weightlifting, shooting, running, and the ever-popular grenade toss event. AEGIS also fields a rugby team, and has an annual "friendly" competition with UNISON (this is affectionately known as "The Blood and Guts Bowl").

Additionally, AEGIS agents are very fond of tactical simulation games, ranging from chess to tabletop war-games. More artistic agents form musical quartets, choirs, or acting troupes, or perform hip-hop acts and improvisational comedy routines.

AEGIS OPTIONS

Some people believe the truth is relative; for such Gamemasters, here are a few changes you can make to AEGIS to fit the tone of the campaign.

THE AEGIS CONSPIRACY

Few things have been more done to death in the comics than the Evil-Sneaky Government agency populated by Evil-Stupid agents, but some Gamemasters like this Iron Age staple. Using this option, AEGIS is a pack of patriotic thugs who spout propaganda while clubbing the good guys, making the real good guys the people who oppose them.

This is *not* AEGIS, a semi-autonomous government agency that's interested in preserving the country against threats internal and external, and who puts the individual's welfare ahead of the system. However,

with only a few changes, a Gamemaster can portray them as red, white, and blue jackboots.

This version of AEGIS sees superheroes as the enemy, an insidious rival power to the United States government; according to this AEGIS' agenda, all secret identities must be uncovered, all superhero technology must be captured and dissected for secrets, and eventually, a way must be found to permanently neutralize all superhuman powers. As such, they represent the greatest threat to superhumans in the world today.

This version of AEGIS employs sneakiness in getting at the hero's secrets, but prefers brute force for everything else.

AGENTS IN BLACK

AEGIS is a very open organization, but what if they were as secretive as SHADOW? This version of AEGIS allegedly works for a minor government agency, and employs complete secrecy when possible. They're at the heart of a thousand conspiracies, but use clever disinformation to hide their activities behind a smokescreen. They use invisibility technology to walk unseen among the masses, and mind control to change people's perception of the truth. Their goal is to keep humans (even superhumans) from peering into a truth that's so shocking the human mind is not equipped to handle it.

Perhaps this truth is related to the Terminus, or perhaps Centurion brought it with him from another world, or it dwells inside the human heart. Small doses of the truth can give a person superpowers, but large quantities turns him into a mad threat to human existence, Only by weaving a web of lies can the veritamancers of AEGIS shield the human mind—and the planet—from forces that would surely destroy it.

THE AEGIS CODE

In order to bolster discipline, Harry Powers developed a code of mantras for agents to recite when they look like they're forgetting their duty. When an agent gets too disrespectful (or too rabid), a commanding officer is advised to stop the troop at the earliest safe opportunity and order the agent to repeat the relevant item.

- Intelligence and combat ability are an equal partnership.

- Disrespect never extends to the mission, no matter how tedious or unimportant it may seem.

- AEGIS is not a video game. Your goal is not to collect bigger "power-ups" and weapons.

- The life of a single hostage is worth more than the lives of a hundred soldiers.

- AEGIS is not God. AEGIS does not judge the people we protect. We provide equal protection to everyone.

- The Constitution of the United States will never be abused as long as an AEGIS Agent breathes.

- When there's trouble, AEGIS takes the initiative. AEGIS does not play it safe.

- When there's trouble, AEGIS uses its brains. AEGIS does not play it stupid.

AEGIS BATTLE CRIES AND CODE PHRASES

An agency can have all the weapons and badass soldiers on the planet, but they aren't officially *cool* unless they have a cool battle cry. Battle cries don't have to be long and complicated; in fact, the simpler they are, the more recognizable they are on a battlefield when mortar shells are exploding all around our heroes and death and carnage are everywhere.

Here are a list of some of AEGIS' battle cries and code words. If the player characters are playing AEGIS agents, tell them that the enemy has compromised the AEGIS playbook and they need to develop some new code words for their operations. In most situations, however, the following code phrases suffice:

- *"AEGIS defend!"* The organization's signature battle cry, the famous battle cry twenty AEGIS agents gave when defending the Capitol Building during the first Operation Inundation. This is the one *everyone* knows and loves; it's the line AEGIS agents say in movies and comic books and cartoons. Anyone who wants to change this one may end up having a little "talk" with Harry Powers.

- *"Shield wall!"* A battle cry for the agents to dig in and hold their position.

- *"Shields high!"* A call to charge.

- *"Turtle formation!"* Move to close quarters and cover a retreat.

- **"Broken arrow!"** An agent is down.

- *"To the wall!"* Do not retreat.

- *"Siege formation!"* Advance slowly and attempt to surround the enemy.

- *"Owl formation"* Agents move back-to-back so they don't get taken by surprise.

- *"Athena says, smite <target>"* Everyone concentrate fire on the specified target.

- *"Calling for Pegasus"* AEGIS requesting air support.

- *"Shield cracked"* (An agent has been telepathically compromised)

- For citizens of the United States, help is only an AEGIS agent away. (And we're good neighbors, too.)

ALERT STATUS

AEGIS uses an alert status scale to tell its agents when a crisis is occurring. A signal on the agent's commlink informs agents of status changes, and a colored diode on the communicator reflects the agency's current state of alert. Alert status ranges from the normal to the apocalyptic. The local commander sets the alert status, but the Director can override any alert status throughout the organization.

- **Condition Green:** Everything's normal.

- **Condition Yellow:** A major situation is expected in the near future. Everyone not on active assignment is to report to home base for a debriefing. Others should finish their current mission, and then report back to base.

- **Condition Orange:** An attack is occurring. Except in situations of life and death, everyone is to group and report to base, preferably in teams. Agents are to expect armed resistance, either getting back to base or at the base itself.

- **Condition Red:** A major attack is ongoing. The city is threatened and in imminent danger. Agents are to defend the local area by any means necessary.

- **Condition Black:** A major catastrophe. Agents are to abandon their base and perform rescue operations. If civil disorder is ongoing, agents are supposed to take control of the situation under martial law conditions.

- **Condition Ultra:** Following the Terminus Invasion, this level was nicknamed "Condition Omega" among AEGIS agents. Human civilization or even reality as we know it is about to cease to exist. The agent's orders are to gather as many able-bodied personnel as possible and travel as a group to a remote wilderness location, where they are to guard the species against extinction. If at some time the United States manages to reassemble itself from the wreckage, the agent's community is to provide assistance, provided the government swears allegiance to the old Constitution; if multiple compatible factions emerge, they are to support unity and the rebuilding of a large American nation. A post-"Omega Event" world could form the basis for an offbeat *Agents of Freedom* series in the rubble.

CHAPTER 4: UNISON

The United Nations International Superhuman Oversight Network, or UNISON, is the world's front line against supervillains. In the United States, AEGIS gets all of the press, but in the far corners of the globe, it's UNISON that takes the risks, putting their lives on the line against supervillains, often without well-stocked arsenals and bases (or even a good medic) at their disposal.

UNISON HISTORY

UNISON is an outgrowth of the UN Peacekeeping forces established in 1956 to deal with the Suez Canal crisis. At the same time as the first peacekeeping forces were established, many people wondered about forces to battle "extra-national security threats" such as the Killer Kaiser, a madman who threatened Germany in the early 1950s. Though supervillains were less common in those days, they were still a concern to international authorities, and when the first peace-keeping forces were established, a provision was added for the creation of a task force to coordinate and hunt supervillains who traveled across international borders.

The task force was inactive for six years, until 1962, when a superhuman called the Leopard King decided the newly independent nation-states of Africa were ripe for takeover. Establishing an army of "Leopard-Men" (brainwashed members of various local tribes), he launched an attack on several states, including Dakana. At the request of King M'Zale, the United Nations sent a peacekeeping force to intervene in the conflict. This was the first recorded use of United Nations troops to fight supervillains.

In 1962, the appearance of SHADOW in the first Operation Inundation posed a worldwide threat, and when AEGIS director Jack Simmons called upon his friends in the military community to battle them, one of the first people to receive a phone call was Edmond Stahl, the Danish head of the Dakana task force. Thanks in large part to Stahl's efforts, many European capitals were spared a SHADOW assault.

INVASION OF THE MALFIDIANS!

In 1969, the United Nation dealt with a new menace: the Malfidians, an expeditionary force from Farside City. They operated out of a small gravel quarry in Central England. Their mission was to procure certain rare elements and assess the planet for conquest.

Uniforce (as it was then called) learned of the menace, and with the help of a mysterious pair called the Associates (time travelers from the future who could possess the bodies of people in the present and work against threats that originated from outside Earth's timestream), the Malfidians were defeated, and the Associates exposed the influence of the time tamperer Zeitgeist, who had possessed the body of Lady Lunar's chief advisor. With her Malfidian Guard defeated, Lady Lunar pledged peaceful coexistence with the Earth.

Unfortunately, Lady Lunar had her own ambitions toward Earth that fit entirely within the normal confines of the timestream. Nonetheless, the incident solidified the creation of Uniforce to guard against alien threats. The Associates have made periodic reappearances in England over the years, explaining it sits on a "dimensional fulcrum," making certain temporal incursions more likely to occur there.

THE THREAT OF MENACE

In the 1960s, a number of terrorist and anarchist groups sprang up around the globe to threaten human freedom and the rule of law. SHADOW is the most infamous of these agencies of evil; however, the now largely forgotten MENACE (Mobile European Network Acquiring Control of Earth) was a group of European lunatics that stole plans for the Inexistence Gun, a weapon that altered causality. This brought about the creation of Team Alphabet (inspired by an offhand comment by the Associates that "you'd need a special agent for every letter of the alphabet to stop MENACE and their super weapon!"). Team Alphabet is an elite team of 26 super-spies who boasted that if they were given a suicide mission, they could solve it "from beyond the grave."

After several years of cat-and-mouse in every corner of the world (and beyond), Team Alphabet managed to cut off MENACE's access to the Arsenal Outside Time, where they had stolen their fantastic weapons, and put an end to their threat.

Although its name often makes eyes roll, the team has always fielded a top-notch contingent. The second-in-command of Team Alphabet, Agent E (Anthony Ellis) is the father of current UNISON chief Colonel Jennifer Ellis. During his mercenary days, Jack Wolf spent a year on the squad as "Agent W" (which, until then, had a reputation for being the "unluckiest letter").

CONVERGENCE

Thanks to the wonders of compartmentalization, Uniforce and Team Alphabet were not the only UN agencies investigating superhuman threats. By 1970, the bureaucracy of the United Nations had developed no less than six different agencies to handle matters relating to aliens and superhuman threats. Clearly, a more unified approach was needed to coordinate these agencies into an effective force.

For years, two sub-agencies, the United Nations Science Advisory Council (UNSAC) analyzed alien technology and the United Nations Paranormal Enclave Committee (UNPEC) advised on dealings with places like Atlantis. Enemy agents interested in sowing dissent had infiltrated both agencies. As a result, convergence of all United Nations concerns did not occur for another 25 years, though the other agencies moved closer to cooperation.

In 1993, everything changed. The Terminus Invasion was a clear signal that the world needed to organize a response to alien threats on a global scale. Major Jennifer Ellis of Great Britain and Major Jahal Daliwhal of India, both experienced Uniforce operatives, again proposed an umbrella organization. When UNSAC opposed the measure, Team Alphabet went undercover and discovered that UNSAC had been infiltrated by a race of alien parasites. With this threat exposed, there was nothing keeping the proposal from going forward. UNISON, a name meant to signify the single-mindedness of the agency to protect humanity, was formally created in 1994 with Spain's Carlos Santiago as its first director.

Despite being created in a favorable world climate, UNISON is not particularly welcome worldwide. Their standard operating procedure is for all national governments to approve their mission before entering. UNISON is supposed to share all intelligence with local authorities and national security agencies, and provide them with regular updates. For the most part, they are allowed to enter a country like the United States when they are on an intelligence-gathering mission to investigate aliens or supervillain threats with a worldwide scope, but they require a special permit to carry weapons.

Fortunately, the fact that Harry Powers and Jennifer Ellis worked together on numerous missions in the past has lowered bar-

> "SUPER-CRIMINALS ARE NOT GOOD STUDENTS OF GEOGRAPHY. THEY HAVE NO RESPECT FOR BORDERS.:
> —CHALCEDONY JOHNSON, UNISON COVERT OPERATIONS

riers between AEGIS and UNISON, though their agents often have a more intense rivalry. In Europe and Canada, they have good relations with most law enforcement agencies, and they are more active in the field. In particular, they have a good relationship with Interpol. In much of Africa and parts of South America, UNISON almost acts with impunity. UNISON has never been granted permission to enter the People's Republic of China, except for a few private meetings between Ellis and Chinese officials.

There is also one worldwide threat where even Powers defers to UNISON's expertise: Overthrow.

NEW THREATS

In the late 1980s, a new terrorist threat surfaced to trouble the world in the absence of SHADOW and MENACE: Overthrow, an alliance of European terrorist cells organized into a terrorist super-organization. This misfit collection of anarchists and political extremists began a campaign of bombing and assassination in Germany, which soon spread to France, Spain, Italy, and Greece, and eventually reached Eastern Europe and even America.

Vehemently opposed to globalization and other market forces driving economies together, Overthrow's skill in hiding itself from sight was matched only by the viciousness of their attacks. In 1999, Overthrow assassinated UNISON Director Santiago, and the following year they assassinated his successor, a capable Jamaican named Harry Smith. In 2002, the UK's Jennifer Ellis was appointed director of UNISON, and has managed to avoid Overthrow bombs and assassins' bullets (though not for lack of trying on Overthrow's part).

In addition to the Overthrow threat, UNISON aided in fighting the Grue invasion of 2003, fielding Uni-Storm, a fleet of ten space-capable heavy fighter planes that UNISON commissioned after the Terminus Invasion. The existence of a small independent space fleet came as something of a shock to members of the Security Council and sparked intense debate on UNISON's role in planetary defense. So far, Ellis has managed to defend her organization from attempts to cripple its independent military capacity, thanks in part to close friends of UNISON like King M'Balla of Dakana (who secretly backed the Uni-Storm program), the Atom Family, and (most notably) the Freedom League.

Atlantis has been a problem for UNISON, as the major world powers realized years ago that the Atlanteans would only accept UNISON as an independent monitoring agency. After long and grueling negotiations with the Atlanteans, they finally agreed to allow UNISON to maintain three monitoring stations within 50 kilometers of Atlantean holdings. Thanks to Atlantean technology, these stations have proven nearly useless in tracking Atlantean activities, but this hasn't prevented them from being targeted three times by Atlantis during recent standoffs with the undersea empire.

Another big test for UNISON came in 2004, when the West African nation of Côte de Liberté attempted to get UNISON involved in controlling its civil war. UNISON went in as an advance force for UN Peacekeepers and became involved in firefights with a number of rebel groups. However, UNISON refused to press the attack or otherwise become involved in a civil conflict. After the death toll mounted, UNISON was heavily criticized, but behind the scenes, they managed to negotiate a cease-fire that has held to this day. The effective combination of restrained force and diplomacy has been one of the hallmarks of Ellis' term as director, but even she admits that she is only one misstep away from a major disaster.

UNISON TODAY

Today, UNISON has something of a split personality. Because its objectives vary depending on the part of the globe in which they are operating, UNISON is much more aggressive in areas of the world that don't have a strong military presence or central authority. Elsewhere, they are investigators who deal with international threats like Overthrow. Their record is excellent; however, they are under intense scrutiny from many quarters.

Overthrow has proven a major source of frustration. UNISON has broken up numerous small cells and stopped dozens of plots, but they have failed to hit the leadership of the organization or discover the secret behind their funding. Years ago, Jennifer Ellis figured Overthrow had to have a powerful player in the world scene supplying it with goods

BUT THE UNITED NATIONS IS BAD!

In certain quarters, the United Nations has a reputation for ineffectiveness and corruption. There are many good reasons for this; even under the best of conditions, diplomacy moves at a deliberate pace. However, too much cynicism is problematic for comic book series, particularly those based on Silver Age comics, where the United Nations represents an ideal of unified world government instead of crushing *realpolitik*; the hope that all men, once they're brought together, can overcome their base nature and solve all of humanity's problems in a peaceful, equitable manner. Most comic book-style UN agencies, be it THUNDER, UNCLE, or UNIT, reflect this idealistic philosophy.

Bronze and Iron Age games allow for different (and more realistic) perspectives. Even these perspectives can be used to present good tests of moral character and cleverness: how an agency handles the frustrations of the United Nations bureaucracy—big countries trying to protect their client states, other countries too scared to commit forces to an operation that's either low on their priority list or which they fear will escalate into a major conflict—can be a challenging element in-game.

Just as AEGIS can be played as a stereotype, so can UNISON. But that's not the way they are in the World of Freedom. Like AEGIS, UNISON agents are the good guys. They exist to take down the bad guys and bring justice to the oppressed. Many who work in UN agencies, particularly health and relief agencies, are dedicated professionals interested in helping people. And, that is also true for members of the fictional UNISON agency. Especially since (due to at least two alien invasions over the last fifteen years), international politics of the world of Freedom City are a *lot* more amenable to cooperation and the need to present a united global front. At one of the chilliest moments of the Cold War in the 1980s, Ronald Reagan speculated an alien invasion could bring the superpowers together almost immediately. In the real world of Freedom City, that cooperation, unknown in our world, is a reality.

and intelligence. After a long investigation, Ellis has ruled out major world government backing, but has no clues, except for the possibility of a connection with Dr. Sin. Defeating Overthrow has almost become an obsession with her, but she is unaware of the greater threat behind Overthrow.

UNISON STRUCTURE

UNISON is based in Geneva, Switzerland, and reports to the Global Special Security (GSS) Sub-committee of the United Nations Security Council. This committee, composed of members of the Security Council, reviews major mission proposals submitted by UNISON staff, approves

UNISON DIVISIONS

Benefit	Military	Investigator	Command	Agency Bonus
1	Private	Officer	Intern	+0
2	Corporal	Lieutenant	Aide	+1
3	Lieutenant	Constable	Senior Aide	+2
4	Captain	Inspector	Deputy Director	+3
5	Major	Chief Inspector	Director	+4
6	Colonel	(none)	(none)	+5

funding, and reports on UNISON activities to the Security Council and the General Assembly. Because UNISON receives much of their funding from "outside" sources like Daedalus, they have more autonomy than one might think; the Security Council, generally understanding the complexities of UNISON's task, rarely raises a fuss.

Members of the organization come from two sources: military forces from member states that volunteer for peacekeeping and security duties, and so-called "extra-nationals," people who volunteer for UNISON duty in a way not unlike the French Foreign Legion. This "floating force" allows UNISON far more flexibility in mission deployment, but is controversial in the western world. In an effort to help UNISON, Dakana has generously agreed to sponsor these troops so they may avoid the bulk of the controversy, even though Dakana does not permit them to enter Dakana unless they remain on the UNISON Earth Defense HQ (the largest UNISON military base in the world, located in Mt. Mgava on the nation's southeastern border), leading some to question its legitimacy.

UNISON has three service branches: Military, Investigation, and Command. The Military branch works in conjunction with UN peace-keeping forces to deal with alien or supervillain threats. The Intelligence branch fights terrorist threats and gathers information on "humanity's common enemies." The Command branch oversees the bureaucracy and works toward meeting the supply needs of UNISON.

The current Director-General of UNISON's operations is Colonel Jennifer Ellis, detailed in **Chapter 4** of *Freedom City*.

OPERATIONS

UNISON's duties include peacekeeping (only in areas where there are active supervillains and the locals can't handle it), preparation for battles against global threats like the Terminus, and controlling dangerous paranormal sites.

ALIEN DIPLOMACY

The United Nations Extraterrestrial Liaison Organization (UNELO) is a United Nations agency set up to allow communications between extraterrestrials and humanity and protect the rights of law-abiding aliens on Earth. UNISON serves as an enforcement arm of the organization, providing security in first contact situations and performing rescue operations when aliens are endangered by human xenophobia (which, after the last two alien invasions, is a more frequent occurrence than most would like to admit).

BORDER CROSSINGS

UNISON's most politically delicate tasks are missions involving supervillains who cross over a border, attack a neighboring state, and then retreat back across the border. Most times, it's up to the supervillain's home country to capture him and extradite him to justice. However, some nation states just don't have the resources to handle them, and the supervillain becomes a major threat to life and liberty.

In this situation, the home country can admit they aren't equipped to handle the situation and formally request UNISON assistance. This is far from a perfect system, as no nation likes to admit they can't deal with their own problems, and neighbors get understandably angry at being victimized. This is why UNBIT exists, the United Nations Border Intervention Treaty, which allows UNISON freer access to their country. During supervillain incursions, when both nations are UNBIT signatories, the complaining nation may take its case directly to the Security Council and get approval for UNISON forces to deal with the threat.

These missions are often the worst part of UNISON's job, particularly when the "supervillain" is actually a covert military operative for the bordering nation and has his home country's backing.

INVESTIGATION

UNISON is far more likely to deploy its forces in an investigative capacity. When they are assigned to investigate an international terrorist agency or "border-crosser," they contact local authorities and request to be brought into a case on an advisory capacity. When the request is approved, the UNISON agent joins the officer on the case, and is supposed to work as their subordinate, allowing the local officer to lead the investigation (coordinate gathering of evidence, conduct interviews, etc.) while UNISON observes. Other times, the local officer attempts to obstruct the investigation. Frequently, however, the UNISON agent's superior training puts them in charge of the case. At the end of the investigation, the UNISON agent prepares a private report for the Security Council.

ASSASSINATION

The most devastating UNISON secret is the H-Treaty, a pact between members of the Security Council authorizing solos, freelance assassins, to "sanction" enemies. These missions occur only with the unanimous consent of all members of the Council, to deal with threats of a worldwide scope (while maintaining plausible deniability). These missions usually target terrorist leaders or dictators (who, unsurprisingly, are not supported by any of the major world powers). Freelance mercenaries and top secret agents are the usual choice for this assignment.

UNISON RESOURCES

Like other UN agencies, UNISON operates largely on the charity of its members. UNISON's private benefactors do give the agency some flexibility and allow it to station a few secret bases around the globe; most of its members rely on the host country to provide its needs. As a result, the resources available to a UNISON agent vary from assignment to assignment and the place where they are stationed.

EQUIPMENT

As with other agents, UNISON operatives rely on their equipment allowance to provide them with the tools of the trade. Typical equipment packages include:

TYPICAL UNISON AGENT (EQUIPMENT 2, 10 POINTS)

Pistol (6 points), cell phone (1 point), digital camera (1 point), notebook computer (2 points)

TYPICAL UNISON TROOPER (EQUIPMENT 4, 20 POINTS)

Assault Rifle (16 points), body armor (Toughness +2, 2 points), cell phone (1 point), night vision goggles (1 point)

TYPICAL UNISON SOLO (EQUIPMENT 10, 47 POINTS)

Holdout pistol (4 points), sniper rifle (13 points), sleep gas pellets (12 points), burglar's kit (2 points), disguise kit (1 point), concealed commlink (2 point), binoculars (1 point), concealed flash goggles (2 points), concealed gas mask (2 points), concealed multi-tool (2 points), night vision goggles (1 point), digital camera (1 point), notebook computer (2 points), broom (1 point), GPS (1 point), plus 3 points worth of additional equipment.

THE UNISON ARSENAL

Unlike AEGIS, UNISON is a grittier, more realistic agency, and that extends to the agency's technology. Comic book technology is rare (or non-existent); instead, UNISON almost exclusively uses real-world tech. Solos and other glamorous operatives, in keeping with the colorful world in which they operate, may also use spy-gear. The run-of-the-mill UNISON agent, however, uses conventional pistols and assault rifles (when they're allowed to carry weapons at all). In places where UNISON assumes a combat role, they may employ heavy weapons.

Similarly, UNISON uses conventional transportation on investigative missions in the United States and Europe (fitted with United Nations plates), and real world military vehicles when stationed on military missions (though they are mostly limited to armed helicopters and ATVs). With the exception of thirteen heavy space fighters stationed at the UNISON Earth Defense Base in Dakana, UNISON does not have access to tanks and fighter jets.

UNISON HEADQUARTERS

As a United Nations agency, UNISON headquarters tend to be small, inconspicuous, and/or mobile, or they operate out of other United Nations facilities (or, in emergencies, the local Dakanan consulate).

MOBILE MILITARY COMMAND

For those who run into UNISON in the field, this is a typical base for a UNISON military camp. Most of these are currently located in Africa, and are set up as a base of operations for UNBIT Treaty Duty.

MOBILE MILITARY COMMAND	HEADQUARTERS

Toughness: 5; *Size:* Huge; *Features:* Communications, Defense System, Garage, Hangar, Holding Cells, Infirmary, Isolated, Laboratory, Living Space, Power System, Workshop.

Agent Complement: 1 Commander (Hard-Nosed Commander), 10 Squads (50 UNISON Agents and 50 UNISON Troopers), 2-3 Field Investigators, 2 Communications/Surveillance Specialists, 2-3 Motor Pool Workers (Grease Monkeys), 3 Combat Engineers, 10-20 Support Staff.

Vehicles: 5 APCs, 5 Military Helicopters.

Cost: Abilities 3 + Features 11 = 14

SECRET UNISON BASE

UNISON also maintains secret bases to serve as command centers for solos and other covert operatives. These offices are centers of UNISON's intelligence network, as data from agents in the field are deposited here for initial analysis.

SECRET UNISON BASE	HEADQUARTERS

Toughness: 5; *Size:* Large; *Features:* Communications, Computers, Cover Identity, Fire Prevention System, Garage, Hangar, Infirmary, Laboratory, Living Space, Security System, Workshop.

Agent Complement: 1 Commander (Spymaster), 2 Squads (10 UNISON Agents), 1 Elite Squad (5 UNISON Troopers), 1-4 Lab Geeks, 1-4 Defense Analysts, 4-6 Support Staff.

Vehicles: 1 Disguising Car, 1 Spy Motorcycle, 1 Spy Sports Car, 1 Surveillance Van.

Cost: Abilities 2 + Features 11 = 13

UNISON CENTRAL HEADQUARTERS

UNISON's main headquarter is located in Geneva, Switzerland. This sprawling estate is an 18th Century castle that belonged to a Swiss noble family (and is haunted by a few family ghosts, although Ellis manages to keep them in line by making them honorary UNISON agents).

UNISON CENTRAL HEADQUARTERS	HEADQUARTERS

Toughness: 10; *Size:* Huge; *Features:* Communications, Computers, Cover Identity, Defense System, Fire Prevention System, Garage, Gym, Hangar, Infirmary, Library, Living Space, Power System, Security System, Think Tank, Workshop.

Agent Complement: 1 Commander (Spymaster), 20 Squads (100 UNISON Troopers), 1 Elite Squad (5 Roughneck Commandos), 5–10 Surveillance/ Communications Specialists, 5–10 Lab Geeks, 10-20 Defense Analysts, 4 Grease Monkeys, 4 Ace Pilots, 30-50 Support Staff.

Vehicles: 1 Disguising Car, 1 Spy Motorcycle, 1 Spy Sports Car, 1 Surveillance Van.

Cost: Abilities 4 + Features 15 = 19

UNISON SPECIAL COMMANDS

Depending on how widespread you want UNISON's structure and influence in your World of Freedom, one or more of the following special commands may exist as part of the organization. These are all optional, and generally secretive enough for most people to be unaware whether they exist or not. Use them as you see fit in your *Freedom City* series.

UNICORN

UNICORN (United Nations International Coalition Ordering the Reality Nexus) is the successor to Uniforce, a little known agency dedicated to fighting threats from beyond Earth's dimension or from other time periods. For their own protection (prolonged exposure to forces that alter the timestream frequently causes psychoses), UNICORN agents are conditioned to forget all operations until they are needed, at which time the memories are telepathically reactivated. At all other times, the agents believe they are UN bureaucrats stationed at a routine data analysis office in London.

UNCOT

UNCOT (United Nations Command On Terrorism) is a branch of UNISON specializing in fighting terrorist agencies like Overthrow. Their trained agents are some of the most capable non-superhumans in the world, but their sometimes-glamorous lifestyle (defeating international terror often requires agents to infiltrate networks of wealth and privilege, which is not cheap) and license to kill (which raises more than a few people's blood pressure) are sources of controversy. UNCOT is primarily made up of British, American, Israeli, and Russian agents who, despite old grudges, work well together.

UNIQUE

UNIQUE (United Nations International Quorum of Unaligned Exceptionals) is UNISON's superhuman branch. This is a Special Forces regiment of superhumans and support staff at UNISON's disposal. These brave men and women specialize in handling crises in the Third World, but they sometimes perform bodyguard duty at important UN functions and conferences. If you want UNISON to have its own super-team, then UNIQUE is it. Its membership and relationship with independent groups like the Freedom League are left for the GM to decide as best suits the series.

UNISON PERSONNEL

UNISON agents come in many shapes and sizes. While the PCs are more likely to meet basic agents, those who travel widely encounter a greater variety.

Among those agents who fit standard archetypes, bases are more likely to be commanded by Spymasters than Hard-Nosed Commanders, and the bulk of agents are basic UNISON Agents, with a smattering of Defense Analysts, Lab Techs, Surveillance/Communications Specialists, and Combat Engineers. Military personnel are basic UNISON Agents or (on rare occasions) Roughneck Commandos, and there's always a chance there'll be a UNISON Solo, Femme Fatale, or Dashing Spy visiting the base.

There are five main options for a UNISON campaign. First, there is a standard Action-Agents game set in Freedom City. Characters should be generated under standard (PL5) guidelines, though spy-gear is not allowed in the team Equipment allowance. For the purposes of the campaign, UNISON Agents are permitted to use firearms; however, the PCs should be aware they will lose the privilege if they are irresponsible with them.

The second option is a UNISON peacekeeper game, set in a foreign country. Their mission is to uproot a supervillain who has established himself in the nation, track him to his hidden stronghold, and remove him—and then deal with the political mess that ensues before they are extracted. This game is also built on PL5 level characters; for the Team Equipment Pool, however, there is no PL ceiling on military ordinance.

The third possibility is a UNICORN game set in London. The heroes are a UNICORN team attached to UNISON, living mundane lives until the Associates show up again with another threat to the nature of reality, and the team is reactivated. This campaign is built on PL5; as with the Peacekeepers campaign, there is no PL ceiling on military ordinance.

Fourth is the super-spy game. Players are glamorous super-spies who wander the globe, battling bizarre criminals in exotic locations. This game should be run at PL6; for the team equipment pool, any conventional weapon and any spy-gear is available, and the characters can re-allocate their equipment points each game session.

Finally, there is the option for the UNISON superhero series, with the players taking the roles of members of UNIQUE, the UNISON super-team. This is a standard *Mutants & Masterminds* series at power level 10 or higher. The characters are likely recruits from different UN member nations around the world, giving the team and the series an international flavor.

UNISON AGENT

The basic UNISON agent is an investigator, often on detached duty from a national law-enforcement organization, although some work full-time for the agency. These agents are not military peacekeepers or soldiers (use the Soldier archetype from *Mutants & Masterminds* for UNISON military assets).

UNISON SOLO

"Solo" is another name for an assassin. While UNISON does not often call upon their services (officially), UNISON solos travel to any part of the globe to complete their mission. This is the flipside of the Dashing Spy, a no-nonsense killer on the side of the angels. Equipped with the latest spy-gear, the solo eschews flash and dazzle in favor of subtlety—and results.

CHALCEDONY JOHNSON

The head of the UNISON covert operations bureau in Freedom City is Chalcedony Johnson, a seemingly young woman who is older than she looks. She is actually the daughter of Captain Griff Johnson, a WWII US Navy Captain and Auriana, a Utopian. When Johnson's PT Boat was destroyed in a Japanese attack, a Utopian woman boating in the waters found and rescued him. They fell in love, and nature took its course. She kept her true heritage a secret from her husband and daughter, but raised Chalcedony with Utopian ideals.

When Chalcedony grew up, a career in UNISON seemed the best fit for her beliefs. She is an idealist (and sometimes an argumentative one, especially when cynicism is expressed within earshot), but there is no question that she backs up her ideals with dedication. She is troubled by her mother's disappearance; Auriana was forced to return to her people when the Utopians chose to cut off contact with the outside world.

UNISON AGENT — POWER LEVEL 3

Str 10	Dex 12	Con 13	Int 15	Wis 14	Cha 10

Skills: Computers 3 (+5), Diplomacy 4 (+4), Drive 4 (+5), Gather Information 4 (+4), Intimidate 4 (+4), Investigate 8 (+10), Knowledge (behavioral sciences) 2 (+4), Knowledge (civics) 2 (+4), Knowledge (current events) 2 (+4), Knowledge (streetwise) 2 (+4), Language 1 (English), Notice 4 (+6), Profession (agent) 3 (+5), Search 5 (+7)

Feats: Benefit (rank) 1, Defensive Roll, Equipment 2

Combat: Attack +3, Damage +0 (unarmed), Grapple +3, Defense +4 (+2 flat-footed), Knockback -1, Initiative +1

Saving Throws: Toughness +2 (+1 flat-footed), Fortitude +4, Reflex +1, Will +6

Saving Throws: Toughness +3 (+2 without helmet), Fortitude +3, Reflex +1, Will +1

Abilities 14 + Skills 12 (48 ranks) + Feats 4 + Powers 0 + Combat 14 + Saves 7 = 51

UNISON SOLO — POWER LEVEL 5

Str 12	Dex 16	Con 12	Int 14	Wis 12	Cha 16

Skills: Acrobatics 2 (+5), Bluff 4 (+7), Climb 2 (+3), Computers 4 (+6), Concentration 4 (+5), Disable Device 8 (+10), Disguise 2 (+5), Drive 2 (+5), Escape Artist 4 (+7), Gather Information 4 (+7), Intimidate 6 (+9), Investigate 4 (+6), Knowledge (current events) 2 (+4), Knowledge (streetwise) 2 (+4), Knowledge (tactics) 4 (+6), Notice 4 (+5), Pilot 2 (+5), Ride 2 (+5), Search 4 (+6), Sense Motive 4 (+5), Sleight of Hand 2 (+5), Stealth 2 (+5), Survival 2 (+3).

Feats: Attack Focus (ranged) 1, Benefit 1, Contacts, Defensive Roll 3, Eidetic Memory, Equipment 10, Evasion, Improved Disarm, Luck, Quick Draw, Well-Informed

Combat: Attack +5 (melee), +6 (ranged), Damage +1 (unarmed), Grapple +6, Defense +4 (+2 flat-footed), Knockback -2, Initiative +3

Saving Throws: Toughness +4 (+1 flat-footed), Fortitude +7, Reflex +10, Will +7

Abilities 22 + Skills 19 (76 ranks) + Feats 22 + Powers 0 + Combat 18 + Saves 19 = 100

MIKOS WEST — POWER LEVEL 5

Str 16	Dex 13	Con 15	Int 19	Wis 14	Cha 14

Skills: Acrobatics 4 (+5), Bluff 8 (+10), Climb 4 (+7), Computers 8 (+12), Concentration 4 (+6), Craft (electronics) 8 (+12), Craft (mechanical) 8 (+12), Diplomacy 4 (+6), Disable Device 8 (+12), Drive 6 (+7), Escape Artist 4 (+5), Gather Information 8 (+10), Investigate 6 (+10), Knowledge (technology) 8 (+12), Language 2 (French, German), Notice 4 (+6), Pilot 4 (+5), Search 4 (+8), Sense Motive 6 (+8), Stealth 4 (+5)

Feats: Attack Focus (melee) 2, Benefit (UNISON rank) 2, Defensive Roll 2, Elusive Target, Equipment 4, Improvised Tool, Inventor, Jack-of-All-Trades, Prone Fighting, Set-Up

Combat: Attack +7 (melee), +5 (ranged), Damage +3 (unarmed) or by weapon, Grapple +10, Defense +7 (+4 flat-footed), Knockback –3, Initiative +1

Saving Throws: Toughness +4 (+2 flat-footed), Fortitude +7, Reflex +6, Will +7

Abilities 31 + Skills 28 (112 ranks) + Feats 16 + Powers 0 + Combat 24 + Saves 15 = 114

CHALCEDONY JOHNSON — POWER LEVEL 8

Identity: Public, the general public is not aware she is half-Utopian

Occupation: Head of UNISON Covert Operations, Freedom City

Base of Operations: Freedom City, USA

Affiliation: UNISON

Height: 6′

Weight: 170 lbs.

Eyes: Brown

Hair: Dark Brown

STR	DEX	CON	INT	WIS	CHA
+7	+4	+6	+2	+4	+3
24	18	22	14	18	17

TOUGHNESS	FORTITUDE	REFLEX	WILL
+7/+6*	+11	+10	+11

*flat footed

Skills: Acrobatics 10 (+14), Climb 6 (+13), Computers 2 (+4), Concentration 8 (+12), Diplomacy 4 (+7), Disable Device 2 (+4), Drive 2 (+6), Escape Artist 8 (+12), Gather Information 2 (+5), Handle Animal 4 (+7), Intimidate 6 (+9), Investigate 2 (+4), Knowledge (behavioral sciences) 2 (+4), Knowledge (civics) 4 (+6), Knowledge (history) 2 (+4), Knowledge (tactics) 2 (+4), Knowledge (theology and philosophy) 2 (+4), Medicine 2 (+6), Notice 4 (+8), Pilot 2 (+6), Profession (agent) 3 (+7), Ride 2 (+6), Search 4 (+6), Sense Motive 3 (+7), Sleight of Hand 2 (+6), Stealth 6 (+10), Survival 6 (+10), Swim 6 (+13)

Feats: Assessment, Attractive, Benefit (UNISON rank) 4, Defensive Roll, Equipment 4, Fearless, Improved Grab, Instant Up, Jack-of-All-Trades, Move-by Action, Precise Shot, Teamwork, Trance

Powers: Immunity 2 (aging, disease, Limited to half effect), **Mind Shield 2, Super-Strength 1** (heavy load: 1,400 lbs.)

Combat: Attack +8, Damage +7 (unarmed), Grapple +15, Defense +8 (+4 flat-footed), Knockback –3, Initiative +4

Abilities 53 + Skills 27 (108 ranks) + Feats 19 + Powers 5 + Combat 32 + Saves 18 = 154

Auriana never had time to say goodbye to her husband or daughter.

In Freedom City, Chalcedony works out of the Dakanan consulate, located in an adjacent building reserved for UNISON (their unofficial headquarters in Freedom City). She is extremely good at charming people, but has some problems with people ruled by realpolitik.

Chalcedony is a beautiful woman and still looks to be in her late twenties, even though she has just turned 50. Six-feet tall, lithe, and smoothly muscled, she has neck-length dark brown hair, almond colored eyes, and a coppery complexion. On the few occasions when she is out of uniform, she usually wears a T-shirt and blue jeans.

MIKOS WEST

Chalcedony's second in command is an oddity: Mikos West, who, despite suffering from dwarfism (inherited from his mother's side of the family), is both a brilliant inventor and a superb hand-to-hand fighter. Mikos is surprisingly laid-back about his size, jok-ingly calling himself "the world's greatest little man of action." Mikos, a more practical man than Chalcedony, often helps her in situations where her idealism might get her into trouble.

CHAPTER 5: SHADOW

Beware SHADOW, the new Reich of Terror! Under the leadership of the infamous Overshadow, this cruel organization's objective is to finish what Nazi Germany began: nothing less than the total domination of the world! Bolstered by legions of clone troopers and some of the most fiendish devices ever invented, SHADOW fights a never-ending war to plunge the world into the darkness of the Overshadow, to rob mankind of the gifts of justice, democracy, and even free will itself!

Most believe SHADOW collapsed from internal struggles during the 1980s and was finally destroyed by AEGIS in 1990. The terrible truth is SHADOW has been lying dormant, planning and scheming for years with virtually no opposition. With the world lulled into a false sense of security and concentrating on other threats (like the terrorist group Overthrow), the day is rapidly approaching when SHADOW shall reemerge to once more darken the light.

SHADOW is the ultimate barbarian at today's gates; like its namesake, this vile organization casts a long shadow that threatens to engulf the ideals of the free world and the liberties of its peoples.

SHADOW HISTORY

The Second World War, much like the First, left many scars. One of the men whose fascist dreams were left in ashes was Sir Jonathan Darke, a British nobleman and Nazi sympathizer who was imprisoned as a German spy during the War. During the 1950s, Darke took bands of disgruntled ex-fascists and banded them together to form a secret army called SHADOW. Darke assumed the identity of the costumed Overshadow. In the early 1960s, this organization struck, launching a simultaneous assault on key targets around the globe. Thanks to the efforts of AEGIS and many superheroes, their scheme was foiled. Darke was tracked down and eventually killed.

SHADOW survived Darke's death—barely. Led by a secret council called the Penumbra, the organization spent years rebuilding its forces, using the DNA of one-time German Olympian Holtz Hellman to make an army of clones. In 1978, this army was unleashed, but they were again defeated by AEGIS and almost completely destroyed.

Again, SHADOW rebuilt. Although they nearly tore themselves apart in the late 1980s, a man named Heinrich Kantor, son of deceased Nazi war criminal Wilhelm Kantor, took possession of the Overshadow name and costume and seized control of the organization.

In 1990, as part of a mad plan to avenge his father, Kantor used advanced battlesuit technology and a mystical artifact called the Tapestry of Fate to invade AEGIS headquarters, where he took control of the agency. Revenge was not as sweet as Kantor had hoped, and eventually he was defeated and killed in a fight with retiring AEGIS-director Jack Simmons. Since Kantor's death, SHADOW has been bereft of leadership, now nothing more than a scattered collection of small local cells committing robberies and the occasional kidnapping and murder, certainly not a major terrorist threat like Overthrow. Some even believe it no longer exists as an organization.

Nonetheless, there are reports that the Nazi supervillain Nacht-Krieger is again active and working for (or even running) SHADOW. Furthermore, AEGIS believes the last surviving member of the old Penumbra, public relations expert Franklin Folkes, is cloistered in a hidden base in the eastern United States. American criminals have reported recent criminal contacts with purported SHADOW agents. The hierarchy of evil, SHADOW, may not be quite as dead as many people believe.

THE REAL HISTORY OF SHADOW

It's funny how careful public relations and a good disinformation campaign can warp the truth. The above history is a carefully crafted fiction. Here's the *real* story of SHADOW.

The year was 1938. The world stood at the brink of the most terrible and bloody struggle in brutal history. One of the key players in that upcoming conflict was Major Wilhelm Kantor of the SS, Himmler's right hand man. Unbeknownst even to the Nazi High Command, this dashing young major had a secondary allegiance as a high-ranking member of the Thule Society, accomplished practitioners of occult magic!

A lifetime of arcane rituals guided Kantor into the desert wastes of Libya, where his destiny lay. Spilling the blood of a dozen of Germany's finest soldiers to empower a ritual, Kantor caused a dead city to rise out of the sand. It was the lost city of Seti-Ab, burial site of the legendary sorcerer Tan-Aktor!

Pronouncing ancient Egyptian curses none had dared to speak aloud for millennia, the vile Nazi opened the wizard's tomb. As the final seal was broken, a black vulture descended from the desert sky and settled on the major's shoulder. This vulture was a *ka*, repository of the old sorcerer's perverted soul, only capable of returning from death to join the reincarnation of Tan-Aktor, Wilhelm Kantor himself!

Thousands of years ago, the sorcerer Tan-Aktor tried to murder Prince Heru-Ra and seize the throne of Egypt. The mortally wounded prince thrust a dagger into the sorcerer's heart, and they died together. Presented for judgment before the gods, Tan-Aktor's *ka* would have been fed to the great Devourer who consumes the souls of all who violate the laws

of *ma'at*. However, even this was not enough for the angry Heru-Ra. The young prince declared no one but he should be allowed to destroy Tan-Aktor, and demanded to be the instrument of divine justice.

The gods, both impressed and affronted by Heru-Ra's presumption, granted his wish. The two souls would never die. Like a pair of scarab beetles reborn in the dung, they would be destined to reincarnate time and again, to battle each other throughout time. In one blinding epiphany, Wilhelm became aware of his origins. He also beheld a hundred past lives, all of which he had spent in the pursuit of evil.

Armed with that accumulated knowledge, Kantor vowed to succeed where his previous incarnations had failed. He would become master of the world. He looked at the long shadows of the city etched in the sand, and vowed the world would fall under his *khebit*, his mighty shadow.

ULTIMA KNOWLEDGE

After blasting Seti-Ab to rubble to protect its secrets, Kantor returned to Germany. As a high-ranking Nazi who embodied the grandest ideals of Aryanhood, Wilhelm used his position to build his own empire of evil. Even the gods of the new age would fall under his shadow. He was appointed Undersecretary of Special Military Projects, giving him access to many of Germany's superhumans: Nacht-Krieger, Nosferatu, der Roter Adler, die Walküre, and many others. Sometimes directly, sometimes through intermediaries, Kantor commanded them all.

Only one fell outside his authority: der Übermensch, the ultimate champion of Nazi might! Conducting investigations through mystical and mundane means, Kantor learned der Übermensch was in fact named Kal-Zed and was a member of the Ultima race that had been discovered by the Thule Society. He was not even Aryan!

Kantor had the knowledge to potentially discredit and humble the mighty der Übermensch, but why engage in petty rivalries when one has an opportunity to gain the knowledge that can change the world? Kantor pretended to abase himself before the mighty hero of the Reich. Gradually, he wrested the secrets of the Ultima from him, and those things he could not learn through guile were unveiled by sorcery. By 1944, Kantor was in full command of the knowledge of the Ultima, but it was already too late. Kantor realized even if he could exploit those secrets, the Allies and their superhumans would seize them before they could be fully implemented.

In 1945, leaving Germany in flames and ruin, Wilhelm Kantor strode over the bodies of the Allies of Freedom and fled to South America, determined to build a new empire, an empire that would learn from the mistakes of Nazi Germany and Tan-Aktor, an Overreich that would never fall, enthroning him as the Master of the Earth for all time!

THE LENGTHENING SHADOW

Only one thing could sway Wilhelm Kantor away from the path of his destiny: the calling of his heart.

In 1945, Kantor fell in love with a young German medical researcher, Dr. Greta Göessler. Greta was one of the most brilliant minds working on Kantor's Projekt Zeugung, his first-generation cloning experiments. As a gift for his beloved, Kantor wanted to give her super-powers, performing the same ritual that transformed Ingrid Hildebrandt into the mighty Nazi villainess, the Valkyrie.

Unfortunately, the powers of the Aesir agreed to a non-interference pact with Earth's Master Mage and would not permit a second Valkyrie to walk the earth. They *did* transform Göessler into one of the Choosers of the Slain, but they declared she must pay a price, and promptly snatched her away to serve the Aesir in Valhalla.

Kantor was enraged at himself for his weakness. He had allowed himself to fall victim to love, and for what? Love was a quality for lesser men, he decided, and devoted himself fully to his plan to build his new Reich. By 1948, his cloning experiments began to bear fruit. He grew hundreds of duplicates of himself and placed them in a huge incubation factory, all but one.

In 1950, Kantor rapidly aged one of his clones to adulthood and trained him as his successor. Dressing him in the garb of Imperial Germany, and christening him "the Killer Kaiser," the Nazi mastermind presented his doppelganger as Kantor gone mad. The hapless clone flew into Germany in a "Battle Blimp" and activated a conditioning protocol Kantor used on thousands of ex-SS soldiers, transforming them into the brainwashed "army of the New Reich."

In spite of his madness, the "Killer Kaiser" possessed enough of Kantor's cunning and intellect to terrorize Europe for two years, far longer than even Kantor anticipated. Some of Kantor's old foes finally destroyed the Battle Blimp in a spectacular dogfight over Dresden. The Kaiser perished in flames and the world breathed a sigh of relief, believing Wilhelm Kantor dead at last.

SUDDEN MOVES

While the outside world wrestled with the Cold War, the amoral monster was left free to plot and scheme in peace. With the power of his sorcery weakened by the counterspell cast by Adrian Eldrich at the end of the war, Kantor turned to technology and the secrets of the Ultima. His clone army matured in vats beneath the Andes, but he had time to develop other projects.

The Monarch, a flying fortress three times the size of anything else in the world in its day, bombed factories on the east coast of the United States before a squad of air aces shot it down. Despite grabbing the headlines, it was only Overshadow's field test in terror.

During the 1950s, Kantor began training units of soldiers using mental conditioning and primitive genetic engineering to fight the "upcoming struggle." These men would be the Umbra, the vast darkness that would swamp the world, and the entire organization would be called SHADOW (Secret Hierarchy of Agents for Domination Over the World).

Kantor delegated his authority when he recruited his "command staff," the Penumbra. First among them were the survivors of the Thule Society, led by an ancient, shriveled Rumanian sorcerer, the Crimson Mask. Colonel Jargon Reinholdt, the Nazi colonel who had been his aide-de-camp since the earliest days of the war, commanded its military wing and was bolstered by a pack of bright young South American military officers. These men would lead Overshadow's forces in Operation Inundation, the day when SHADOW would overwhelm the unsuspecting West and finally take control of the world! To increase the agency's influence, Overshadow incorporated the survivors of the Invisible Empire, a movement of American fascists of the 1930s and '40s. The Invisible Empire's secret bases provided SHADOW with a network of headquarters in the continental United States that would have taken years to build on their own.

Like a chess grandmaster, Kantor planned to build up his forces slowly and carefully, waiting until his first generation of clones became fit for duty before he struck. In 1961, something forced his hand: the Scarab appeared in Freedom City.

To others, the Scarab was just another colorfully costumed crime-fighter, a throwback to the masked mystery men of the Second World War. Kantor, on the other hand, recognized him for what he truly was the

reincarnation of Heru-Ra! Despite his oft-repeated claim that "emotions are for the common herd," rage filled the Overshadow's dark soul. He *knew* he had to destroy the Scarab (and the society he protected) without delay!

OPERATION INUNDATION AND ITS AFTERMATH

Giving his Penumbra less than a week to gather their forces, Kantor ordered Operation Inundation to commence. Around the world in Paris, France, New York, Washington DC, Freedom City, and thirty world capitals, SHADOW mobilized its troops and attacked major government, commercial, and media centers. It was an audacious plan, and for a few hours, the free world was plunged into chaos. Several major European cities were forced to surrender to SHADOW. In America, three of the largest military bases were in flames, and more than two-thirds of the country's major military resources were disabled or destroyed.

Unfortunately for Kantor, SHADOW's Freedom City cell had already been compromised by the Scarab, who tipped off the newly founded AEGIS organization. Kantor had dismissed AEGIS as a band of troublemakers and misfits. The "contraterror cowboys" (as the first generation of AEGIS agents were called) proved him wrong. As a result of their actions, SHADOW was unable to gain control of America's nuclear arsenal, the one thing that would have ensured success.

In the end, SHADOW captured less than 15% of its intended targets; of those it captured, it couldn't hold any for more than a few days. The unexpected intensity of the counterattack forced a retreat on all fronts.

Overshadow didn't have time to brood over his defeat; sensing a moment of weakness, one of the Penumbra, a disgraced British noble named Dr. Jonathan Darke, seized his opportunity. Formerly second-in-command of the Invisible Empire, Darke believed it was *his* destiny to rule SHADOW (and through it, the world). He mobilized the surviving SHADOW forces and launched an attack on Kantor's headquarters. With his back against a wall and a gun against his head, the Overshadow survived only by transferring his mind into one of his immature clones at the exact moment that Darke pulled the trigger.

Displaying Kantor's body as a trophy, Dr. Darke seized control of SHADOW. Unfortunately, there was no recovery from the failure of Operation Inundation, and Darke's victory proved to be a Pyrrhic one. Within a year, AEGIS demolished Darke's version of the organization, and AEGIS Director Jack Simmons declared, "there are no more shadows left for these creeps to hide in." Nearly everyone assumed Dr. Darke was the mysterious "Overshadow" who headed the organization, and with his demise, the world believed SHADOW could never recover. Only the Scarab remained unconvinced that the threat was over.

SHADOW'S SCHEMES

Less than two years after Operation Inundation, the Scarab's fears were realized with a new campaign of terror. A resurgent SHADOW reappeared in the United States and Western Europe, using I-Bots (imposter robots) to replace key military personnel and foment conflict. The nefarious androids brought the United States and the Soviet Union to the brink of nuclear annihilation before SHADOW's plot was foiled by the unlikely alliance of Centurion and Bogatyr.

Despite this setback, Overshadow (who now considered Wilhelm Kantor as dead as his other previous incarnations) continued to enact grandiose schemes. He took over city governments by polluting their water supply with a mind control drug; he turned nuclear power plants into giant bombs; he bred mutant animal packs and let them loose; he took over army vehicles by remote control. No scheme was too mad.

A MORE VISIBLE SHADOW

This history assumes SHADOW has not yet reemerged in the campaign world. If, on the other hand, SHADOW has been an active villain in your campaign world for some time, simply retcon it so a few years after Heinreich's supposed death, SHADOW was believed destroyed, but reemerged (with a new Overshadow) sometime before your campaign started. This is a pretty minor deviation from the "official" story, whose sole purpose is to keep an aura of mystery around the agency.

Of course, if it's no big secret that Overshadow is Wilhelm Kantor, that's fine too. The "official" story takes a back seat to player enjoyment any day of the week.

Time and again, AEGIS and other superheroes nipped these schemes in the bud, usually with a daring commando raid. But while AEGIS celebrated victory after victory, Overshadow's true goals advanced unhindered: the theft of information, the acquisition of new technology, and the construction of a suit of battle armor that would set him among the gods. Overshadow was engaging in the most elaborate game of misdirection in history. Using the Penumbra as a front, no one even came close to penetrating his identity.

THE SCARAB FALLS

In the early 1970s, Overshadow received a visit from the universe's hippest time traveler: the "Tick-Tock Doc" and his time traveling companions, the Counter-Clock Culture. The archvillain seized control of "the grooviest time machine in the universe" and attempted to rewrite his past defeats. Multiple incarnations of the Scarab stopped him with the aid of Dr. Tomorrow, but the evil genius learned enough about time manipulation to cut the growth time of his clone armies in half.

In 1978, Overshadow attempted a second Operation Inundation, this time using the first of his cloned armies. Unfortunately, too many of the clones considered themselves the Overshadow rather than mere foot soldiers; his army, instead of obeying its master's commands, tore itself apart. The second Operation Inundation was an even bigger debacle than the first. Many people heroically resisted the clone army, but the hero of the hour was the Scarab. Overshadow's old nemesis discovered the weakness in the clones and, pushing his telepathic powers to their limits, fomented dissent in thousands of soldiers, ensuring SHADOW's defeat across the globe.

Overshadow realized he needed to improve the indoctrination techniques for his clones. He also knew that before he had any chance for success, he had to eliminate his old foe, the Scarab, at all costs.

Returning to his occult roots, Overshadow summoned the Scions of Sobek, ancient sorcerers who had been rivals to both Tan-Aktor and Heru-Ra, and charged them with the destruction of the Scarab. Declaring that they took commands from none except Sobek or Set, the Scions immediately turned on Overshadow and destroyed his cloned body. Of course, Overshadow had anticipated their treachery, and once again transferred his consciousness into another body.

The Scarab had no such recourse. He had not recovered from straining his abilities during the second Operation Inundation, and was unprepared for an attack by foes as powerful or determined as the Scions. Storming into Freedom City like the locusts of antiquity, the Scions left a trail of carnage as they headed for the city center.

The Freedom League intervened, but the Scions seized control of them, and the city's defenders became the vanguard of the assault on the Scarab's Pyramid Plaza headquarters. Rookie hero Brainstorm was able to use his mental powers to delay the Scions, but he was no match for their power. The Scarab, arriving at the battle as Brainstorm gave his final breath, finally broke the Scions' control over the Freedom League, but the strain on his powers was too great, and he died, freeing his allies.

Using Eldrich's magic to shield their minds from a second takeover, the Freedom League tracked down the Scions, who were performing a ritual to send Freedom City back to the time of ancient Egypt, where they would use its advanced technology to rule the ancient world. In the subsequent battle, the League destroyed all but a handful of the Scions.

Although he had lost a base and a body, Overshadow was pleased. The death of his archenemy (and the humiliation of his other enemies) was more than adequate compensation for the loss of one body. Unfortunately for Overshadow, one archenemy was about to be replaced by another.

RAGNAROK

Overshadow's highest goal was godhood. He had used advanced science in unspeakable ways, genetically engineering the Kantor form into the most powerful body possible without marring its physical appearance. Most intellects would be proud at such an achievement, but Overshadow was unsatisfied, for he knew "greater gods than I still walk the earth." Overshadow, predictably, went to extreme lengths to achieve his goal. Once he even hijacked Centurion's body, but the transfer proved unstable. If Centurion was unsuitable, might there be a more suitable, and powerful, host body?

Once again, Overshadow turned to dark sorcery to locate the most powerful compatible form in existence and summoned it to him. The ritual complete, a figure strode into Overshadow's view from beyond the worlds, a huge, handsome man with flowing blond hair.

"Father!" the stranger called, instinctively recognizing Wilhelm Kantor.

Overshadow didn't give the man's claim a second thought before he struck to complete the psychic transfer. In fact, the man *was* Wilhelm Kantor's son. Unbeknownst to Overshadow, Greta Göessler was pregnant when the Aesir took her to serve them. In Valhalla, she gave birth to a boy, Albrecht. The Valkyries raised the child, nursed him with the milk of divine goats, and the power of Asgard strengthened him. Raised as a god, the boy gained extraordinary powers, including a will strong enough to resist his father's attempt to possess his body.

A grizzly oedipal conflict ensued. Rushing to their leader's defense, three platoons of SHADOW agents sacrificed themselves to cover Overshadow's escape. Leaving the ruins of the SHADOW base behind, Albrecht Kantor declared war against his treacherous father, taking on the name Ragnarok, the Twilight of the Gods. Whenever he found a SHADOW base, he left only devastation, and he didn't particularly care if innocent bystanders got in the way. Unfortunately for Overshadow, Ragnarok (together with AEGIS and an emerging generation of superheroes) cost his organization whatever advantage it might have gained from the death of the Scarab.

Still undaunted, Overshadow remained focused on his goal of world conquest. In 1984, the mastermind made contact with the Curator and attempted to interface with him to access the entire knowledge of the cosmos. Thanks to a meddling superhero, the resulting data stream fried the villain's brain, putting him in a coma for years.

With their leader out of action, the Penumbra was forced to take over the reins of SHADOW. Throughout the remainder of the 1980s, SHADOW ran more like a business than a world-conquering organization, and members of the Penumbra lined their pockets from stolen goods. Making money wasn't SHADOW's only concern; using the public relations genius of Franklin Folkes, SHADOW embarked on Operation Blackguard, the systematic destruction of the reputation of every superhero on the planet. It was a major catalyst for the decline in popularity of superheroes at large during the 1980s.

THE SHADOW SYNDICATE

The "Corporate Period" of SHADOW was arguably its most successful. The practical men of the Penumbra bought munitions plants, trucking and shipping networks, communications companies, banks, even security firms, and it was this "infrastructure of evil" that allowed the organization to expand, virtually unchecked, to a level beyond anything Kantor ever imagined. For obvious reasons, Overshadow preferred the centralization of power. A new attitude brought SHADOW new prosperity.

It was not to last, however. Within the Penumbra, that simplest and deadliest form of corruption—sheer greed—reared its ugly head, and by the end of the decade, SHADOW was on the verge of destroying itself in internecine conflict. This was the so-called "Shadow War," where SHADOW bases fought each other in the heart of America's cities, with AEGIS and many superheroes caught in the middle.

To save SHADOW, the Crimson Mask stole the Mirror of Souls from Eldrich's sanctum and used it to restore Overshadow's broken mind. The mastermind easily regained control of his organization, and immediately removed those who had lined their pockets and polluted the "purity" of SHADOW with "crass commercialism." Of course, Overshadow was happy to add the now-deceased members' fortunes to SHADOW's coffers, the organization kept the infrastructure the Penumbra had built, and (despite being at the center of the corruption) Franklin Folkes stayed on as a trusted advisor.

In SHADOW, success is sometimes more than its own reward.

THE DEEPENING SHADOW

In 1990, Overshadow managed to contact Greta Göessler in Valhalla. Their love was now just an old, distasteful memory to him, but Greta had achieved a high status among the Valkyries, so he exploited their old love (which *she* had not forgotten) to trick the Norn into giving him access to the Wheel of the Skein, the source of their power. Then Overshadow kidnapped a blind seamstress, Roz King, and forced her to weave the Tapestry of Fate, an artifact giving its possessor almost unlimited control over reality.

Armed with the Tapestry, Overshadow walked into AEGIS headquarters at the retirement party for his old enemy, aging AEGIS director Jack Simmons. He forced the AEGIS agents to prostrate themselves before him. Overshadow should have been satisfied with his triumph, but it wasn't enough. He wanted to see Simmons suffer for his defiance. He ordered AEGIS' top agents (Simmons' closest friends) to hunt him down and kill him. However, Simmons still had a few tricks up his sleeve, and with the help of Greta Göessler and Roz King, the aging AEGIS leader managed to gain control of the Tapestry of Fate.

Simmons used the artifact to transform himself into a young man, simultaneously wishing Overshadow out of his battlesuit. With the playing field leveled, the two old adversaries engaged in a brutal hand-to-hand struggle on the gondola of a rebuilt Battle Blimp, which Overshadow had transformed into a devastating weapon of war with the Tapestry. In the ensuing struggle, Overshadow fell to his death (of course, he transferred his mind into another clone). Simmons destroyed the tapestry ("Thanks for the birthday present, Overshadow, but it clashes with every room in the house"), accepted his mortality, and went into retirement on a high note.

The world believed SHADOW was finally destroyed, true to its roots, in a manner befitting an old Republic serial. Bloodied but unbowed, Overshadow decided it was to his advantage if the world continued to believe him dead. Again, he turned his attention to rebuilding his empire and using the wealth it had accrued to expand it on a vast scale. He recruited new members for the Penumbra, upgraded his battle armor, and authorized an ambitious program to build bases on every continent.

His program was interrupted, however, by a much graver threat than any AEGIS had ever provided: invasion from beyond.

TERMINUS

Earth had experienced invasions before, and Overshadow treated them like a vulture treats a corpse: opportunities to scavenge for new technology. However, the Terminus Invasion was different. This was no mere military exercise or glorified scavenger hunt. This was a fight to the finish for the fate of the universe.

Early in the crisis, Overshadow recognized the extent of Omega's power. He attempted to win his support, only to lose another body at the negotiating table. Realizing diplomacy would never succeed with such a nihilistic entity, Overshadow covertly deployed some of SHADOW's resources in an attempt to end the threat. Of course, even in a fight for survival, Overshadow remained true to his roots—he hijacked a squad of Omegadrones captured by AEGIS and dissected them to discover the secrets of Omega's technology.

There were several capable lieutenants in the Penumbra, but Overshadow lacked someone with a reputation for ruthlessness to serve as his enforcer. The archvillain remedied this by turning to his past: Nacht-Krieger, second only to der Übermensch in the hall of shame reserved for Nazi supervillains. The Scarab had imprisoned Nacht-Krieger under Pyramid Plaza in 1967; now Overshadow made contact with his old lackey and persuaded him to destroy the ring that granted him his powers. This act freed Nacht-Krieger from imprisonment, but condemned him to an existence as a living shadow.

Driven mad by decades of solitude, Nacht-Krieger was easily manipulated into rejoining the fold of SHADOW. Since his release, Nacht-Krieger has spearheaded most of SHADOW's most important operations and murdered dozens of AEGIS agents. The world knows Nacht-Krieger is at large once more, but no one has (yet) connected his reappearance with Overshadow. AEGIS believes that Nacht-Krieger is drawing on some of SHADOW's old resources, but no one suspects his true level of involvement.

OVERTHROW

A key to SHADOW's goals was its collaboration with the Foundry in the early 1990s to develop its teleportal technology. Overshadow used it to connect his bases so they could secretly transfer goods and materials without being detected. The efficient transport of goods reduced

SHADOW's need to commit open robberies, allowing them to plunder resources in remote locations, away from the public eye.

During the 1980s, SHADOW had drifted from its world-conquering roots, becoming a group of thieves. Because thieves were a lower priority for law-enforcement agencies than overt threats to national security, it served Overshadow's purposes to perpetuate that façade. However, SHADOW still needed a terror arm, so he gathered various European terrorist cells and combined them into a new organization, Overthrow. In the guise of a high-tech anarchist group, Overthrow would perform actions that advanced SHADOW's goals, but wouldn't lead AEGIS or UNISON back to their door. Overthrow would distract the world, allowing SHADOW to advance its goals in secret.

SHADOW TODAY

Overthrow played its role to perfection. Today, most people believe Overthrow poses a far greater threat to civilization than SHADOW (and many people doubt that SHADOW still exists at all), which is precisely what Overshadow wants them to believe.

Since 1990, SHADOW has taken to the shadows and vanished from public awareness. Only AEGIS continues to warn that (despite their inactivity) SHADOW remains one of the world's preeminent threats. With each passing year, however, fewer people take that warning seriously. It's amazing how quickly even something as terrible as SHADOW can fall off the public radar.

RESOURCES

n the late 1990s and early part of the new millennium, Overshadow became obsessed with three projects that were key to his plans for world conquest. First, he needed an impenetrable base of operations. Second, he wanted to grow his clone armies on a vast scale. Third, he wanted to reliably mutate clone agents into superhumans.

The construction of Nifelheim, SHADOW's huge hidden Antarctic stronghold (see *Freedom City*, **Chapter 6**) achieved the first goal. Nifelheim is SHADOW's crowning technical achievement. Never again (or so Overshadow hopes) will enemies ever break down the doors of his fortress and interrupt a plan just as it is coming to fruition. Now his designs could proceed in perfect security.

On every continent, SHADOW used the vast wealth it had amassed in the 1980s and '90s to purchase dummy corporations whose major purpose was to hide SHADOW's clone vats. The second goal has been

HOLTZ HELLMAN

Born in 1911, Holtz Hellman was Germany's most outstanding athlete in the late 1920s and 1930s. Tall, blond, with an Olympian physique, Hellman was a polymath: scholar, philosopher, musician, and athlete (as a boxer, he was a favorite sparring partner of Max Schmeling). Secretly, Hellman was also a member of the Thule Society. Obsessed with success, he made a pact with diabolic forces to win a gold medal at the 1936 Berlin Games, though his performance was overshadowed by Jesse Owens in several events.

A dedicated Nazi, Hellman was a notorious SS Colonel during the War (he was particularly fond of having boxing matches with underfed Allied POWs, until he was knocked out cold by a bare-knuckled young Arrow). Hellman fled to South America with Kantor and a number of other Nazis at the end of the war.

In many ways, Hellman's career paralleled Kantor's—they even looked like they could be brothers—however Hellman enjoyed the limelight far more than the future Overshadow. In South America, Hellman assisted in the creation of SHADOW. He also tried to get revenge on Tim Quinn after the American became the second Bowman, but his deathtrap backfired, and the once-athletic German was crippled.

Despite his infirmity, Hellman remained a key player in SHADOW until the first Operation Inundation, when he summoned demons to support the plot. His old foe Bowman broke the summoning circle with an anti-magic arrow provided by Eldrich, and a demon grabbed the SHADOW sorcerer and dragged him down into the Inferno. The aptly named Hellman has not been seen since.

Hellman's DNA was substituted for Kantor's in the records of SHADOW's cloning experiments, so experts have identified SHADOW's clones as his genetic offspring. This mistaken belief has ensured the name of Holtz Hellman continues to live in infamy.

achieved. A new generation of clone soldiers awaits the third Operation Inundation.

Many of SHADOW's resources have been dedicated to biological research. With an army of thousands of loyal volunteers at its disposal, SHADOW is the perfect place to explore the wonderland of superhuman genetics. It has made remarkable progress in giving short-term mutations to clones, though these mutations inevitably destroy the subject.

ALLIANCES AND OPERATIONS

Nacht-Krieger is not the only supervillain in the Penumbra. The Crimson Mask has been recruiting young sorcerers to rebuild the Thule Society. Furthermore, at the Mask's urging, Overshadow has reconciled with his son. Tired of being hunted by the authorities as a destructive vigilante, Ragnarok accepted his father's invitation to join him. The world is unaware of Ragnarok's change in allegiance, which was also motivated by his new bride: Anya Datsyuk, the Russian-born granddaughter of the original Valkyrie, who inherited a small fraction of her grandmother's powers (and more than a fraction of her beauty, arrogance, and ambition, which Overshadow finds quite charming).

Since the Terminus Invasion, Overshadow pays far more attention to diplomacy than he has in the past. He realizes that Earth's master criminals share common enemies as well as common ambitions, so he

has forged relationships with some of his more sociable rivals. Taurus and Dr. Sin are both considered "associate members" of the Penumbra, consulted on major operations, and their plans are to be respected (and even assisted) by SHADOW. Moreover, Overshadow is actively courting Superior—the former Nazi Übermensch (who's unaware Overshadow is the same Wilhelm Kantor he despised in the Second World War).

One recent attempted alliance has gone disastrously awry. Several years ago, Overshadow brought together himself, Dr. Sin, Taurus, Mastermind, Una, Gamma, Baron Samedi, Lady Lunar, and Talos to form a collective known as "the Council of Evil." This powerful but unstable collective fell apart thanks to efforts of the Freedom League and the betrayal of Talos, who tried to create a "Chimera of Evil" android out of the combined powers of the villains.

At some point in the near future, Overshadow plans two major operations. He still believes the only way to conquer the world is to overwhelm its defenses in one devastating blitzkrieg, so he plans a third Operation Inundation. First, however, he intends to remove one of the biggest thorns in his side. He plans to destroy every support mechanism the Scarab might have left his successor—even if he has to destroy all of Freedom City to do it. He has authorized increased SHADOW activity in Freedom City to prepare for the operation, even if it exposes SHADOW's renewed presence to his old enemies.

SHADOW ORGANIZATION

SHADOW's organizational structure is a simple one: a pyramid with vast numbers of indoctrinated clone troopers at the bottom, the Penumbra and Directorate in the middle, and Overshadow at the summit. Overthrow and the Thule Society are organizations that fall under the wider SHADOW umbrella.

Unlike other agencies, SHADOW has no rank structure, no complicated chain of command. In SHADOW, people know their place, and those who forget, from Jonathan Darke to the unfortunate Penumbra members who died in the Shadow War, don't survive long enough to regret their error.

OVERSHADOW

At the top of the pyramid is Overshadow, the clone of Wilhelm Kantor carrying his twisted mind and spirit. He is the unquestioned commander of SHADOW and one of the most powerful supervillains on Earth.

The general public has known the name "Overshadow" since 1962, when AEGIS uncovered it after the first Operation Inundation. However, thanks to Kantor's mind transfer trick (combined with a disinformation program), Overshadow's identity is shrouded in mystery. Even today, his true identity is known only to a handful of longtime associates in the Penumbra.

Public opinion holds that many people have worn the Overshadow costume over the years. AEGIS believes Dr. Darke was the original Overshadow, and other Overshadows include German athlete and one-time Nazi poster boy Holtz Hellman, various members of the Penumbra, and even Kantor's vengeful son Heinrich (a fictitious cover identity posthumously invented for the Overshadow who was defeated by Jack Simmons).

Throughout time, Overshadow has been a hundred faces of evil. He was a Philistine commander who plundered ancient Canaan, a cruel prince of medieval Russia, a leader of the Spanish Inquisition, the last (and bloodiest) high priest of the Aztec sun god Huitzilopochtli, a Hessian mercenary captain during the American Revolution, a sadistic

plantation owner during the Civil War, and many others. Only when he became Wilhelm Kantor, using the magic of the Thule Society to explore his mystical roots, did he become aware of his infamous role in history.

Overshadow is the eternal conqueror, the enemy of liberty. Ruling SHADOW from his seat of power in Nifelheim, Overshadow monitors the world, looking for weaknesses, and nurturing a hundred tyrannical schemes. Never fond of a fair fight, Overshadow prefers to supervise his operations from a safe distance. He only leaves Nifelheim for his annual inspection tour of each of his major bases (which is probably the best opportunity for heroes to directly confront him), to have face-to-face meetings with the Penumbra, or to deal with emergencies that can't be handled by Nacht-Krieger or his other lieutenants.

Beyond tending plans of conquest, Overshadow spends time with technical research (usually analyzing other people's work) and arcane study (poring over stolen ancient tomes). Overshadow is a brilliant analyst, but not especially creative; as the years and repeated failures have worn at his mind, he's become much better at implementing other people's ideas than devising his own.

Overshadow also keeps a vigilant eye out for the return of Heru-Ra. He knows a reincarnation of the Scarab is out there somewhere, and he intends to kill him *before* he can become a threat or find the resources his predecessor undoubtedly left for him. However, because of the magic of Eldrich (who promised the Scarab he'd cast a shielding spell in the event of his death), all attempts to track down that reincarnation's whereabouts have proven futile.

Overshadow's closest allies are Nacht-Krieger and the Crimson Mask. He enjoys Dr. Sin's company (they have had many long philosophical conversations). Taurus knew several of his past incarnations, so Overshadow's discussions of history take on the overtones of pleasant (if sometimes gruesome) nostalgia. Still, the master of SHADOW considers no one his equal; it is the reason why he and he alone is destined to rule the world as its immortal emperor, and none shall stand in his way.

THE DIRECTORATE

Overshadow doesn't manage the day-to-day operations of SHADOW; that task has been left for the Directorate. The Directorate is a mix of bureaucrats, analysts, and think-tank wonks, huddled together in the Antarctic cold of Nifelheim. Their primary jobs are to service SHADOW cells around the world, manage the organization's finances, and monitor the globe for situations worthy of Overshadow's attention.

Additionally, the Directorate is in charge of SHADOW's espionage program. If SHADOW needs someone to quietly gather information or perform a kidnapping, then the Directorate calls the shots. If a local SHADOW cell is present in the area, the Directorate calls the presiding Penumbra officer and the operation is delegated to him. If no local cell exists, then SHADOW gets Overthrow to do its dirty work. If Overthrow is not available, SHADOW deploys free-lance agents or supervillains (or clone agents trained as spies).

HILDA REINHOLDT

The head of the Directorate is Hilda Reinholdt, granddaughter of Kantor's original aide-de-camp. Although she has no superpowers (and has turned down opportunities to acquire them), she is an extraordinarily capable woman who is an excellent organizer and a physical equal for the best AEGIS agent. This is unsurprising; Hilda was once a high-level AEGIS operative (romantically involved with AEGIS Field Captain Michael Hughes before she was revealed as a double agent) and loathes the organization she once served. She is a loyal servant of Overshadow, but her hatred of AEGIS knows few boundaries, and she has often used SHADOW resources to further her personal vendetta without Overshadow's knowledge or consent. So far, she has gotten away with it.

Hilda is also the head of the Freedom City SHADOW headquarters, traveling between Nifelheim and Freedom City via teleportal. As the Freedom City base becomes more and more active, she will spend more of her time in the city. For her game stats, use the Hard-Nosed Commander archetype from **Chapter 1**. Hilda is a Caucasian woman in her early 30s, beautiful—except for severe burns that cover the left side of her face and her left hand. She wears her blond hair long enough to cover the scarred side of her face.

STORN

OVERSHADOW		POWER LEVEL 15
Identity: Public		**Occupation:** Terrorist organization leader
Base of Operations: Munich, Germany		**Affiliation:** Overthrow, SHADOW
Height: 5'11"		**Weight:** 175 lbs.
Eyes: Blue		**Hair:** Red

STR	DEX	CON	INT	WIS	CHA
+12	+2	+2	+14	+7	+7
34/14	14	14	38	24	24

TOUGHNESS	FORTITUDE	REFLEX	WILL
+17/+2*	+9	+8	+15

*without battlesuit

Skills: Computers 16 (+30), Craft (electronic) 16 (+30), Disable Device 16 (+30), Diplomacy 8 (+15), Drive 5 (+7), Gather Information 4 (+11), Intimidate 8 (+15), Investigate 4 (+18), Knowledge (arcane lore) 8 (+22), Knowledge (technology) 16 (+30), Notice 8 (+15), Pilot 5 (+7), Search 6 (+20), Sense Motive 8 (+15)

Feats: Assessment, Equipment 20, Improvised Tools, Inventor, Master Plan, Ritualist, Second Chance (saves vs. Mind Control effects), Skill Mastery (Computers, Craft (electronic), Disable Device, Investigate)

Powers: Device 24 (battlesuit, hard to lose)
Battlesuit: **Blast 15, Enhanced Strength 20, Force Field 10** (Continuous, Impervious), **Immunity 9** (life support), **Protection 5, Super-Senses 13** (blindsight [radio, extended x2], darkvision, direction sense, distance sense, infravision, radio, time sense), **Super-Strength 5** (heavy load: 50 tons)

Equipment: Give Overshadow up to 100 points in equipment, particularly headquarters and vehicles.

Combat: Attack +15, Damage +12 (unarmed), +15 (blasters), Grapple +32 (+17 without armor), Defense +13, Knockback –13, Initiative +2

Abilities 68 + Skills 32 (128 ranks) + Feats 27 + Powers 96 + Combat 56 + Saves 21 = 300

DOMINIC DOWD

Implementing many of Reinholdt's commands is her chief assistant, Dominic Dowd, a financial wiz kid and one of the brightest currency traders and financial advisors in the world. Dowd is an unscrupulous playboy who spends half of the year traveling the globe, frequenting gambling meccas, drinking, womanizing, and partying. Law enforcement agencies suspect his connections to SHADOW and to the European criminal underworld, but no one has ever been able to prove anything. Because of his high public profile, Dowd is probably the most easily accessible connection to the Penumbra, someone heroes can track to get to SHADOW'S inner circle.

On the other hand, anyone who has crossed swords with him has disappeared under mysterious circumstances, including a pair of French superheroes, so Dowd is not someone to trifle with.

For his game stats, use the Dashing Spy archetype from **Chapter 1**.

"BLACK" JACQUES DELACOURT

Military matters are left to Overshadow. However, the Directorate has input into them in the person of "Black" Jacques Delacourt, a traitor in the French Foreign Legion who is an archenemy of current AEGIS director Harry Powers (an enmity that extends from assorted betrayals, one of which forced Delacourt to wear an artificial hand, the perfect accessory for bitter ex-mercenaries who lose a struggle over a pit of crocodiles). For his game stats, use the Tough-as-Nails Mercenary from **Chapter 6**.

THE PENUMBRA

The Penumbra is SHADOW's advisory council. The full Penumbra is forty-nine members strong; it consists of twenty-two cell leaders from around the world, seventeen regional administrators, and the Council of Ten, Overshadow's chief advisors. The Penumbra coordinates the day-to-day activity of SHADOW cells and keeps the organization running as a unified whole. The Penumbra usually corresponds by a secured transmission, the Internet, or (in extreme situations) through telepaths like those of Project Mimir.

The seventeen regional leaders and twenty-two cell leaders run SHADOW cells in major cities and world capitals. They are usually ex-military or disgraced law enforcement officers, or descendents of Kantor's old Nazi and Thule Society associates.

The ten advisory members of the Penumbra are not cell leaders; they are people whom Overshadow views as valuable advisors or allies, even though he is mindful that many come with their own agendas. These include the following.

DR. SIN

Years ago, Dr. Sin came to Overshadow with a challenge: whoever lost a game of chess would become the other's servant. Overshadow agreed and won the game, but agreed to be "magnanimous" (that is, he wanted to keep Sin at arm's length while still keeping an eye on him), so instead of forcing Sin to work as his servant, he brought him in as an "advisory" member of the Penumbra, treating him as a respected ally.

Dr. Sin is the *de facto* head of SHADOW and Overthrow in Asia, promoting and protecting their cells (except, of course, when it conflicts with his personal agenda). Sin, abiding by the letter of his deal, handles the cells with exceptional efficiency (though not kindness; if anything, he seems to enjoy heaping abuse on clone troopers). Within SHADOW, Dr. Sin is known as the Scourge Emperor (if the PCs encounter SHADOW in the Far East, they won't recognize the true master of the hands of darkness until a suitably dramatic moment).

TAURUS

Another supervillain considered an ally and not a full member of the organization, Taurus sees SHADOW as a useful ally and a good source for guinea pigs. Like Sin, he uses his position with SHADOW to keep the agency from interfering with his personal schemes, and when Overshadow makes his next move, Taurus' loyalty is by no means assured.

However, Taurus and Overshadow are willing to leave that confrontation for the future. For the moment, they are collaborators; Taurus has shared samples of his genetic brilliance with SHADOW, helping to develop some of the short-term mutations SHADOW uses to turn clones into mutates. In return, SHADOW does not interfere—and occasionally assists—in the Labyrinth's schemes.

NACHT-KRIEGER

Not particularly respected for his intellect, the Nazi villain is SHADOW's preeminent symbol of terror, absolutely loyal to Overshadow. His presence on the Penumbra reinforces the archvillain's control of his agency. Sometimes, other members of the Penumbra employ Nacht-Krieger as an assassin, though no one really enjoys working with him. The Crimson Mask, who knew him and liked him in the old days, is surprisingly cold toward him; the Mask knows there are powers in the *Shattenwelt* that could corrupt even a servant as loyal as Nacht-Krieger, and worries that even if he is loyal to SHADOW now, the forces of that dimension might find a way to use him as their puppet.

HILDA REINHOLDT

The head of the Directorate, she is an Overshadow loyalist. See her description previously.

THE CRIMSON MASK

He is the head of the Thule Society, and is also an Overshadow loyalist. See his description in **The Thule Society** section.

PRINCE VULTORR THE CRUEL

The greatest of SHADOW's allies among the Serpent-People, this inhuman creature pays lip service to the Brotherhood of the Yellow Sign, but serves only himself. He is the Serpent-People's appointed ambassador to our world (who view SHADOW as the only thing in our world worthy of diplomatic contact). Vultorr's sole interest in SHADOW is using it for personal gain: especially gold, jewels, comforts, and magical artifacts. Vultorr is a powerful sorcerer who uses his powers and his alliances to open a foothold into our world. Unsurprisingly, he is a rival of the Crimson Mask, as he covets the Mask's magic and occult connections.

Beyond this, Vultorr's game stats and his background are being left deliberately vague, so the Gamemaster can customize him as best fits his plots. See the Serpent Person template in *Freedom City* for details.

DOMINIC ASHE

The head of Overthrow, his opinions probably garner even less respect than Nacht-Krieger's. Even so, he uses bluster and bravado as a cover for more insidious plans, and is one of the few members who might someday lead a revolt against Overshadow. See his description in the **Overthrow** section.

FRANKLIN FOLKES

Once the *enfant terrible* of SHADOW, this aging public relations master spends most of his time on Capitol Hill, where, under the guise of a leading political lobbyist, he cultivates crooked politicians and works against major law enforcement agencies, particularly AEGIS. As cunning as he is corrupt, he has become even more adept at not taking the fall than he was back in the 1980s. He is loyal to Overshadow, but would abandon him if it looked like he was about to be deposed. He is currently in charge of the Midnight Invective.

RAGNAROK

Kantor's prodigal son and former adversary, Ragnarok has reconciled and now sits on the Penumbra. He is being kept in reserve as a high-grade enforcer. See his description later in this chapter.

THE TENTH MAN

This is the name given to the mysterious and final (tenth) member of the Penumbra. He is so mysterious, in fact, even this book's author has no idea who "the Tenth Man" is; only the Gamemaster knows his true identity (or what mysterious influence he holds over the organization and Overshadow). In other words, this spot is for the GM to fill as desired.

The Tenth Man might be another clone of Wilhelm Kantor (maybe he is the "real" Overshadow, ruling from behind the scenes), a host body possessed by Zeitgeist, the time-traveling Nazi mastermind (see the *Golden Age* sourcebook for details), a pawn of Dr. Sin or Taurus, or whatever else you would like.

THE CLONES

The vast bulwark of SHADOW is comprised of legions of cloned troopers. The clones are raised through a rigorous process. Conceived in a laboratory, the clones are kept in stasis in vats until they have reached the biological age of seven. At this point, they are removed from the vats for a two-week acclimation and assessment period; the cloning process produces numerous imperfections, and clones that do not meet set standards are destroyed. They are returned to the vats, tested again at bio-age 14, returned to the vats again, and released at 21. Only 10% of clone candidates survive to adulthood. There are clone vats hidden in SHADOW installations on every continent; the number of clones in each facility numbers in the tens of thousands.

While in stasis, clones receive subliminal training and a *lot* of indoctrination. Those who have interviewed captured clones describe them as intelligent, but shallow; they are essentially human robots more fanatically brainwashed than the worst cult members. Most clones are programmed to inject a lethal poison into their veins in the event of capture (or if someone attempts to make telepathic contact with any of SHADOW's secrets buried in their minds), so such interviews are rare.

Clones live sheltered, soulless lives as members of their SHADOW cell. Days are spent training, and nights are spent in eight-hour sleep-indoctrination sessions. Clones don't know enough to expect anything more out of life, though there have been at least two escapes by clones who rebelled against the system.

The general public is aware SHADOW uses clones, but (thanks to SHADOW's disinformation campaign) believes they were taken from the body of the 1930s Nazi star athlete, Holtz Hellman.

A handful of exceptional clones are removed from the development process to receive special training. These are SHADOW's espionage corps, trained experts at infiltration and sabotage. The clone's appearance is surgically altered for the mission, sometimes radically (including changes to gender and ethnicity).

A few clones are extensively programmed and put into place as sleeper agents; they have no memory of their lives as agents, and appear as normal, capable people—until their programming is triggered.

SEND IN THE CLONES?

One reason SHADOW troopers are clones is frankly so heroes can beat up on large numbers of them without feeling bad, since the clones aren't "real" people, but little more than biological robots programmed with unthinking loyalty to SHADOW. In the typical light-hearted, four-color style *Freedom City* game, you don't have to worry too much about the origin or the fate of SHADOW troopers: they're faceless minions you specifically *don't* need to worry about.

If you're running a more post-modern game, and want to address issues like whether clone troops can develop their own sense of awareness or morality, or if taking them out in combat is really a bad thing, by all means feel free. Otherwise, don't worry about it.

SHADOW WORLDWIDE

SHADOW has bases on every continent and in every major world capital. Each world region has a coordinator, and that coordinator is a member of the Penumbra. SHADOW is truly a global threat. They tend to scale back their bases where their allies are active (such as continental Europe, where they defer to Overthrow, or the Far East, where they stay out of Dr. Sin's way). The "seventeen parts of SHADOW" are:

I: WESTERN UNITED STATES AND WESTERN CANADA

SHADOW's facilities are mostly a few conventional bases, as well as hidden vehicle storage bases in desert or wilderness areas. Their major activities here include infiltration of the Canadian drug trade, money laundering, and muscling into natural resources firms. Also, a few factory farms supply the food needs of hundreds of thousands of clones.

II: EASTERN UNITED STATES AND EASTERN CANADA

SHADOW has large bases throughout the eastern seaboard. There are large clone storage bases hidden under industrial facilities that went bankrupt in the 1980s and '90s. Some of America's largest steel mills are running (at a loss) just to provide cover for a hidden SHADOW base buried fifty to a hundred feet below the site. As these are traditional company towns, folks are used to not asking too many questions about the boss as long as they can pay their mortgages, unaware they are working for enemies of their country.

III: MEXICO AND CENTRAL AMERICA

There are more clone storage bases as well as munitions plants in Mexico. SHADOW is also involved with supplying weapons and vehicles to Central American drug smugglers.

IV: THE CARIBBEAN, VENEZUELA, AND COLOMBIA

SHADOW is only a minor player in the region's narcotics trade, but supplies weapons, vehicles, and uses drug dens and smuggler's hideouts as safe havens.

V: SOUTH AMERICA

SHADOW has major bases in Brazil, Paraguay, and Argentina. SHADOW cells operate in rural areas, and SHADOW has used folk religions to recruit locals for slave labor. Brazil is a center of SHADOW's genetic research

VI: UK, NETHERLANDS, AND SCANDINAVIA

This is where the bulk of SHADOW's European operations take place, and SHADOW is a major player in the British underworld. SHADOW is also building a backup Nifelheim-sized base beneath the island of Soroya near Hammerfest, Norway.

VII: CONTINENTAL WESTERN EUROPE

Here, SHADOW takes a back seat to Overthrow. At least one aging German industrial magnate is an old associate of Kantor's, and actively collaborates with SHADOW by supplying the agency with industrial and storage facilities. Overshadow has a surprisingly sentimental attachment to this base.

IX: EASTERN EUROPE

Overthrow operations take priority here. However, the Thule Society is actively recruiting sorcerers from small cults and the region's remaining gypsy clans.

X: THE MIDDLE EAST

Here SHADOW's forces are led by an Egyptian high priest of the Cult of Set and closely tied to the Serpent-People, who have enclaves in the area.

XI: NEAR EAST AND INDIA

SHADOW has an interest in India's burgeoning high-tech sector. A few of India's tech support centers are really SHADOW cells, gathering information on multinational corporations and their customers for SHADOW databases.

XII: THE FORMER SOVIET UNION

As Russia and the former Soviet republics have opened up, SHADOW has tried to infiltrate its criminal networks. They have been largely unsuccessful (though Overthrow has enjoyed much success with Soviet military and security vets), but they have made great progress in plundering some of Russia's mystical treasures.

XIII: SOUTHEAST ASIA AND OCEANIA

The bulk of SHADOW's heavy industry can be found in this area, particularly in Malaysia and Indonesia.

BEHIND THE CURTAIN

The incarnations and divisions of SHADOW are meant to reflect the comic books of the era corresponding to their history, with the caveat that agent books such as *Nick Fury, Agent of S.H.I.E.L.D.* tended to be a little grimmer than many comic books of the same era, and their heroes were more willing to use deadly force on their enemies.

- The Killer Kaiser of the proto-SHADOW period is a silly villain in the style of late Golden Age and early Silver Age comics.

- The grandiose failures of 1960s' SHADOW reflects agency plots in Silver Age comics (especially Steranko's run on *Nick Fury, Agent of S.H.I.E.L.D.*), with a touch of the 1980s' *GI Joe* and the more flamboyant *James Bond* films.

- Overthrow is a thoroughly Iron Age group. They are ruthless, do not play with kid gloves, and invariably create a body count. The same is largely the case with the "corporate" period of SHADOW in the 1980s.

- The history of the Thule Society is a cross between 1970s Horror books such as *Tomb of Dracula* or *Man-Thing* and early Vertigo titles (or pre-Iron Age Britpunk books like *Captain Britain* and *Marvelman,* published as *Miracleman* in America).

Within the timeline of SHADOW, there is room for scenarios with many different tones. Games do not *need* to be set in the present. Just set your campaign in the appropriate historical era, and have fun! Plus, there is always the potential for flashbacks and time travel to visit those other eras for anything from a scene to a whole series.

XIV: CHINA AND JAPAN

This is Dr. Sin's domain, although SHADOW is active in China's computer industry, whose expertise they are using to develop computer combat programs. They have also siphoned off resources from China's recent building boom and transferred them to their own building projects (including Nifelheim).

XV: WEST AFRICA

SHADOW is involved in the diamond and precious metal trade, often using slave labor (and mercenaries to keep government forces at bay). SHADOW also exploits some tribal magical traditions to further their own ends.

XVI: EAST AFRICA

SHADOW views the regional conflicts with distaste, but has one deep interest in the region: *daka* crystals. Stolen *daka* crystals were used in the construction of Overshadow's battle armor, and he would dearly like a steadier supply so he can build even more powerful devices.

XVII: AUSTRALIA AND NEW ZEALAND

SHADOW used the Australian outback as a major base in the 1970s and early 1980s, but when they tried to seize control of several of the most powerful mystical sites, they were dealt a major defeat by Australia's superheroes. SHADOW transferred most of its resources to Antarctica and has yet to rebuild in Australia.

Antarctica might constitute an 18th regional zone; however, it is wholly the province of Overshadow, as it is the location of SHADOW's main headquarters.

OVERTHROW

Overthrow, the fanatical terrorist cartel, is a secret wing of SHADOW. Whereas SHADOW tends toward colorful costumes, huge operations, and grand schemes, Overthrow agents have no costumes, no huge plans, and want to cause havoc and disrupt society. Under the leadership of Dominic Ashe, a European left-wing terrorist of the 1980s, Overthrow views modern society with dismay. Modern day anarchists, they use high-tech weapons (particularly explosives) in their fight against the corruption of 21st Century life. Once society is destroyed, Ashe promises that Overthrow will emerge from the ashes and rebuild the world in a "purer" form.

When his movement wavered in the 1980s after the collapse of the Soviet Union, Ashe received an offer from SHADOW to back his cause. Overshadow told him that he shared Ashe's concern over the direction of society, and promised that if Ashe cooperated, SHADOW would help reorganize the scattered splinter cells of Europe's left wing terror cells and bring them under his command. Ashe agreed to the deal.

In 1991, the revitalized Overthrow made its first attack, destroying a monument in Paris to the French superheroes of WWII. This was the first stroke in a bombing campaign that swept across Europe. Throughout the 1990s and the early years of the new millennium, Overthrow was responsible for hundreds of acts of violence: assassinating generals, cabinet ministers, and college professors, setting bombs and luring European superheroes into traps, as well as numerous kidnappings. It was the breadth of their activities that attracted UNISON's attention; clearly, Overthrow was more than just another small band of extremists.

In 1998, Overthrow expanded out of Europe in a big way, planting a huge cache of explosives under a globalization conference in Freedom City that might have killed hundreds of people, except for the intervention of a plucky novice hero. Since then, Overthrow (with SHADOW's blessing) has established a cell in the mighty metropolis, and attacked commercial interests around the city.

There are dozens of Overthrow cells around the world, and while the press sometimes exaggerates their threat, there is no question that Overthrow is dangerous. Overthrow cells are small, typically consisting of between 6–12 operatives (or a single brainwashed suicide bomber carrying explosives). They prefer stealth, sabotage, and surgical strikes to flamboyant commando raids (that's SHADOW's style—Overthrow is for tense, grittier espionage adventures). Overthrow Prime, the organization's headquarters, is based in Munich, hidden inside the political studies department of a small German university.

Cells communicate with each other through coded communications or secure Internet chat sites. Overthrow cells rarely use a central headquarters, though they will often rent space to store equipment. Overthrow does control several shipping companies and telecommunications networks. Eschewing typical superheroics, the group has only one melodramatic touch; at the scene of each of their crimes, Overthrow likes to mark their crime with a "circle T" symbol spray-painted on a convenient wall or floor section.

Ashe's closest confidante in Overthrow is Rebecca Ward, a former European terrorist with links to the Russian Mafia and various terror cells in the former Soviet Bloc. Ward is Overthrow's recruiter, seemingly able to find willing volunteers at a moment's notice, be they a competent Russian ex-special forces agent or a fanatic willing to blow himself up. Ward is looking for new recruits: those who wish to enter the elite ranks of Overthrow Prime must commit three acts for the cause: a kidnapping, a murder, and an act of terror.

In addition to Ward's superb recruiting skills, even regular Overthrow operatives are surprisingly well trained due to Overthrow's think-tank device, which inserts useful knowledge into the subject's short-term memory. Stats for a typical Overthrow agent can be found in **Chapter 4** of *Freedom City*. Advanced Overthrow agents can also use the Femme Fatale archetype from **Chapter 1** and the Capable High-Tech Adversary archetype from **Chapter 6**.

DOMINIC ASHE

While in his early 20s, university student Dominic Ashe became involved in the violent world of European political activism. He became a leader of student protest and dedicated himself to "waking up" society from its complacency. Supervillains and Marxist theory provided potent inspiration.

In 1989, he became leader of a small, active, and vicious terrorist circle he called "the Overthrow of Western Civilization." After the fall of the Berlin Wall, his attacks intensified, as he sought to "punish" Eastern Europe for joining with the decadent West, drawing disaffected

DOMINIC ASHE — POWER LEVEL 6

Identity: Public

Occupation: Terrorist organization leader

Base of Operations: Munich, Germany

Affiliation: Overthrow, SHADOW

Height: 5'11"

Weight: 175 lbs.

Eyes: Blue

Hair: Reddish brown

STR	DEX	CON	INT	WIS	CHA
+0/+6	+2	+1	+4	+3	+4
10/22*	14	13	19	16	18

TOUGHNESS	FORTITUDE	REFLEX	WILL
+6/+4**	+6	+4	+9

* right arm only **flat-footed

Skills: Bluff 6 (+10), Computers 6 (+10), Concentration 6 (+9), Diplomacy 6 (+10), Disguise 4 (+8), Drive 4 (+6), Escape Artist 4 (+6), Gather Information 6 (+10), Handle Animal 4 (+6), Intimidate 6 (+10), Investigate 6 (+10), Knowledge (business) 6 (+10), Knowledge (civics) 6 (+10), Knowledge (current events) 6 (+10), Knowledge (streetwise) 6 (+10), Knowledge (tactics) 6 (+10), Language 4 (French, German, Italian, Russian), Notice 6 (+9), Pilot 4 (+6), Search 4 (+8), Sense Motive 6 (+9), Stealth 6 (+8), Survival 2 (+5)

Feats: Beginner's Luck, Defensive Roll 2, Eidetic Memory, Equipment 20 (100 points, includes personal equipment and headquarters), Improved Initiative, Leadership, Luck 2, Master Plan, Minions 10, Seize Initiative, Ultimate Effort 2

Powers: Cybernetic Arm (**Enhanced Strength 12, Super-Strength 1**, Limited to One Arm), Sub-Dermal Armor (**Protection 3**)

Combat: Attack +6, Grapple +13 (+6 without cybernetic arm), Damage +6 (unarmed), Defense +6 (+3 flat-footed), Knockback –3, Initiative +6

Abilities 30 + **Skills** 30 (120 ranks) + **Feats** 42 + **Powers** 10 + **Combat** 24 + **Saves** 13 = 149

Ashe is not the fool most of the Penumbra take him for. He is playing a role, and biding his time until he can make a move to either gain independence from SHADOW, or (if he builds his confidence too much) take over the organization.

Ashe is now in his late 40s, though he maintains himself in good physical condition, with (thinning) reddish brown hair, dark brown eyes, a pointed beard, and (most notably) a cybernetic right arm, courtesy of an accident that occurred in a clock tower (during the one time UNISON nearly captured him). The few superpowers he possesses are courtesy of that arm and some sub-dermal armor implants.

THE THULE SOCIETY

Devastated by their defeat in the Great War, in 1918, a group of thirteen German officers gathered to form a coven with the intention of placing a curse on the nation of France at the moment that the armistice was signed. To better facilitate their dreadful spell, the soldiers revived the spirits of three ancient magicians: the Hungarian vampire Count Varney Orloff; the spirit of Scandinavian winter, the Winter King; and the haunted sorcerer known as the Crimson Mask.

The Three wanted to do more than just place a curse on France; they wanted to remain in the mortal realm and seize control of Earth's occult community. To prevent the soldiers from dismissing them as easily as they had been summoned, they bound the officers to a mystic compact in exchange for their help; if any of the Three were dismissed, the entire coven would die. Nonetheless, the sorcerers employed carrots as well as sticks, and the coven learned to enjoy the benefits provided by the Three: wealth and political power even during disasters of the 1920s and early 1930s. For their part, the Three found themselves comfortable in Germany, and the alliance went smoothly for decades.

Once they were settled, the Three pursued greater ambitions. The Winter King spoke of an enclave of supermen that troubled his dreams, the Hyperboreans of legend, and he believed Germany's rightful conquest could be attained if they formed an alliance with them, whom he believed were the Progenitors of the Aryan People. They lived in a hidden place called Ultima Thule, and the coven dedicated themselves to its discovery. To fully dedicate themselves to this quest, they branded themselves the Thule Society.

Between the wars, the Thule Society had two main objectives: to expand their mystical knowledge and power, and to patronize German expansion. In particular, they sought to back German adventurers and

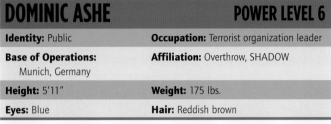

members from leftist organizations like the Red Brigade to his cause. This behavior attracted Overshadow's attention, and the supervillain decided to become Ashe's patron.

Running a global terrorist agency has not been easy. While Ashe delights in the small victories and the infamy he has obtained, he is frustrated that he does not seem to be winning his battle with western society. Worse, he has come to realize his patrons in SHADOW are using him (and his dream) for their own, decadent designs. At meetings of the Penumbra, Ashe is dismissed as a fanatic who is irrelevant to the greater plans of SHADOW. However, explorers, increasing their expertise so they could find Ultima Thule. They desired to be the powers behind the throne, and those who showed magical aptitude would be taken directly into their ranks.

Obsessed with the Northern spirit of the legendary Teutonic Golden Age, the Thule Society quickly tied itself to the Nazi party, seeing them as the force that most embodied that spirit of nationalism. Rather than work directly with Hitler, the Society looked for an intermediary whose first loyalty would be to *them*. They found it in a young Austrian sorcerer and adventurer named Wilhelm Kantor.

The Thule Society achieved their goal when they discovered Ultima Thule in 1938. Unfortunately, the Hyperboreans were not receptive to the Winter King's arguments for an alliance to ensure Aryan supremacy, and they erased all memories of the encounter, sending the intruders on their way.

It was a memorable year for another reason; Wilhelm Kantor visited the lost city of Seti-Ab and discovered his true nature as an eternally reincarnating scion of evil. Armed with the knowledge of a hundred lifetimes, Kantor went to the Three, claimed preeminence, and demanded obeisance. The Three, recognizing Kantor for who and what he truly was, offered to share their power with a kindred soul. Kantor agreed, and the Three became Four without bloodshed or even rancor.

World War II saw numerous triumphs for the Thule Society, but ultimately Allied sorcerers defeated them. As the vampire Nosferatu, Count Orloff was slain by the Bowman. After an attempt to bring a *Fimbulwinter* down upon the British Isles, the Winter King was defeated and imprisoned by Eldrich and Spitfire Jones within an artifact called the Summer Rose (an undying flower planted by Queen Elizabeth I at the start of her reign). Toward the end of the war, Eldrich cast a spell that undid the work of the Thule Society, negating the power of many Nazi superhumans. Kantor fled to South America. As for the Crimson Mask, Eldrich's counterspell also broke the spell that prevented him from being pursued by the spirit of Stefan Báthory, and he was forced to flee to the ends of the Earth to escape his wrath.

Most of the sorcerers who belonged to the Society died in the war. The few survivors went into exile with Kantor, and struggled to regain their power in the aftermath of Eldrich's spell. They were little more than Kantor's lackeys during SHADOW's first climb to power in the 1950s. Nonetheless, they made slow but steady progress in rebuilding what they had lost.

In 1962, following the failure of the first Operation Inundation, Overshadow realized he needed to bolster his resources (including his magical ones), so he formed a new Thule Society. He tracked down the Crimson Mask and worked a ritual that freed him from Báthory's curse. The Crimson Mask was charged with the task of rebuilding the Society.

No longer haunted by a centuries old Transylvanian Prince, the Mask was finally free to pursue his own ambition—to become the new Master Mage. He has slowly and carefully built up his forces, meticulously breaking the bonds Eldrich had placed on the old magic. Though ever loyal to Overshadow, he wonders if the years haven't taken too much of a toll on him, whether he hasn't sacrificed his passion to the clockwork precision of technology and genetic alchemy. The Mask is prepared to abandon SHADOW and set the Thule Society on its own course, but only if Overshadow looks like he is about to falter.

Based in a small castle on the outskirts of modern Budapest, the modern Thule Society is composed of thirty mages, three archivists, several alchemists, and an oracle. Their primary pursuit is the acquisition of arcane knowledge, but they also travel the globe to ensnare demons and elementals, which they plan to unleash *en masse* during the next Operation Inundation. They have also kidnapped at least fifty children from around the globe and press-ganged them into Hurstboer's Academy for the Gifted, a black arts academy hidden in a pocket dimension. Several hundred SHADOW clones have been consigned to "spell mills," where they recite incantations certain to eventually kill them, but the pronunciation of these dooming spells enhances the power of the Society.

Each year, seventeen Thule Society mages are designated as wandering agents, going into the occult communities to find out what is going on in the occult world, and work it into their designs.

More disturbing is their research into RMDs ("Rituals of Mass Destruction"). Last year, a German city was nearly destroyed when an experimental anti-pentagram weakened dimensional barriers and flooded it with demons. This caught the attention of a number of Earth's prominent mages, but they have not identified who is responsible yet. The Thule Society is becoming a major threat in the mystic world, a shadow within SHADOW.

The Thule Society is expanding. Each year, five sorcerers are nominated into the ranks; whoever wins a test of magic is initiated (the test is nearly always fatal for the losers). The initiate is drained of blood, which is replaced with demon ichor. Although the body eventually replaces the lost blood, the Mask believes few white magicians would willingly sully their veins with the stuff of demons, making it an effective test of loyalty.

THULE SOCIETY SORCERER					POWER LEVEL 8
Str 10	Dex 10	Con 12	Int 16	Wis 16	Cha 13

Skills: Concentration 8 (+11), Craft (artistic) 4 (+7), Diplomacy 4 (+5), Disguise 4 (+5), Gather Information 8 (+9), Intimidate 8 (+9), Knowledge (arcane lore) 8 (+11), Knowledge (current events) 4 (+7), Knowledge (theology and philosophy) 2 (+5), Notice 6 (+9), Search 4 (+7), Sense Motive 8 (+11), Sleight of Hand 4 (+4)

Feats: Attack Focus (ranged) 4, Connected, Ritualist

Powers: Magic 8 (*Spells:* Eye of Compulsion [**Mind Control 8**], Fog of Forgetfulness [**Area Mental Transform 8**], **Mystic Blast 8**, **Mystic Bonds 8**, Mystic Blinding [**Visual Dazzle 8**], **Mystic Passage 8**, Mystic Shield [**Force Field 8**], Truth of Night [**Telepathy 8**]), **Mind Shield 3**, **Life Control 5** (*Alternate Powers:* **Boost 3** [any one biological trait, Ranged], **Drain 3** [any one biological trait, Ranged], **Healing 5**), **Regeneration 1** (+1 Recovery, Regrowth)

Combat: Attack +4 (melee) +8 (ranged), Grapple +4, Damage +0 (unarmed), +8 (Mystic Blast), Defense +7 (+4 flat-footed), Knockback –4 (–0 without Mystic Shield), Initiative +0

Saves: Toughness +9 (+1 without Mystic Shield), Fortitude +6, Reflex +2, Will +8

Abilities 17 + **Skills** 18 (72 ranks) + **Feats** 6 + **Powers** 51 + **Combat** 22+ **Saves** 12 = 126

THE CRIMSON MASK — POWER LEVEL 14

Real Name: Alexandru Movilâ	**Identity:** Secret
Base of Operations: Mobile	**Affiliation:** The Thule Society, SHADOW
Height: 6'1"	**Weight:** 175 lbs.
Eyes: Red	**Hair:** White

STR	DEX	CON	INT	WIS	CHA
+0	+1	+2	+9	+6	+1
10	12	14	28	23	13

TOUGHNESS	FORTITUDE	REFLEX	WILL
+12/+2*	+12	+5	+14

* without force field

Skills: Bluff 4 (+5), Concentration 12 (+18), Craft (artistic) 4 (+13), Diplomacy 8 (+9), Intimidate 12 (+13), Investigate 4 (+13), Knowledge (arcane lore) 11 (+20), Knowledge (current events) 2 (+11), Knowledge (tactics) 1 (+10), Knowledge (theology and philosophy) 2 (+11), Notice 10 (+16), Ride 2 (+3), Search 4 (+13), Sense Motive 12 (+18), Stealth 10 (+11), Survival 2 (+8)

Feats: Artificer, Attack Focus (ranged) 5, Connected, Inspire 2, Fearsome Presence 5, Ritualist

Powers: Immunity 3 (aging, necromantic effects), **Magic 10** (Spells: **Force Field 10**, **Mind Control 10**, **Mind Reading 10**, **Mystic Blast 10**, **Mystic Passage 10**), **Mind Shield 4**, **Nauseate 14** (Ranged, *Alternate Powers:* **Boost 9** [any one biological trait at a time, Ranged], **Drain 9** [any one biological trait at a time, Ranged], **Disintegration 7**, **Fatigue 9** [Ranged], **Healing 9** [Ranged]), **Regeneration 1** (+1 recovery, Regrowth)

Combat: Attack +7 (melee), +12 (ranged), Grapple +7, Damage +0 (unarmed), +10 (Mystic Blast), Defense +9 (+4 flat-footed), Knockback –6 (–1 without Mystic Shield), Initiative +1

Abilities 40 + **Skills** 25 (100 ranks) + **Feats** 15 + **Powers** 94 + **Combat** 32 + **Saves** 22 = 228

THE CRIMSON MASK

A prince in Fifteenth Century Bucharest, Alexandru Movilâ was involved in the desperate struggle to keep Eastern Europe under the control of Christianity. He was not otherwise a good man, as he asked a high price for his service in money and favors from the crowned princes of Christendom and from the Holy See itself.

Movilâ dabbled in the occult, developing curses for his (many) enemies as well as ways to sustain his life and increase his influence. He was also an extraordinarily bad neighbor: an unreliable ally and a repulsively cruel enemy, even by the standards of that time and place.

In the most desperate battle, the defense of Transylvania against the Turks, Alexandru accepted a bribe from the Turks and betrayed its lord,

Stefan Báthory to his death. Unfortunately, Báthory was a sorcerer of great power who was said to sit at the devil's left hand, and he placed a terrible curse on Movilâ. He would not die, but live so Báthory's spirit could torment him forever. Movilâ found himself chased nightly by a terrible apparition he had no power to resist.

Alexandru ran—straight into the arms of Báthory's closest ally, Vlad Dracula. The monster punished Movilâ with the death of ten thousand cuts; each day, a hundred tiny, precise cuts were cut on Alexandru's face, and then washed with vinegar. Each day for a hundred days, the process was repeated. Alexandru was supposed to go mad from the pain and eventually die from infection. His face became a puss-ridden blight; always bleeding from his sores, they mockingly called him the Crimson Mask.

However, death never came. Alexandru lived. When Dracula set him on a tree and impaled him, Alexandru crawled off the spike and fled into the night, still pursued by the haunting spirit. Wherever he went, he heard the voice of Stefan Báthory whispering, "Traitor, traitor," in his ear, filling him with horror. In desperation, Alexandru entombed himself and put himself to sleep, "until the time of one whose power can break this curse." Whether such a day would ever come was a matter for debate, for Báthory was more powerful than any sorcerer had been for generations.

Movilâ awoke in 1918, when the founding members of the Thule Society needed three masters of the arcane to empower their Armistice Day curse on France. His disfigurement was not cured by the centuries, so when they asked Alexandru his name, he simply replied, "The Crimson Mask." He assumed a position of power within the Society, using the other sorcerers to keep Báthory's ghost at bay.

For twenty-five years, the Society built up its magical talents, only to have them destroyed by Adrian Eldrich at the end of the Second World War. Báthory's ghost afflicted the Crimson Mask once more, so he fled Germany and took shelter within an artifact known as the Cabinet of Grim Silence, where Báthory's voice could not assail him. He stayed in the cabinet for over a decade, until Wilhelm Kantor released him and put an end to the curse. Kantor had been a Báthory in one of his previous lifetimes of evil, and in that family line, blood is stronger than magic. After five hundred years, Stefan Báthory was silenced.

The Crimson Mask has sworn never to be so tormented or humiliated ever again. Since his release, all of his energies are devoted to becoming Earth's new Master Mage—which he sees as an unassailable position—and heaven help anyone who gets in his way.

THE CORONA

The Corona is a branch of the Directorate, five scientists who have joined Overshadow to form a council devoted to advancing SHADOW's technological capabilities. The members are:

- **Dr. Ibn Al-Assad** is the head of SHADOW's high-technology program, dealing with computers, robotics, and battlesuits; he is based at a major SHADOW base hidden under the desert sands of Tunisia. Allegedly the white sheep of a Saudi family in prison for activities against the Saud Royal Family, this greedy and bitter young researcher dreams of a day when the Middle East is united under his heel.

- **Dr. Gemini Jones** is the head of SHADOWs genetics program; her laboratory is located on a hidden Pacific atoll. She is a true believer in Overshadow's promised world government whose medical experiments would horrify most sociopaths.

- **Dr. Winston Baker** heads SHADOW's special materials project, which is disguised as a Pennsylvania research facility for a legitimate company. Baker is an engineer who was fired by major defense contractors after AEGIS uncovered his secret sales to overseas military dictatorships.

- **Rudolf Heinz** is head of SHADOW's vehicles engineering group. He is a former Luftwaffe pilot who became immortal through a sorcerous pact.

The fifth member of the Corona is the head of the energy weapons group; that person's identity and location is left open for the needs of the Gamemaster.

These are not the only areas where SHADOW is conducting research (there are rumors of a lab in Tokyo dedicated to developing new poisons, for example), just the most prominent ones.

THE ECLIPSE GUARD

The Eclipse Guard is made up of Nacht-Krieger and his personal retainers, a squad of six mutates: four Shadow-in-SHADOW mutates, an Eye-in-SHADOW mutate, and a Gate-in-SHADOW mutate. Their job is to gather intelligence on AEGIS operatives, choose the most strategically valuable agent, lure him into a trap, and kill him without drawing attention or leaving a trail that can be traced back to SHADOW.

Even less known (but equally important to SHADOW), the Eclipse Guard has quietly arranged the deaths of nearly a dozen archeology and history students who have shown an aptitude in Egyptian studies, and another ten young men and women who were born between 1978-1979 and who moved to Freedom City from Egypt. Overshadow believes killing them can nip the return of the Scarab in the bud.

These murders are the backbone of SHADOW's Midnight Invective campaign, but they are only the beginning—now that he has honed his squad's techniques, Nacht-Krieger would like to test his murderous methods on more challenging prey.

THE SCIONS OF SOBEK

Although only tangentially associated with SHADOW, these sorcerers are useful tools for SHADOW. Their leader, Ka-Khemet, was a sorcerer who struck deals with numerous powers of the Black Land, from Set to the great serpent Apep. Set told him he would grant his wish, provided he corrupted the guardian crocodile Sobek into his service. Sobek was a benign deity, but not beyond ambition. He wished to have power equal to the sons of Ra, so he ordered Ka-Khemet to steal the Milk of the

HUNT 06

Sun, whose sustenance could elevate a demi-god to the status of the Eight Great Gods. In exchange for the milk, Sobek would lay a clutch of eggs wherein Ka-Khemet and his fellow sorcerers could place their *ka*, their souls. When the eggs hatched, they would be reborn as Scions of Sobek.

Ka-Khemet did as he was told, and stole the Milk of the Sun from the great temple of Ra. The theft of the milk attracted the notice of Heru-Ra, Prince of the Kingdom, and his good friend, Tan-Aktor, the sorcerer-champion. They interrupted Ka-Khemet's ritual, defeated an army of crocodiles, and prevented them from feeding the Milk of the Sun into the mouth of the guardian crocodile.

A magical duel between Ka-Khemet and Tan-Aktor ensued. Ka-Khemet was the victor, but the duel weakened Sobek's champion to the point where Heru-Ra could strike him down. Ka-Khemet and his guard were forced to flee their bodies, and their kas entered the divine crocodile eggs laid by Sobek, where they hoped to unite with the divine offspring and hatch with the power of gods. However, Tan-Aktor laid a curse on the clutch, preventing them from ever hatching. The Scions of Sobek were trapped within the eggs for eternity.

The cooperation between Tan-Aktor and Heru-Ra proved short-lived, replaced with eternal enmity. Millennia later, remembering the power the Scions possessed, the reincarnation of Tan-Aktor removed his curse from the eggs and allowed them to hatch. When they did, they indeed took the form of the Scions of Sobek, crocodile-headed sorcerers.

Sensing the presence of Tan-Aktor, the Scions immediately killed (and ate) the clone body that tried to negotiate with them. However, Overshadow told them of the existence of Heru-Ra as the Scarab, so the Scions next struck against their old enemy. They descended on Freedom City and used the Freedom League as their puppets, which led to the

Scarab's death. Once freed from their control, the Freedom League fought back, destroying all of the Scions except for Ka-Khemet and his two chief lieutenants.

Ka-Khemet fled to what was once southern Egypt (now the Sudan), where he enslaved several villages and had them build a hidden magical tower amid the swamps of the Nile. He began to search the world for magical artifacts, using a flying, cloaking pyramid as his base.

Overshadow knows of Ka-Khemet, his whereabouts and allegiances, and it is not hard to get messages to his ancient enemy and manipulate his hatreds so that the Scions dance according to his tune. The Scions are, and will likely continue to be, a useful weapon in SHADOW's arsenal.

The Corrupt Sorcerer archetype in **Chapter 11** of *Mutants & Masterminds* is a suitable template for the abilities of Ka-Khemet. For the other Scions of Sobek, reduce power level and major traits like Magic by three.

SHADOW OPERATIONS

The hands of evil are seldom idle. SHADOW's wide range of interests—robotics, energy systems, genetics, and the occult—means the organization dabbles in *everything*. With its combination of both science and sorcery, SHADOW encompasses a wide range of potential plots. They can be modern-day Nazis searching for the Holy Grail or the Spear of Destiny, or builders of mind-control or death-ray satellites. They can be spies who infiltrate the heroes' lives, sabotage their headquarters, and uncover their secrets, or mad scientists who build doomsday devices they plan to unleash on an unsuspecting world, or all of the above!

Some typical SHADOW operations include the following:

MYSTICAL ARTIFACTS

SHADOW, especially the Thule Society, does not believe there is *anything* Man Was Not Meant to Know. Knowledge, particularly arcane knowledge, is power, and SHADOW wants to seize it. So the organization is interested in sources of occult lore and mystic power, particularly ancient artifacts.

If an artifact is at the site of an archeological dig, SHADOW might kidnap an archeologist (perhaps a hero's secret identity or friend). If rival archeologists are trying to get at something they want, they may try to scare them off (if they are trying to avoid attention) or kill them (if they don't care about attracting attention).

When SHADOW's researchers fail to understand something they have uncovered, they will kidnap experts who might be able to do the job (or serve as cannon fodder or a handy sacrifice in case a demon unexpectedly breaks lose).

Artifacts can come in all shapes and sizes: books, statues, furniture, the relics of saints and anti-saints, bowls, urns, seals, ever-burning flames, weapons that never rust, idols that compel people toward certain behavior, the staffs of wizards, and the crowns of god-kings. The tactics SHADOW employs to take possession of these artifacts vary, but usually they send a six-man recovery team, one technical expert (an archeologist for digs or a security expert in case they need to break into a museum), and a sorcerer from the Thule Society as an advisor. If SHADOW's expecting trouble—or if Overshadow *really* wants the artifact, the complement is increased accordingly.

TECHNOLOGICAL SECRETS

SHADOW loves gadgets. The researchers of SHADOW are clever folks, and SHADOW never has a shortage of new technology to develop, field test, or smuggle to their cells.

Technological devices range from the conventional (new compact guns, weapons that can be dismantled and easily reassembled, communications signal hijackers) to the insidious (devices that turn cell phones into remote control bombs, brainwashing devices attached to televisions, auto-computer hackers that send data from any source, "discord rays" to make normally calm people argumentative and irritable, or even "behavioral reversal rays" designed to turn boy scout superheroes into temporary psy-

chopaths) to the bizarre (freeze guns, devolution guns, shrinking rays) to the terrifying (weather control machines, earthquake generators, time stop fields, or mass attractors designed to pull asteroids towards earth).

These devices require three things: development (either through research or theft), testing, and implementation. The more deadly the device, the more important it is for the heroes to stop it early in its development. With small-scale devices such as new guns, the crux of a scenario will involve preventing its distribution (usually with a raid on a warehouse or docks) or stopping its production (usually by a direct assault on a munitions plant). With bizarre devices, the Gamemaster wants to showcase their effects, so either a player character or a sympathetic non-player character will be set up as a victim, and the focus of the scenario will be on preventing SHADOW from using the device again.

SHADOW's most important lab facilities will be located under a base and use the base's facilities as security.

When a weapon goes to test, SHADOW's needs become trickier. The larger and showier the effect, the more likely someone will notice it (such as a casual observer from a distance or a satellite) and inform the authorities that something unusual is going on (of course, the more information that gets leaked, the more likely the heroes will get involved, so the Gamemaster *wants* the information leaked). And, of course, a mad scientist may decide to test a particularly bizarre device on a superhuman subject.

ESPIONAGE

Spying is SHADOW's *raison d'être*. They engage in industrial sabotage, stealing plans and sabotaging the plants building major defense projects. They have managed to set back some key projects by years, without being detected (or deflecting the blame to other villains or rival defense contractors). They are particularly active in computer and satellite espionage, and sometimes alter records of spy satellites to feed their enemies false intelligence.

THE MIDNIGHT INVECTIVE

If SHADOW were solely concerned with world domination, it wouldn't be nearly as dangerous. Unfortunately, Overshadow is as vengeful as he is power-hungry; anyone who has ever "wronged" him has a death sentence hanging over their head. The biggest target, of course, is AEGIS.

With the help of the ever-reliable Franklin Folkes, Overshadow devised a three-pronged plan to destroy AEGIS. This plan is the Midnight Invective, the systematic elimination of SHADOW's enemies, one agent at a time, if necessary. Over the last three years, SHADOW has secretly killed or arranged the deaths of nearly fifty AEGIS agents (and a dozen UNISON agents). Some have been ambushed during "routine missions," others were telepathically commanded to commit suicide, some came too close to a human bomb, and some have been ripped to shreds by a mysterious attacker (i.e. murdered by Nacht-Krieger). The targeted agents were amongst AEGIS' most capable, those who would normally mentor the next generation of operatives. SHADOW is chipping away at AEGIS' mid-tier leadership, the ones who would take control in the event of a major crisis.

The second part of the Midnight Invective is subtler. Thanks to the Crimson Mask's spells, off-duty AEGIS agents have been losing their temper in public places, resulting in injury and property damage, usually when the press is nearby. Most people believe this is simply an example of agents getting a little rowdy, and no one has detected a pattern in their behavior, not even that it seems to spike when the press is nearby, or when AEGIS' budget is being debated in Congress. With the combination of bad press and SHADOW influence within the halls of government, a few strategically placed memos are threatening to reduce AEGIS' budget for the first time since the Terminus Invasion. Clearly, this plan has Franklin Folkes' fingerprints all over it; the most cunning member of the Penumbra hopes AEGIS will be forced to close half of their bases within the next five years.

The third part of the Midnight Invective involves manipulating the selection process for new AEGIS agents. AEGIS agents have always had a cowboy streak, but thanks to SHADOW interference, recruiters often end up with the most wild, undisciplined agents they can find: people guaranteed to disrupt the organization from within. Almost sounds like a group of player character heroes....

PROJECT MIMIR

SHADOW, as noted earlier, does not have a major interest in psionics, but from small acorns do mighty oaks grow. Project Mimir is SHADOW's nascent psionics program, based in the parapsychology program of a major American university (left to the discretion of the Gamemaster). The program uses a special psionics detector to weed out real telepaths from charlatans and performs experiments on them.

SHADOW's goals are to develop more powerful psionic detectors, psionic field neutralizers for their bases, drugs to amplify or diminish a target's psionic abilities, and techniques people can use to trick mind-readers into believing false, implanted memories. The last project caused a serious security leak when a telepath lost control of her powers and began shifting people's consciousnesses between bodies at a frat party. SHADOW covered the incident by placing hallucinogens in the punch of the party and poisoning anyone whose minds could not be restored.

Other Project Mimir priorities are to increase the abilities of the Eye-In-Shadow mutates and identify (and recruit) clairvoyants and precognitives. One of these mercenary telepaths, the project's namesake, Mimir, is already active in SHADOW trouble spots; the organization trusts him enough that he may fill the next vacancy on the Penumbra, provided they can a find a way to reliably shield themselves from his telepathic powers.

I-BOTS

One of the oldest weapons in SHADOW's arsenal are the Imposter-Bots, or I-Bots. They have been used many times to impersonate SHADOW's enemies and deal crippling blows from the inside. Imposter-Bots have been in use since the early 1960s; the first models were molded to a specific appearance and had a remote operator providing the intelligence. Since the early 1980s, I-Bots can change shape between human forms and operate independently of human control (though they can still be operated remotely as well).

Imposter-Bots are expensive, so they are rare. They are sometimes found as prisoners in the cells of SHADOW bases, waiting to be taken as Trojan horses into the heart of the enemy camp. A few have been captured and reprogrammed by AEGIS. There has already been one attempted assassination on Harry Powers that was foiled because the target turned out to be an I-Bot duplicate. (Unfortunately, AEGIS has not captured a replacement Imposter-Bot in some time.)

The original designer of the Imposter-Bot is for the Gamemaster to fill-in to fit the needs of the series. If nothing else, they may originate with Talos and the Foundry (see *Freedom City* for details).

SHADOW SLEEPER AGENT

Like any good espionage agency, SHADOW's success often depends on their ability to place agents in important places. To carry out this twisted goal, SHADOW has developed a special type of operative: the Telepathic Sleeper Agent.

Many SHADOW Sleeper Agents do not realize they are actually SHADOW agents. They work until they have achieved a position where they can access sensitive information (state, military, or corporate secrets). The information is then stored in their brains until accessed by an Eye-in-Shadow who gives the appropriate telepathic trigger via mental communication. Most opponents do not even realize they have been raided.

There are instances of a few deep cover operatives who have become so horrified at the realization that they are SHADOW Agents that they enlist in the fight against SHADOW, so this agent can serve as a template for that rarest of creatures: the renegade SHADOW agent.

IMPOSTER-BOT				POWER LEVEL 8	
Str 26	Dex 14	Con —	Int 14	Wis 14	Cha 16

Skills: Acrobatics 3 (+5), Bluff 6 (+9), Climb 3 (+11), Computers 6 (+8), Concentration 3 (+5), Craft (electronic) 6 (+8), Craft (mechanical) 6 (+8), Diplomacy 2 (+5), Disable Device 3 (+5), Disguise 6 (+9), Drive 3 (+5), Escape Artist 2 (+4), Gather Information 6 (+9), Intimidate 2 (+5), Investigate 2 (+4), Knowledge (current events) 2 (+4), Knowledge (popular culture) 4 (+6), Knowledge (streetwise) 2 (+4), Knowledge (tactics) 2 (+4), Knowledge (technology) 2 (+4), Notice 6 (+8), Profession (choose one) 5 (+7), Search 2 (+4), Sense Motive 6 (+8), Stealth 6 (+8)

Feats: Attack Focus (ranged) 1, Eidetic Memory, Instant Up, Precise Shot, Stunning Attack

Powers: Communication 5 (radio), Morph 5 (any humanoid), Immunity 30 (Fortitude Effects), Protection 8

Combat: Attack +8, Damage +8 (unarmed), Grapple +16, Defense +8 (+4 flat-footed), Knockback –4, Initiative +2

Saves: Toughness +8, Fortitude —, Reflex +10, Will +10

Abilities 24 + Skills 24 (96 ranks) + Feats 5 + Powers 53 + Combat 32 + Saves 16 = 154

SHADOW SLEEPER AGENT				POWER LEVEL 6	
Str 10	Dex 12	Con 12	Int 14	Wis 14	Cha 16

Skills: Acrobatics 3 (+4), Bluff 6 (+9), Climb 3 (+3), Computers 2 (+4), Concentration 3 (+5), Diplomacy 4 (+7), Disable Device 3 (+5), Drive 3 (+4), Escape Artist 2 (+3), Gather Information 6 (+9), Intimidate 2 (+5), Investigate 2 (+4), Knowledge (current events) 2 (+4), Knowledge (popular culture) 4 (+6), Knowledge (streetwise) 2 (+4), Knowledge (tactics) 2 (+4), Knowledge (technology) 2 (+4), Notice 6 (+8), Profession (undercover agent) 5 (+7), Search 2 (+4), Sense Motive 6 (+8), Stealth 6 (+7).

Feats: Attack Focus (ranged) 1, Defensive Roll 3, Eidetic Memory, Fascinate (Bluff), Instant Up, Precise Shot, Stunning Attack. Teamwork

Combat: Attack +5 (melee), +6 (ranged), Damage +1 (unarmed), Grapple +5, Defense +6 (+3 flat-footed), Knockback –2, Initiative +1

Saves: Toughness +4 (+1 flat-footed), Fortitude +7, Reflex +6, Will +7

Abilities 18 + Skills 19 (76 ranks) + Feats 10 + Powers 0 + Combat 22 + Saves 16 = 85

SHADOW RESOURCES

Both SHADOW and Overthrow have developed huge arsenals of weapons and unusual devices to help them commit crimes. Overthrow uses ballistic weapons and a few high-tech spy gadgets designed to mask their presence.

EQUIPMENT

A typical SHADOW agent has an Equipment allowance, which can be spent in numerous ways. Here are some packages for each of the major archetypes:

TYPICAL SHADOW AGENT (EQUIPMENT 3, 15 POINTS)

Blaster pistol (10 points), body armor (Toughness +4, 4 points), commlink (1 point).

TYPICAL ADVANCED COMBAT AGENT (EQUIPMENT 4, 20 POINTS)

Blaster rifle (16 points), body armor (Toughness +3, 3 points), commlink (1 point).

TYPICAL ADVANCED INFILTRATION AGENT (EQUIPMENT 5, 24 POINTS)

Blaster pistol (10 points), body armor (Toughness +2, 2 points), commlink (1 point), multi-tool (1 point), cleaner's kit (1 point), investigator's kit (1 points), video camera (2 point), PDA (1 point), camouflage field (4 points), burglar's kit (1 points).

OVERTHROW TERRORIST (EQUIPMENT 7, 30 POINTS)

Hold-out pistol (5 points), holo-disguise (8 points), radio scrambler (3 points), commlink (1 point), burglar's kit (1 points), gas mask (1 point), sleep gas grenades (11 points).

SHADOW WEAPONS

Classification	Weapon Type
Gremlin	Blaster Pistol
Demon	Blaster Rifle
Hades	Blaster Heavy Cannon
Tartarus	Autoblast Rifle
Blackguard	Entropy Rifle
Craven	Fear Pistol
Exile	Fear Rifle
Viking	Force Field Projector Rifle
Impaler	Leech Pistol
Vampire	Leech Rifle
Raven	Neuro-Paralyzer Pistol
Vulture	Neuro -Paralyzer Rifle
Tarantula	Net Rifle
Nocturne	Tranquilizer Pistol
Nightmare	Tranquilizer Rifle
Morpheus	Sleep Gas Pellets

SHADOW WEAPONS

All conventional modern military weapons are available in SHADOW's arsenal. In addition, these comic book weapons are assigned to agents when they fit the mission profile (lethal weapons for assassination missions, restricting weapons for smash and grab missions, etc.).

Some other weapons are listed as experimental. They are allowed, but may malfunction at the GM's discretion.

No other exotic weapons are in SHADOW's arsenal, though at the Gamemaster's option, they might steal something from another agency. Overthrow only has conventional weapons, plus disguised and spy-gear equipment (see **Chapter 1**).

SHADOW VEHICLES

SHADOW, being a secretive organization, does not field many heavy military vehicles unless they are launching a major operation (or even another Operation Inundation). As befits its name, SHADOW prizes vehicles with stealth capabilities. Recently, however, SHADOW has devised a way to use its teleportal technology to move vehicles from its bases to teleport points hidden at small security bases. Though the teleport network is untested, Overshadow hopes it will allow the agency to field larger air and armor forces in relative security (though it remains to be seen whether most of these vehicles make it back intact).

Vehicles fielded by SHADOW are listed on the table below.

SHADOW EXPERIMENTAL WEAPONS

Classification	Weapon Type
Omega	Disintegration Pistol
Terminus	Disintegration Rifle
Downfall	Gravity Rifle
Chalice	Hypno-Rifle
Cyclops	Inertia Rifle
Charybdis	Vertigo Rifle
Whisper	Silence Grenade

SHADOW VEHICLES

Classification	Vehicle Type
Dagon	Armored Hovercraft (ports only)
Satan	Military Helicopter
Tiamat	Combat Speedboat (ports only)
Charon	Flying APC
Stygian	Flying Platform
Nyx	Cloaking Truck
Cereberus	Combat Van
Typhon	Fighter Jet
Apophis	Stealth Attack Helicopter
Sobek	Cloaked Gunship
Sutekh	Tank

OVERTHROW EQUIPMENT

Overthrow does not have huge cloning vats, teleport machines, genetically engineered agents, or death rays, but they have every item on the spy-gear equipment list. Additionally, they have a number of fantastic inventions that put them on the cutting edge of the espionage world.

THINKTANK MACHINE

This plot device justifies Overthrow agents having advanced skills and training they should not have. The device can implant the following skills at whatever rank the GM deems appropriate: Computers, Disable Device, Investigate, Knowledge (civics), Knowledge (current events), Knowledge (history), Knowledge (technology), Notice, and Survival.

BRAINWASHING MACHINE

Sometimes the weakest spot of an enemy is their mind. Overthrow's brainwashing machine is meant to exploit this; bombarding the senses with messages subliminal, overt, and obscene, the brainwashing machine has bent many fragile minds to its will. It has a Mental Transform 10 effect and requires at least an hour to work on a subject.

ORIGAMI ESCAPE GLIDER

When an operative who breaks into a tall office tower needs an escape route, this is the tool of choice. Stored in one's belt, removing the belt and pushing on the belt buckle causes it to expand in a few seconds into a small hand glider with a plastic sheathe. The glider cannot fold back into a belt once it is used, making it a one-shot item.

Origami is a nickname for the device, however Overthrow researchers have in fact developed a piece of paper that rapidly expands when sprayed with a special chemical. It is theoretically possible to make an appropriate origami sculpture (such as a crane), spray it, and use it as an escape craft. It is Flight 3 with the Gliding modifier and the Collapsing feature.

Size: Medium (Diminutive when folded), **Toughness:** 5, **Cost:** 4 equipment points

POWER OVERLOAD BOX

This small but powerful bomb hooks into any electrical system within 30 feet through the nearest wiring. When activated, it generates a pulse of electricity guaranteed to take all but the most heavily protected electrical system offline (Nullify Electronics 8, Full Action, Limited to Connected Targets). Both Overthrow and SHADOW use this device to take out electrical systems prior to sending in an intrusion team.

Size: Small, **Toughness:** 8, **Cost:** 4 equipment points

SHADOW HEADQUARTERS

Local SHADOW cells exist to carry out orders from SHADOW Command. A Cell Leader runs each cell and reports to his region's Penumbra officer. There are twenty-two Penumbra officers scattered across the globe, each led by the Leader of a cell in a large city, who also administrate a number of smaller, adjacent cells.

Supposedly, SHADOW is under orders to maintain a low profile until the next Operation Inundation. Standing orders call on SHADOW cells to limit themselves to relatively minor crimes like information gathering, sabotage, and the occasional kidnapping/brainwashing operation. However, there are many times when a local SHADOW Leader or Penumbra officer can't resist using his men to perform a robbery, lining their pockets on the quiet. As long as the Leader in question doesn't

PINNING THE TECH ON THE AGENCY

Matching the technology and equipment to an agency to give it the right feel can be tricky, especially for SHADOW and Overthrow, who have a lot in common, but *not* their technology.

If it would look too bizarre and otherworldly for a modern issue of *Batman*, do not use Overthrow. SHADOW, on the other hand, employs any technology it can get its hands on; if it exists in the campaign world, SHADOW either wants it, or already has it.

An Overthrow adventure should feel like a spy drama like *Alias* (without the Renaissance miracle tech), one of the grittier *James Bond* flicks, or a *Jason Bourne* movie. Overthrow scenarios are about teams of good guys figuring out what the bad guys are doing and stopping them before someone gets hurt (or, if they're too late to stop the plan, tracking them down before they can make a getaway). Overthrow adventures are about using one's investigative skills to make sure you are in the right place at the right time.

SHADOW, on the other hand, is all about sneaking around until you get to a big, rollicking firefight and set piece battle.

disrupt SHADOW's long term plans—and gives the Command a cut of the profits—Command turns a blind eye to the practice.

SHADOW has two additional headquarters features. One is the Clone Tank, where clones are manufactured, tested, and grown to adulthood. The second is the Teleportal, a system of teleportation gates controlled from SHADOW's main base in Antarctica. Teleportals have Teleport 9 with the Long Distance Only and Portal modifiers.

SMALL SHADOW CELL

Small SHADOW cells, found in small or unimportant cities, typically have a few operatives who receive instructions via computer from a Penumbra officer stationed in another city. They have a small office space to meet and store their records, protected by a cover identity. This is used to conduct small-scale operations or serve as a fallback position when a larger base is compromised.

SMALL SHADOW CELL	HEADQUARTERS
Toughness: 5; *Size:* Tiny; *Features:* Communications, Computers, Cover Facility, Fire Prevention System, Garage, Security System.	
Agent Complement: 1 Commander (Advanced Trooper), 1 Squad (5 Basic Troopers).	
Vehicles: Automobile (mid-sized), SUV, Motorcycle.	
Cost: Abilities –1 + Features 6 = 5	

MEDIUM SHADOW CELL

Medium SHADOW cells, found in major cities, typically have a small base with a local leader and a pair of strike teams permanently on station, as well as an additional strike team in reserve. Typically, they are remodeled warehouses or industrial complexes, isolated from other establishments. They receive their instructions via computer, though for the most important operations, a Penumbra Officer briefs them in person (often bringing his personal strike squad with him).

MEDIUM SHADOW CELL	HEADQUARTERS
Toughness: 10; *Size:* Large; *Features:* Clone Tanks, Combat Simulator, Communications, Computers, Cover Identity, Fire Prevention System, Garage, Gym, Hangar, Holding Cells, Infirmary, Library, Living Space, Power System, Security System, Self-Destruct Device, Workshop.	
Agent Complement: 1 Commander (assistant to a Penumbra officer), 4 squads of Basic SHADOW troopers. 1 squad of Advanced Troopers, 1 squad of Infiltrators, 1 Mutate.	
Vehicles: 2 Cloaking Trucks, 2 Disguising Cars, 2 Spy Surveillance Vans, 5 Flying Platforms, 3 Stealth Attack Helicopters, 2 Combat Vans.	
Cost: Abilities 3 + Features 17 = 20	

LARGE SHADOW CELL

Large SHADOW cells, found in major capitals or important cities like Freedom City, have a Penumbra Officer, their personal assistant, and four strike teams permanently on station.

These secret bases are located in isolated areas, usually an underground area hollowed underneath an industrial complex or a sub-division. They are repositories for the amazing high tech weapons that are SHADOW's trademark.

LARGE SHADOW CELL	HEADQUARTERS
Toughness: 10; *Size:* Huge: *Features:* Animal Pen, Clone Tanks, Combat Simulator, Communications, Computers, Concealed, Defense Systems, Fire Prevention System, Garage, Gym, Hangar, Holding Cells, Infirmary, Laboratory, Library, Living Space, Power System, Self-Destruct Device, Security System, Teleportal, Workshop	
Agent Complement: 1 Penumbra officer, 8 squads of Basic Troops, 2 squads of Advanced Troops, 2 Umbral agents (Nifelheim attachés), 3 squads of Infiltrators, 3 Mutates.	
Vehicles: 4 Cloaking Trucks, 2 Disguising Cars, 4 Spy Surveillance Vans, 6 Stealth Attack Helicopters, 2 Combat Vans, 2 Cloaked Gunships, 4 Tanks, 10 Flying Platforms, Flying APC.	
Cost: Abilities 4 + Features 21 = 25	

SHADOW DEATHTRAP

When SHADOW kidnaps someone and puts them in a deathtrap, they usually haul them off to a facility away from their operations where they will be crunched in the jaws of death, drowned in a slow-rising tide of water, or gently lowered into a pit of crocodiles or vat of molten bronze. More crazed (or inventive) SHADOW leaders may strap captured agents to a metal table attached to a giant lightning rod as a thunderstorm approaches. The communications gear broadcasts the results back to the SHADOW base.

The following statistics represent a typical SHADOW deathtrap installation.

SHADOW DEATHTRAP	HEADQUARTERS
Toughness: 10; *Size:* Small; *Features:* Communications, Cover Facility, Death Trap	
Agent Complement: None	
Vehicles: None	
Cost: Abilities 1 + Features 3 = 4	

Stats for SHADOW's main headquarters in Antarctica, Nifelheim, can be found in *Freedom City*, **Chapter 6**.

MAJOR SHADOW BASE

Secret Elevator from Cover Facility

Garage/Workshop

Living Quarters

Living Quarters

Upper Security Center

Mess/Meeting Hall

Kitchen

Storage

Holding Cells

Infirmary

Briefing Room

Combat Arena

Gymnasium

Interrogation Chamber

Storage

Library

Clone Tanks

Laboratory

Portal Room

Leader's Quarters

Computer Room

Guest Quarters

Guest Quarters

Communications Room

Power Core

SHADOW PERSONNEL

If there is one thing SHADOW has in abundance, it is personnel. All over the world, clone tanks are bursting with agents trained as mindless drones, with a few select agents trained for more complex tasks.

Alas, SHADOW Agents are not a good choice for an agents game, especially since playing mindless drones is not a lot of fun. Players who want to run a "bad guys" game would probably be better off running a team of mercenary spies associated with Overthrow (who run into both UNISON and AEGIS). The "heroes" would infiltrate businesses to perform sabotage, assassinate politicians and military leaders, and race their opposite numbers across the globe to grab various McGuffins.

As with any Super-Spies game, this should be run at PL6; for the team Equipment pool, any conventional weapon and any spy-gear is available for the PC's use, and they can change the pool every session.

AGENTS

SHADOW deploys a number of agents on its operations, sometimes augmenting them with advanced mutagenic processes.

Whenever possible, SHADOW agents are organized in squads of six, with each squad member given a partner. The partners are supposed to watch each other's backs, while each pair watches out for the other two pairs in the triad.

All SHADOW troopers are programmed with "the Umbral Protocol:" if an agent ever rebels against Overshadow, or is about to give information that will compromise SHADOW (including failing to resist telepathic interrogation), a toxin is released into the agent's brain, and he dies instantly. This is a 0-point Drawback; obviously, it is a disadvantage to the agent, but it is compensated by its benefit to the organization, and it is ultimately more of a plot device.

SHADOW Troopers should be considered minions. The GM can make other SHADOW agents minions or not as the scenario demands.

SHADOW TROOPER

SHADOW Troopers are the drones of SHADOW, faceless troops that Overshadow sends into battle. They guard SHADOW bases and work as the muscle for SHADOW operations. They are easily trained and low-maintenance. They comprise about 95% of the agents that survive to adulthood.

SHADOW TROOPER		POWER LEVEL 5/MINION RANK 3			
Str 12	Dex 12	Con 12	Int 10	Wis 10	Cha 10

Skills: Knowledge (Tactics) 5 (+5), Notice 5 (+5), Profession (soldier) 5 (+5), Sense Motive 5 (+5)

Feats: Equipment 3

Equipment: Blaster pistol (**Blast 5**), body armor (Toughness +4), commlink

Combat: Attack +5, Damage +1 (unarmed), Grapple +6, Defense +5 (+3 flat-footed), Knockback –2, Initiative +1

Saving Throws: Toughness +5 (+1 without armor) Fortitude +3 Reflex +2 Will +1

Drawbacks: Umbral Protocol self-destruct (0 points)

Abilities 6 + Skills 5 (20 ranks) + Feats 3 + Powers 0 + Combat 20 + Saves 4 = 38

SHADOW INFILTRATOR

SHADOW Infiltrators are drones with the capacity for special training; their job is intrusion and espionage. Equipped with a cloaking device to blend into the shadows, they spy on SHADOW's targets, determining weak spots, uncovering secrets that can later be used in blackmail, and planting explosive devices for intrusion and diversion.

SHADOW INFILTRATOR		POWER LEVEL 5/MINION RANK 3			
Str 12	Dex 12	Con 12	Int 10	Wis 10	Cha 10

Skills: Acrobatics 2 (+3), Climb 2 (+3), Concentration 2 (+2), Disable Device 2 (+2), Drive 2 (+3), Intimidate 4 (+4), Knowledge (tactics) 5 (+5), Notice 5 (+5), Profession (agent) 4 (+4), Search 2 (+2), Sense Motive 5 (+5), Stealth 5 (+6)

Feats: Equipment 4, Instant Up

Equipment: body armor (+2 Toughness), plus 18 points in other equipment, particularly spy-gear.

Combat: Attack +5, Damage +1 (unarmed), Grapple +6, Defense +5 (+3 flat-footed), Knockback –1, Initiative +1

Saving Throws: Toughness +3 (+1 without armor), Fortitude +3, Reflex +2, Will +1

Drawbacks: Umbral Protocol self-destruct (0 points)

Abilities 6 + Skills 10 (40 ranks) + Feats 5 + Powers 0 + Combat 20 + Saves 4 = 45

SHADOW ADVANCED TROOPER

SHADOW Advanced Troopers are agent leaders. These are the blank templates that receive short-term mutations, sacrificing a long lifespan for short-term power and the good of their cause. Select troopers are used as squad leaders, and a few are surgically altered and deployed as deep cover agents.

SHADOW ADVANCED TROOPER		PL 5/MINION RANK 5			
Str 14	Dex 14	Con 14	Int 14	Wis 14	Cha 10

Skills: Acrobatics 3 (+5), Climb 3 (+5), Concentration 3 (+5), Disable Device 3 (+5), Drive 4 (+6), Intimidate 6 (+6), Knowledge (tactics) 6 (+8), Knowledge (technology) 2 (+4), Medicine 2 (+4), Notice 6 (+8), Profession (agent) 5 (+7), Search 4 (+6), Sense Motive 6 (+8), Stealth 6 (+8), Survival 3 (+5), Swim 2 (+4)

Feats: Attack Focus (ranged) 1, Equipment 4, Instant Up, Precise Shot 1, Teamwork 1

Combat: Attack +5, Damage +2 (unarmed), Grapple +7, Defense +5 (+3 flat-footed), Knockback –2, Initiative +1

Saving Throws: Toughness +5 (+2 without armor), Fortitude +7, Reflex +5, Will +5

Drawbacks: Umbral Protocol self-destruct (0 points)

Abilities 20 + Skills 16 (64 ranks) + Feats 8 + Powers 0 + Combat 20 + Saves 11 = 75

SHADOW UMBRA GUARD

Agents of the Umbra Guard are the best of the best, clones given intense training and genetic enhancements. These are the bodies Overshadow uses when he wants to transfer his intellect into a new body. For the most part, they are kept in stasis, though some are released to work as elite guardsmen in Nifelheim.

SHADOW UMBRA GUARD		POWER LEVEL 6/MINION RANK 6			
Str 14	Dex 14	Con 14	Int 12	Wis 12	Cha 12

Skills: Acrobatics 3 (+5), Climb 3 (+5), Concentration 3 (+4), Disable Device 3 (+4), Drive 4 (+6), Intimidate 6 (+7), Knowledge (current event) 2 (+3), Knowledge (tactics) 6 (+7), Knowledge (technology) 2 (+3), Medicine 2 (+3), Notice 6 (+7), Pilot 2 (+4), Profession (agent) 5 (+6), Search 4 (+5), Sense Motive 6 (+7), Stealth 6 (+8), Survival 3 (+4), Swim 2 (+4)

Feats: Attack Focus (ranged) 1, Equipment 5, Inspire 1, Instant Up, Leadership, Precise Shot 1, Teamwork 1

Equipment: body armor (+4 Toughness), plus 21 points in other equipment.

Combat: Attack +6, Damage +2 (unarmed), Grapple +8, Defense +6 (+3 flat-footed), Knockback –3, Initiative 2

Saving Throws: Toughness +6 (+2 without armor), Fortitude +9, Reflex +7, Will +7

Drawbacks: Umbral Protocol self-destruct (0 points)

Abilities 18 + **Skills** 17 (66 ranks) + **Feats** 11 + **Powers** 0 + **Combat** 24 + **Saves** 18 = 88

SHADOW MUTATES

Ordinary SHADOW agents, while formidable against conventional forces, fall like ninepins before the mighty fists of your average super-hero. To counter this, SHADOW and Taurus have collaborated on a process to augment SHADOW's clones to give them superpowers. These special SHADOW agents comprise only a tiny fraction of SHADOW's complement, but they can be a nasty surprise for heroes expecting an easy fight.

They are not, however, without their drawbacks. Not wishing to undermine his own (clearly superior) efforts, Taurus made sure the SHADOW mutates were built with two serious flaws. First, only one clone in five survives the mutation process. Having a superhuman at your disposal is handy, but SHADOW would rather have hordes of agents than a handful of minor league supers, so their numbers are limited.

Second, if they ever roll a natural 1 on an attack roll or check for their powers, they die. For powers without an attack roll (such as a perception range power), a natural 20 on the target's Saving Throw has the same effect. Casual uses of power (such as an Eye-In-SHADOW's mental communication) are not subject to this drastic effect, although for story purposes, the Gamemaster can assume every six months to a year, a mutate dies from casual power use.

Thus, all SHADOW mutates are living on borrowed time. Fortunately, when you are a clone thoroughly indoctrinated since birth, little things like life and death do not matter very much compared to the glory of your cause. And while Overshadow would like to reduce the mortality rate, mutates (and all forms of life except his own) are disposable.

EYE-IN-SHADOW

The world of psionics is largely a mystery to SHADOW, but where there's power, SHADOW dabbles. The primary duty of the Eye-In-SHADOW is to relay telepathic messages between their home base and Nifelheim.

Because of the range, it requires a relay network of several telepaths to transmit the information to its final destination, but they offer the ability to send secure messages that cannot be matched by any other method.

EYE-IN-SHADOW				POWER LEVEL 8	
Str 14	Dex 14	Con 14	Int 14	Wis 14	Cha 12

Skills: Acrobatics 3 (+5), Bluff 2 (+3), Climb 3 (+5), Concentration 3 (+5), Disable Device 3 (+5), Drive 3 (+5), Intimidate 2 (+3), Knowledge (behavioral sciences) 6 (+8), Knowledge (current event) 2 (+4), Knowledge (tactics) 6 (+8), Knowledge (technology) 2 (+4), Medicine 2 (+4), Notice 6 (+8), Pilot 2 (+4), Profession (agent) 5 (+7), Search 4 (+6), Sense Motive 10 (+12), Stealth 6 (+8), Survival 1 (+3), Swim 1 (+3)

Feats: Attack Focus (ranged) 1, Equipment 4, Inspire 1, Instant Up, Leadership, Precise Shot 1, Teamwork 1

Powers: Comprehend 1 (Languages), **Telepathy 8** (*Alternate Powers:* **Confuse 8**, **Fatigue 5** [Ranged], **Mental Blast 4**, **Illusion 8** [visual])

Combat: Attack +6 (melee), +7 (ranged), Grapple +8, Damage +2 (unarmed), Defense +8 (+4 flat-footed), Knockback –2, Initiative +2

Saving Throws: Toughness +5 (+2 without armor) Fortitude +7 Reflex +8 Will +12

Drawbacks: Living on Borrowed Time (–1 point); Umbral Protocol self-destruct (0 points)

Abilities 22 + **Skills** 18 (72 ranks) + **Feats** 10 + **Powers** 22 + **Combat** 28 + **Saves** 21 – **Drawbacks** –1 = 120

FIST-IN-SHADOW

Also known as the Hellman Tank (after the Nazi athlete who is (mistakenly) believed to be the father of all SHADOW clones), this mutate is a human brick-house who leads SHADOW's charge in open confrontations with its enemies. They are usually not attached to a squad; instead, they are often unleashed on an enemy to cause random destruction and distract the opposition.

FIST-IN-SHADOW				POWER LEVEL 8	
Str 18/26	Dex 14	Con 12	Int 12	Wis 12	Cha 12

Skills: Acrobatics 6 (+8), Climb 4 (+12), Computers 2 (+3), Concentration 5 (+6), Disable Device 2 (+3), Drive 2 (+4), Escape Artist 2 (+4), Gather Information 2 (+3), Intimidate 10 (+11), Investigate 2 (+3), Knowledge (streetwise) 4 (+5), Knowledge (tactics) 4 (+5), Notice 5 (+6), Profession (agent) 5 (+6), Search 4 (+5), Sense Motive 5 (+6), Sleight of Hand 4 (+6), Stealth 6 (+8), Swim 2 (+10)

Feats: Equipment 3, Improved Disarm, Improved Grab, Improved Grapple, Improved Pin, Instant Up, Skill Mastery (Acrobatics, Escape Artist, Intimidate, Swim)

Powers: Enhanced Strength 8, **Protection 8**, **Super-Strength 8** (heavy load: 117 tons; *Power Feats:* Shockwave, Super-Breath, Thunderclap)

Combat: Attack +8, Damage +8, Grapple +24, Defense +7 (+4 flat-footed), Knockback –4, Initiative +2

Saving Throws: Toughness +8, Fortitude +7, Reflex +8, Will +5

Drawbacks: Living on Borrowed Time (–1 point); Umbral Protocol self-destruct (0 points)

Abilities 20 + **Skills** 19 (76 ranks) + **Feats** 9 + **Powers** 35 + **Combat** 30 + **Saves** 16 – **Drawbacks** –1 = 128

FLAME-IN-SHADOW

The mutate most likely to be encountered in a group of agents is the Flame-in-SHADOW. The Flame-in-SHADOW is a support trooper who uses his fire control powers to cover troops as they move and provide distractions (particularly if he can find something flammable to put on fire).

FLAME-IN-SHADOW				POWER LEVEL 7	
Str 14	Dex 14	Con 14	Int 14	Wis 14	Cha 12

Skills: Acrobatics 3 (+5), Bluff 2 (+3), Climb 3 (+5), Concentration 3 (+5), Disable Device 3 (+5), Drive 3 (+5), Intimidate 2 (+3), Knowledge (behavioral sciences) 6 (+8), Knowledge (current event) 2 (+4), Knowledge (tactics) 6 (+8), Knowledge (technology) 2 (+4), Medicine 2 (+4), Notice 6 (+8), Pilot 2 (+4), Profession (agent) 5 (+7), Search 4 (+6), Sense Motive 10 (+12), Stealth 6 (+8), Survival 1 (+3), Swim 1 (+3)

Feats: Attack Focus (ranged) 1, Equipment 4, Inspire 1, Instant Up, Leadership, Precise Shot, Teamwork

Powers: Fire Control 7 (*Alternate Powers:* **Blast 7**, **Blast 5** [Line Area], **Blast 5** [Trail Area], **Teleport 7** (Medium—flames), **Insubstantial 3** [flame form]), **Flight 3** (Gliding), **Immunity 5** (fire damage)

Combat: Attack +5 (melee), +6 (ranged), Grapple +7, Damage +2 (unarmed), +7 (flame blast), Defense +7 (+4 flat-footed), Knockback –3, Initiative +2

Saving Throws: Toughness +6 (+2 without armor), Fortitude +8, Reflex +7, Will +7

Drawbacks: Living on Borrowed Time (–1 point); Umbral Protocol self-destruct (0 points)

Abilities 22 + Skills 18 (72 ranks) + Feats 10 + Powers 28 + Combat 26 + Saves 17 – Drawbacks -1 = 120

GATE-IN-SHADOW

SHADOW's technological gate network is one of the keys to its recent success. Naturally, they'd like to imitate it with natural powers. The Gate-In-SHADOW is the perfect conveyance for SHADOW agents to get to and from an operation without being traced.

GATE-IN-SHADOW				POWER LEVEL 6	
Str 14	Dex 14	Con 14	Int 14	Wis 14	Cha 12

Skills: Acrobatics 3 (+5), Bluff 2 (+3), Climb 3 (+5), Concentration 9 (+11), Disable Device 3 (+5), Drive 3 (+5), Intimidate 2 (+3), Knowledge (current events) 2 (+4), Knowledge (tactics) 6 (+8), Knowledge (technology) 2 (+4), Medicine 2 (+4), Notice 6 (+8), Pilot 2 (+4), Profession (agent) 5 (+7), Search 4 (+6), Sense Motive 10 (+12), Stealth 6 (+8), Survival 1 (+3), Swim 1 (+3)

Feats: Attack Focus (ranged) 1, Equipment 4, Inspire 1, Instant Up, Leadership, Precise Shot, Teamwork 1

Powers: Immunity 5 (teleportation effects), **Teleport 6** (Accurate, Portal; *Power Feats:* Progression 2 [portal size])

Combat: Attack +5, Grapple +7, Damage +2 (unarmed), Defense +5 (+3 flat-footed), Knockback –3, Initiative +2

Saving Throws: Toughness +6 (+2 without armor) Fortitude +6 Reflex +8 Will +6

Drawbacks: Living on Borrowed Time (–1 point); Umbral Protocol self-destruct (0 points)

Abilities 22 + Skills 18 (72 ranks) + Feats 10 + Powers 37 + Combat 20 + Saves 14 – Drawbacks -1 = 120

SHADOW-IN-SHADOW

For those occasions when SHADOW needs complete stealth, the Shadow-in-SHADOW is an almost Platonic ideal of an operative. These agents are sometimes attached to Nacht-Krieger's assassination squads.

SHADOW-IN-SHADOW				POWER LEVEL 7	
Str 14	Dex 18	Con 12	Int 12	Wis 12	Cha 10

Skills: Acrobatics 6 (+10), Climb 6 (+7), Computers 2 (+3), Concentration 2 (+3), Disable Device 2 (+3), Drive 2 (+6), Escape Artist 10 (+14), Gather Information 2 (+2), Intimidate 10 (+10), Investigate 2 (+3), Knowledge (streetwise) (+6), Knowledge (tactics) 5 (+6), Notice 6 (+7), Profession (agent) 5 (+6), Search 6 (+7), Sense Motive 5 (+6), Sleight of Hand 6 (+10), Stealth 10 (+14), Swim 2 (+3)

Feats: Equipment 4, Improved Disarm, Instant Up, Skill Mastery (Escape Artist, Search, Sleight of Hand, Stealth), Stunning Attack

Powers: Darkness Control 8 (*Alternate Powers:* **Blast 8**, **Drain Constitution 8** [Ranged], **Fatigue 5** [Ranged], **Strike 8**, **Teleport 8** [Medium—shadows]), **Invisibility 2** (Passive), **Regeneration 8** (+8 recovery bonus, Source—shadows)

Combat: Attack +7, Grapple +9, Damage +8 (unarmed), Defense +8 (+4 flat-footed), Knockback –3, Initiative 4

Saving Throws: Toughness +6 (+2 without armor), Fortitude +8, Reflex +10, Will +7

Drawbacks: Living on Borrowed Time (–1 point); Umbral Protocol self-destruct (0 points)

Abilities 16 + Skills 24 (94 ranks) + Feats 8 + Powers 29 + Combat 30 + Saves 19 – Drawbacks 1 = 125

WHEEL-IN-SHADOW

When the Wheel-In-SHADOW turns, destruction follows. Another good team player, the Wheel is the bane of conventional military forces, as his powers can easily shield advancing agents from most conventional ballistic weapons.

WHEEL-IN-SHADOW				POWER LEVEL 8	
Str 14	Dex 14	Con 14	Int 14	Wis 14	Cha 12

Skills: Acrobatics 3 (+5), Bluff 2 (+3), Climb 3 (+5), Concentration 3 (+5), Disable Device 3 (+5), Drive 3 (+5), Intimidate 2 (+3), Knowledge (behavioral sciences) 6 (+8), Knowledge (current events) 2 (+4), Knowledge (tactics) 6 (+8), Knowledge (technology) 2 (+4), Medicine 2 (+4), Notice 6 (+8), Pilot 2 (+4), Profession (agent) 5 (+7), Search 4 (+6), Sense Motive 10 (+12), Stealth 6 (+8), Survival 1 (+3), Swim 1 (+3)

Feats: Attack Focus (ranged) 1, Equipment 4, Inspire 1, Instant Up, Leadership, Precise Shot 1, Teamwork 1

Powers: Telekinesis 5 (Damaging, *Power Feats:* Precise, *Alternate Powers:* **Blast 8**, **Deflect 5** [all projectiles and thrown weapons, Ranged], **Disintegration 4**, **Snare 8**), **Flight 5**

Combat: Attack +6 (melee), +7 (ranged), Grapple +8, Damage +2 (unarmed), +8 (blast), Defense +8 (+4 flat-footed), Knockback –3, Initiative +2

Saving Throws: Toughness +6 (+2 without armor), Fortitude +5, Reflex +6, Will +8

Drawbacks: Living on Borrowed Time (–1 point); Umbral Protocol self-destruct (0 points)

Abilities 22 + Skills 18 (72 ranks) + Feats 10 + Powers 30+ Combat 28 + Saves 13 – Drawbacks –1 = 120

RAGNAROK

Almost since the moment of his conception, Albrecht Wilhelmsson was bound for a great and terrible fate. His mother, Greta Göessler, was given the powers of a Valkyrie while he was still in the womb, and Albrecht shared in her powers, and then some. Given to the Aesir as an infant and raised as one of their own, the power of the Nine Worlds thundered in his veins, rivaling the gods themselves.

Even so, as a boy living among the Aesir, life was far from easy. He was made a servant to young gods, and abused as "mortal-spawn." To defend himself, he became a fighter, a moody berserk brawler, and taught himself how to beat his oppressors. After their children began coming home beaten and humiliated by one who barely had divine blood, Albrecht was quietly returned to the Valkyries, where he assisted them in their duties.

His mother was overjoyed to see her son. She taught him about the great cities of Midgard, and the great German nation. She also taught him about his father, the handsomest, smartest man on Earth, a father who would give him all the love and respect he ever wanted, should they be reunited. His interest piqued, Albrecht made a perilous journey to the Norn to find a way to reach Midgard without the Aesir's knowledge. The Norn warned him to stay away, or it would cost him his soul. He didn't take the advice.

Years later, with Albrecht now grown as tall and broad as a true Prince of the Aesir, he was summoned by his father to Midgard. When he felt the summons to Earth, he was overjoyed— then his father tried to steal his body.

For a man whose life had been a struggle against abuse and the betrayal of trust, this was the final straw. He vowed revenge on Overshadow and the mother who had lied to him about his father. He named himself "Ragnarok" after the twilight of the gods. He was a force of rage and destruction, mostly aimed at SHADOW, but not particularly respectful of anything (or anyone) who got in his way.

The Aesir, citing Albrecht's half-human heritage, decided he was not subject to the non-interference pact between the Aesir and Earth's Master Mage, and chose to wash their hands of the whole affair.

Well over a decade passed, and the rage that consumed him faded. He spent less time pursuing SHADOW and more running from the authorities, who considered him a destructive

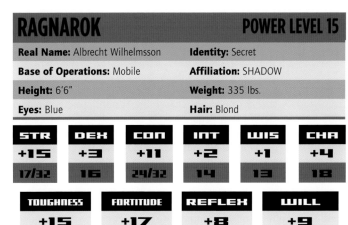

RAGNAROK — POWER LEVEL 15

Real Name: Albrecht Wilhelmsson	Identity: Secret
Base of Operations: Mobile	Affiliation: SHADOW
Height: 6'6"	Weight: 335 lbs.
Eyes: Blue	Hair: Blond

STR	DEX	CON	INT	WIS	CHA
+15	+3	+11	+2	+1	+4
17/32	16	24/32	14	13	18

TOUGHNESS	FORTITUDE	REFLEX	WILL
+15	+17	+8	+9

Skills: Acrobatics 2 (+5), Climb 1 (+12), Concentration 4 (+5), Diplomacy 2 (+6), Handle Animal 2 (+6), Intimidate 14 (+18), Knowledge (arcane lore) 3 (+5), Knowledge (current event) 3 (+5), Notice 12 (+13), Perform (singing) 1 (+5), Ride 6 (+9), Sense Motive 10 (+11), Stealth 1 (+4), Survival 10 (+11), Swim 1 (+12)

Feats: Blind-Fight, Chokehold, Fearless, Grappling Finesse, Improved Grab, Improved Grapple, Improved Pin, Power Attack, Stunning Attack, Rage 5 (+8 Str, +4 Fort for 15 rounds), Takedown Attack 1

Powers: **Enhanced Strength 15, Enhanced Constitution 8, Flight 5** (250 MPH), **Immunity 18** (aging, alteration effects, critical hits, magic), **Mind Shield 4, Impervious Toughness 10, Protection 4, Super-Strength 5** (heavy load: 102 tons), **Regeneration 1** (Resurrection)

Combat: Attack +15, Grapple +31 (+35 while raging), Damage +11 (unarmed, +15 while raging), Defense +15 (+8 flat-footed, +1 while raging), Knockback –12, Initiative +3

Drawbacks: Power Loss (requires a monthly sacrifice or loses all powers, –3 points).

Abilities 42 + Skills 18 (72 ranks) + Feats 15 + Powers 80 + Combat 60 + Saves 19 – Drawbacks 3 = 231

vigilante, as well as a thief (he committed robberies when he needed any goods), and he began to see why SHADOW and his father opposed the authorities of Midgard.

In recent years, Ragnarok has fallen in love with Anya Datsyuk, the granddaughter of the original Valkyrie, while investigating connections between Overshadow and Overthrow in Eastern Europe. Anya, seizing an opportunity for power within SHADOW, convinced Ragnarok that one "misunderstanding" didn't justify a decades-old vendetta, and helped negotiate a deal with SHADOW. Ragnarok would join the Penumbra, providing the organization with one of the most physically powerful superhumans on Earth. He would give his father everything but his body. Overshadow agreed.

Now, a hundred infant "Sons of the Slain" grow in a hidden crèche in Nifelheim. With SHADOW's time acceleration technology, these clones, perhaps the deadliest secret weapons yet, will be ready within a decade.

SHADOW IN FREEDOM CITY

Freedom City is of immense interest to SHADOW, being the home of Overshadow's now deceased archenemy, the Scarab. There is a single large base located in Port Regal under a construction site called the Valus Tower project. Ten years ago, a corrupt developer absconded with millions in funds, and the property is in limbo while the courts decide its fate. Legal motions keep the project from being developed (providing the perfect cover).

Hilda Reinholdt, who frequently commutes by teleportal between the Valus Tower base and Nifelheim, heads SHADOW's Freedom City operations. Hers is not the only important base in Freedom City, as the agency also maintains a headquarters in the downtown core (as detailed in the scenario *Return of SHADOW*), and the Thule Society secretly operates out of the cellar of *Neither Hide Nor Heirloom*, an antique store on Lantern Hill.

SHADOW AND OTHER AGENCIES

SHADOW is a now a unified, dangerous whole, secretly waiting for the right moment to strike at an unsuspecting world. But, what do the other villains know of their plans, and will they aid or thwart them?

TAURUS & DR. SIN

Taurus and Dr. Sin, as noted earlier, are allies and titular members of the Penumbra. They know most of the agency's secrets, though even they don't suspect its current size. Any help they offer SHADOW is likely to be half-hearted at best, and neither is likely to want the next Operation Inundation to succeed, though they are poised to benefit if it does.

BROTHERHOOD OF THE YELLOW SIGN

The Brotherhood of the Yellow Sign considers SHADOW a potential rival it can manipulate into doing its bidding. They see Prince Vultorr as their leader in this regard, unaware he does not share their goals. Beyond that, the Serpent-People's relationship with SHADOW is a strange dance. They recognize Overshadow as Tan-Aktor reborn, and honor him as an agent of the god Set, whom many of them still revere. Likewise, the symbolism of shadow has deep significance in the occult practices of the Serpent-People. On the other hand, SHADOW is still made up largely of humans, interlopers on the surface of the great world-egg, destined for death or enslavement.

THE CRIME LEAGUE

The Crime League (in any of its incarnations) has never respected SHADOW (in any of *its* incarnations). SHADOW does not even presently register on the Crime League's radar. Their response to a new Operation Inundation would be to wait for the heroes to crush it, and then take advantage of the chaos (particularly if the Freedom League suffered any losses).

THE FACTOR FOUR

The Factor Four have worked as mercenaries for SHADOW in the past, but have no close ties to them. As far as they are concerned, SHADOW is a pack of washouts, though they would work for them again, for the right price.

TALOS

Talos is currently on the outs with SHADOW, owing to his actions during the League of Evil fiasco. However, Overshadow respects Talos' skill, and will almost certainly reconcile when he needs more Foundry technology. Talos is one of the few individuals with an advantage over SHADOW, as he can override the Foundry teleportal technology they employ, and every time Overshadow uses a teleportal, Talos' loyal servant Scylla knows and logs it. SHADOW is one of the Foundry's best customers, and a SHADOW victory would be profitable for Talos.

THE PSIONS

The Psions have always been bitter enemies of SHADOW; not only does Professor Psion recognize their Nazi roots, they are as big a threat to his planned utopia as any government or superhero. The Professor suspects the organization is not nearly as defunct as it appears, but has no knowledge of their current operations.

THE TYRANNY SYNDICATE

The Tyranny Syndicate recognizes SHADOW as this world's version of LIGHT (Liberty's Insurgency for Goodness, Hope, and Truth). Even though they understand SHADOW is far more compatible with their goals than LIGHT, and Overshadow is in every way the opposite of Highlight (LIGHT's true leader), the Syndicate just cannot bring themselves to join forces with a version of an ineffectual group they so utterly crushed on their own world. Plus, they don't like the idea of any potential rivals.

HADES

Hades views SHADOW as barely worthy of his notice. Although, he has taken a mild interest in Ragnarok, given his connection to the Aesir and his potential as a "god-killer" (given the right guidance and motivation).

LADY LUNAR

Lady Lunar sees SHADOW as one of numerous potential Earthly allies who could help her regain her rightful throne. She would like to get in their good graces, but will not stoop to beg, although she might offer Overshadow an alliance.

MALADOR

Malador is a rival of the Crimson Mask (although he would say no one rivals his occult power). Each seeks the destruction of the other. Other than wanting to tear apart the Crimson Mask and anyone in the Thule Society who supports him in his bid to become Master Mage, Malador couldn't care less about SHADOW.

MASTERMIND

Mastermind sees Overshadow as a pale imitation. He watches his efforts to conquer the world and is amused by them, in a pathetic sort of way. He is also one of the few who recognizes the extent of SHADOW's current power, but does not believe they are capable of conquering the world, let alone consolidating such a conquest, so he leaves them to play their little games, for now.

MR. INFAMY

Mr. Infamy? Who knows? Does anyone really want to know how *that* creature thinks? The only "relationship" of note is that Mr. Infamy has never offered one of his famous deals to anyone in SHADOW, Overshadow included. His reasons remain his own.

OMEGA

Omega sees SHADOW as little more than dust specks caught in the maelstrom that is the Terminus. If asked, he might express bewilderment over why anyone would want to know about his opinion of a nest of termites. SHADOW will be swept away along with the rest of creation when the time comes.

TERRA-KING

Terra-King considers SHADOW just another potential intruder into his underground realm. He knows nothing else about them.

UNA

Una sees SHADOW as a potential ally (or pawn) in her great plan to destroy Eldrich, to be subjugated or discarded once the Master Mage is removed as an obstacle in conquering Earth's dimension. Fortunately, Overshadow is well aware of her duplicity, and has wisely declined any overtures to an alliance with the Netherworld.

THE BIGGEST CHALLENGE OF SHADOW

You know how in the comics, villains can degrade over time? A villain who seemed like an invincible badass in their first appearance can, after the fortieth time they are used as a hero's punching bag, seem incredibly lame?

SHADOW—like any "they've been a dominant agency/conspiracy despite decades of failure" organization—has this problem. And, SHADOW *is* built to lose. Unless the Gamemaster wants to run a "World of SHADOW" campaign where the third Operation Inundation is a complete success, they *have* to lose. SHADOW exists in part so players can enjoy the special comic book thrill of having their characters wade through hordes of agents. However, if the players do not respect the in-game threat (and you are not intentionally playing them as incompetent buffoons strictly for laughs), your scenario's in trouble.

MYSTERY

There are a number of ways to prevent this. First, portray SHADOW with an aura of mystery, especially as your heroes are starting their careers. SHADOW agents who proclaim their eternal loyalty to SHADOW, are forced to gasp their secret, and die before they can spit out what the players need to know are a wonderful way to separate SHADOW from other superhero game agencies. The players find the local SHADOW base? The first time they meet them, have the local commander blow up the SHADOW base just as the PCs are about to enter. Prolong the anticipation of that first big encounter. Don't delay it so long the PCs lose interest, but don't give your players what they want as soon as they want it. Make them wait and work for it.

Don't forget that the heroes don't read sourcebooks, so information in this chapter (and in the *Freedom City* book) that is obvious to you, the reader, is still a mystery for the heroes (and perhaps the players, depending on how much they've read). So in addition to not knowing SHADOW still exists, they may not know its troops are primarily clones, that they're clones of Overshadow (or that he, himself, is a clone), about the makeup of the Penumbra, the location of SHADOW's bases, and much more. There's plenty of potential mystery to play out where SHADOW is concerned.

IMPROVEMENT

What do you do when the mystery is gone? There are two answers. One is to reboot with a different agency. Overthrow is one possibility, of course. And, what if Omega could project energy clones onto the earth (which evaporate into the ether when they're knocked out)?

The second way to make the PCs respect SHADOW is to revamp and upgrade them as they go along. Don't have the rank and file agents grow in power along with the players; that's very unsatisfying. You should, however, reveal SHADOW a piece at a time. Your first SHADOW story arc should not end with a climactic invasion of Nifelheim, the simultaneous death of Overshadow and all of his clones, and the complete dismantling of the organization. When they defeat the local SHADOW cell for the first time, drop hints of other elements of the organization, such as the Thule Society or the Corona. Build anticipation for the next stage in the conflict.

A good next stage threat is the introduction of the "elite adversary:" a legendary agent commander, special squad, or supervillain who is coming to town to give the local SHADOW cell reinforcements and deal with these troublesome new heroes. The villain comes in, performs a few ruthless acts off-camera, and builds his reputation. After a while, he directly sets his forces against the heroes. If SHADOW was a nameless, faceless threat in their first encounter, then the elite adversary's job is to give them a face and make sure the conflict becomes *personal*.

Whenever possible, point out SHADOW has seriously mobilized all of their resources only twice in their history; they have been defeated on numerous occasions, but *their real plan is unchanged by most setbacks*. By saying "SHADOW wasn't employing all their resources at the time," we can justify most of these defeats and maintain the credibility of the organization for some time.

CHAPTER 6: THE AGENT SERIES

Agent scenarios can be a lot of work. They pose special challenges, which, if ignored, can result in a disastrous game session. This chapter addresses some of those challenges and proposes solutions that not only make your adventures less troublesome, but also suggest interesting twists. How do you make agents a threat? How do you efficiently run agent battles? How do you handle hostages? The answers are here.

Archetypes for important agent types from comic books, movies, and cartoons are also presented. If you need a quick NPC hero, a quick character for a guest player, or a *villain du jour*, just drop in an archetype, modify a few traits, add an equipment package, and you're ready to go.

POWER LEVEL VS. TONE

Mutants & Masterminds attempts to reproduce the tone of comic books with an emphasis on how they felt during the classic Silver Age. Unfortunately, there are two contradictory ways agents are presented in the source material.

Sometimes agents were more than a credible threat, they were a challenge. When the hero was caught in a *mano a mano* struggle against a single opposing goon, especially when there was a convenient nearby deadly obstacle (a cliffside precipice, a buzz saw, a burning building, the stuff of pulp cliffhangers), the enemy agent became a credible, dramatic threat. In this case, the dramatic tension of the fight was more important than making our hero look cool and impressive.

In other circumstances, particularly when there's only a few pages left in the story and a lot of agents between Our Hero and the final goal (bad guy, doomsday switch, etc.) the bad guy's minions suddenly lose all fighting skills (and would probably get trounced in a fight with the cast of *Scooby Doo*).

Gamemaster Fiat and the awarding of hero points help to make these things happen in *M&M*. In the initial scenes of an adventure, you can liberally use GM Fiat and setbacks to give the heroes a suitable challenge, even from agents they would normally walk all over. The enemy agents have a plan, and oftentimes a secret advantage of some kind, be it a new device, a mole in the heroes' agency, or simply a fiendishly clever plot. This allows you to make things tough for the heroes, giving them a chance to show off their skills and really earn their successes.

In the concluding scenes of the adventure, particularly the climatic scene, the heroes should have a respectable number of hero points built up. Then it's time for the tide to turn; make less use of GM Fiat, and encourage the players to spend those hero points doing what their heroes do best: kicking enemy agent butt!

THE NUMBERS GAME

Sometimes the things that promise to be the most fun end up being the biggest hassle. Agent scenarios, wonderful in theory, can be one of these. Adventures with large numbers of agents have the potential to produce two game-killing situations.

The first is the lucky hit. When you have a lot of agents on a battlefield and the Gamemaster's playing with hot dice, odds are good that your heroes are going to lose a fight they should really win.

The second is the nightmare of logistics. Even when you're not playing with a battle mat, figurines, or attacks of opportunity (options detailed in the *Mastermind's Manual*), when you've got 20-40 agents on the field, it's going to be a chore taking care of them.

The minion rules from *Mutants & Masterminds,* **Chapter 8**, can help limit these problems. Another way to handle the situation is with the Field Battle rules from *Golden Age,* setting up large groups of agents as combined forces and dealing with them all at once rather than individually.

The toughness of minions depends on a combination of implemented rules, GM tactical play, and the luck of the dice. If you want tougher minions and don't mind slower battles, don't use the minion rules or Field Battle rules, but use the combined action rule. If you want faster battles and to give the heroes the rush of throwing around minions like confetti at a political convention, then use the minion rules and Field Battle forces as much as possible.

KNOCK 'EM OUT

Another problem with agent combats is when the Gamemaster decides to play out the following scene, "The heroes get mobbed by seemingly endless numbers of agents. Despite fighting heroically, the odds catch up with them, and one by one they fall..." Then the Gamemaster decides to play out that scene... and the dice don't go where the script wants them to go, or worse, it takes forever to get the desired result.

There are better ways to handle this situation. The most obvious is to tell the players they are being knocked out now, and everyone can take a hero point they can use in the escape. This isn't particularly satisfying, but at least it's in genre and more entertaining than a long drawn out fight. However, there are other things you can do and still get the desired result.

One alternative is the hero point quota fight. Tell your players the following, "Okay, you're going to lose this fight; there are too many agents, you won't win. After twenty agents are decked, you're going to be swarmed by a dog pile of agents, and we'll fade to black. However, we're going to have a little competition..."

This competition might include things like:

- Whoever drops the most agents gets a hero point. (Or, less competitively, anyone standing at the end of the fight gets a hero point).

- Whoever gives the most entertaining description of how they beat up their minion gets a hero point. Alternately, whoever gives the most entertaining description of how their hero *loses* gets a hero point.

- There is one very tough agent on the battlefield. Whoever takes him out gets a hero point.

- One of the agents is actually a mole, and (using the fight as a cover) he needs to slip someone on the team a hidden message. If he can do so without being caught, everyone gets a hero point.

- Somewhere on the battlefield is a hidden objective. Maybe one of the commanders is wearing a disguise belt to mask his identity. Maybe somewhere off to the side of the battlefield, someone is taking readings of the heroes' powers. Tell the players that something is going on out there, but let them figure it out for themselves. Whoever solves the hidden objective gets a hero point.

Another alternative is the Throw A Fight scenario. The player characters are fighting an agency and need to get inside the bad guys' HQ, but they don't know where it is. The personality profile of the agent leader says he is the type to capture people, hold them in cells, torture them, and gloat. Therefore, the heroes need to throw the fight in a convincing manner. The mission becomes a challenge to escape a villain's trap with the information you need to solve the scenario. Plus, the players get to figure hammy ways to be taken out.

THE HOSTAGE DRAMA

Okay, you have the heroes lined up ready to take out the bad guys... when suddenly you notice they've got their weapons trained on the very pack of hostages the PCs were meant to save. What do you do?

There are two potential problems with a hostage standoff scenario: first, a player character may say, "Why do I give a flying fig about hostages?" and fire away, completely ignoring the fact that their character is supposed to be a hero and a professional who follows rules of engagement. The second problem is when the situation becomes completely paralyzed and no one takes action. To remedy these situations, try the following:

THE MISSION CHECK

If the players are ignoring the risk to the hostages and their characters have orders to save them, the GM has the option of asking the team leader if he wants to force a Mission Check to preserve the situation. The mission leader has to be present and aware of the situation. A Mission Check forces the attacker to make a Will save, DC 10 + the leader's Intimidate modifier; if they fail, they hold their action for that round.

Mission Checks are not just applicable to hostage situations. They can apply to any situation where it is against a mission to take an aggressive action and someone in the chain of command is about to "foam out". Are you parleying with an enemy and someone gets bored, stupid, and unprofessional? The team leader can enforce a Mission Check to keep them in line.

The Mission Check option is not meant to prevent the player from doing something stupid. It is meant as a reminder to the player that their role demands a professionalism that needs to be taken seriously, and the rules of engagement should not be broken on a whim. It is a speed bump, not a brick wall.

SITUATIONAL BREAKDOWN

Alternatively, a player can always spend a hero point to cause a situational breakdown that gives them a reasonable excuse to fire without making a Mission Check. Are you caught in a hostage situation and you *really* want to fire? Spend a hero point, and one of the following situations (or something similar) occurs:

*   A hostage makes eye contact with the player character, nods in approval, and ducks out of the way just as the hero fires.

*   You recognize a hostage as a known terrorist. The hostage is a fake!

*   The villain primes their weapon, and is about to fire. Unless you attack *now,* the hostage is dead anyway.

THE STRESS CHECK

Alternatively, sometimes a hostage situation goes too long, and player indecisiveness robs a situation of drama. In these cases, the Gamemaster can enforce Stress checks to make sure people don't break down and start firing. A Concentration Check or Will save (whichever has the higher bonus, DC 5) is required from all parties in the situation; if every-

one succeeds, the situation continues, but further stress checks (with cumulative increases in DC) may be called upon to force the situation. Again, a hero point can be spent to turn the situation into something where the use of force is justified or the hostage can be protected.

HOW HEROES CAN BEAT UP MINIONS

Heroes can deal with agents pretty effectively if the Gamemaster uses the minion rules from *Mutants & Masterminds,* **Chapter 8**. Furthermore, make sure the player characters know they are heading into a campaign where there are going to be a *lot* of agents, so they can adjust their characters to fight them more effectively (particularly with area attacks and the Takedown Attack feat). Heroes with enough Impervious Toughness can fight lower power level foes like agents all day long without any risk of damage, so long as the agents aren't doing anything more than ineffectually firing away at them with attacks that can't hurt them.

Give agents some bad luck you normally wouldn't give to PCs. *Mutants & Masterminds* doesn't pay much attention to fumbles or ammunition, but let the minions run out of ammo on an attack roll of "1" (or jam, if it's early in the fight and it makes no sense for them to be out of bullets).

Poor tactical choices can make for easy agent battles: position minions close together when the heroes have Area attacks, or (more cinematically) near obstacles that can be conveniently brought down to eliminate several minions at once, like under stacks of pipes or near ammo dumps. For other cinematic treatments, use things like cells with electrified force fields to throw agents into and shock them unconscious.

The true classic, however, is the crossfire dodge technique. This is where two agents are positioned on opposite sides of the hero; when they fire, the hero ducks and the two agents blast each other and take each other out. This is an application of the trick option for Bluff (*M&M*, page 42). Encourage players to spend hero points on the Bluff check.

HOW AGENTS CAN TAKE DOWN HEROES

If you really want to make for a more competitive fight between superheroes and agents, here is some advice.

First, there is the basic teamwork technique: the Neutralize/Damage technique. One agent hits the opponent with an attack that neutralizes the hero's defense (such as Dazzle or Snare), then other agents attack when the opponent cannot defend himself. Alternatively, use attacks like Drain or Nullify to negate some of the hero's toughness, then attack.

Next, Aid, and Combined Attacks are the friends of those in a mass battle. It is arguable that Combined Attacks are too effective in some circumstances; unless you want minions to be dangerously effective, consider reducing the damage bonus for each successful attack that comes within 5 points from +2 to +1. Elite agents and commanders still get the +2.

An agent who is being attacked can get a good defense with a combination of another agent doing an Aid while he is doing a Defensive stance. Likewise, if the agents have numbers on their side but are finding it difficult to hit the mark, why not go to an aggressive stance?

The dirtiest technique is to force the heroes to Interpose. Why aim at a hero, when they can aim at a hostage and have the stupid costumed lug dive in the way and take the hit?

Finally, you can cheat. The agents have some sort of plot device weapon that negates a major PC advantage (anti-teleport fields, anti-invisibility cloaks). If you need to give the agents one of these on the fly or you won't even have a remotely competitive fight, award the player a hero point for negating the advantage.

SUB-GENRES

There are also many agent sub-genres worth mentioning. Some of these spotlight certain character archetypes; you can run them as solo runs for characters in the campaign (casting other players in the role of the character's supporting cast).

For example, Joe, the AEGIS' squad's team pilot, may spend most of his time ferrying passengers and taking surveillance photos. A GM can run a scenario where his old squadron commander gets shot down in a hostile country, and he can take his plane on an unauthorized mission to rescue him (and the various former squad mates are the other players).

ACES IN THE SKY

This is a genre where the heroes are a squad of aviators dispatched to deal with trouble spots around the globe. Since air squadrons are heavily regimented in the real world, this campaign is often set in a future time when mercenary pilots with a retro-WWI vibe work for corporations or other quasi-feudal entities. It also tends to focus on wartime squadrons, particularly during the First and Second World Wars.

This is essentially a mercenary/special forces campaign set in the skies. Obstacles include enemy mercenaries, employers who won't pay the heroes (in mercenary campaigns), or evil "ally" dictators who try to force the heroes into doing their dirty work, then betray them at the first opportunity.

In between missions, there are fierce rivalries between mercenary squadrons, which often involve soap opera theatrics involving plucky young pilots, rival aviators, and the girl.

Appropriate Archetypes: Ace Pilot, Hard Nosed Commander, Communications/Surveillance Specialist, Grease Monkey.

Inspiration: The *Blackhawks, Enemy Ace, Robotech, Top Gun, Area 88,* to some extent *Battlestar Galactica.*

ASSASSIN

This is a gritty variation of the secret agent genre where characters are professional secret agents carrying out assassinations. In fact, most player characters *are* assassins and the adventure involves a caper to perform an assassination (even when things go horribly wrong), and how the heroes overcame adversity and kill off the right (or in some cases more deserving) target.

Even in this campaign, there is a lot of variety in tone (contrast some of the grittier Sean Connery *Bond* films with the campier Roger Moore outings). What unifies the genre is that it casts the PCs in the roles of unrepentant killers with a job to do. In gritty games, all ballistic weapons do lethal damage, and characters are limited to a maximum of one hero point each. In more fanciful settings, only the main bad guys and their lieutenants have lethal weapons, and characters have the same hero point limits as a standard *Agents of Freedom* game.

Appropriate Archetypes: Dashing Spy, Femme Fatale (the standard female hero of the genre), Sharpshooter.

Inspiration: *24,* grittier *James Bond* movies, *The Bourne Series, Le Femme Nikita.*

HARDCORE MILSPEC

Characters are soldiers, a special missions force like the Navy SEALS, the United Kingdom's SAS, or Canada's JTF-2. They fight the enemies of their country, often by being more brutal than their foes.

Life is cheaper than beer or watered-down gasoline. You get to know your squad mates long enough to mourn them when they die. Your country sends you on thankless missions, then spits on you when you return.

The idea of having a code against killing makes you laugh. Your only loyalty is to the corps, and the only moral code you have is your refusal to leave a man behind. If you get a good commander, he becomes your god; poor officers are to be treated like lepers, or even fragged if they become a danger to the squad.

To use *Mutants & Masterminds* to run a milspec game, use these guidelines as a start:

- All weapon attacks do lethal damage. If you are playing in a world with guns, people die.

- Superhuman abilities are only present if you are running a milspec horror game, and even then, they are not available to the player characters. The bad guys might have powers, weird, disturbing powers. You have guns. That's all you need.

Appropriate Archetypes: Roughneck Commando, Combat Engineer, Communications Specialist, Defense Analyst, Sharpshooter, Navy SEAL.
Inspiration: Tom Clancy novels and military special-ops films.

MARTIAL ARTS

This is the martial arts campaign of modern popcorn movies. This genre involves player character martial arts masters traveling the globe, battling mercenaries, ninja, and evil martial artists, and eventually having a climactic fight scene where they are pitted against each other in a fight to the death (naturally they have to escape and kick people's butts) or face the Unstoppable Martial Artist in a fight to the death.

Popular venues in this campaign include the local Zen garden (attached to the local martial arts master's house), the dojo, and the arena. The local crime boss always has a gang of martial artists at his disposal. The really big tournaments, such as the *kumite*, happen overseas. Thailand is a forbidding land of evil martial arts, where people cover their hands in broken glass (which make punches do lethal damage) and fight to the death.

For this campaign, martial arts are king. The limit on an attack is double the campaign's power level, provided the attack comes as part of a feat associated with a fighting style. Non-martial arts weapons, especially firearms, are limited, and nobody uses a gun when they can fight hand-to-hand.
Prominent Archetypes: Martial Artist, Con Artist.
Inspiration: Numerous American 1980s and 1990s martial arts films such as *Kickboxer* and, more recently, *Ong Bak*.

OUTLAW MERCS

They are... Outlaw Mercenaries, On the Run For A Crime They Didn't Commit. In this sub-genre, the characters are a band of outlaws who have decided to use their explosive whoop-ass abilities to help people in need against evil cults and corrupt local businessmen. In the meantime, they are pursued by the most ineffectual and stereotypical officers the military has to offer. The goal is to find out the bad guys' plans, stop their thugs from terrorizing innocent people, and pull off elaborate schemes that inevitably "come together" in a shootout with improvised explosives.

In this particular sub-genre, nobody gets hurt. Weapons do not inflict normal damage. Instead, a bruised result imposes a –1 penalty to further saves, a stunned result has its normal effect, a staggered result means the target runs away (if a bad guy; if he's a good guy, he says "We can't stay here..." and heroically retreats), while an unconscious result means they surrender (and whatever vehicle they're riding in flips over and explodes for good measure). Explosions trigger checks from everyone in the affected area, and improvised explosions should be given substantial bonuses.

If the players get bored with this set-up, declare it "a later season" episode, which functions as a normal *Agents of Freedom* game where real injuries happen and the military guy chasing the team is a little more competent and less of a cardboard character.
Prominent Archetypes: Con Artist, Elite Commando, Combat Engineer, Strong Guy.
Inspiration: *The A-Team* and, to a lesser extent, *Alias Smith and Jones*.

SUPER-SPIES

In a Super-Spies campaign, the heroes are glamorous, globe-trotting agents seducing beautiful women (and men) and making clever quips as they battle nefarious evils of all shapes and sizes. It should not be confused with espionage in the real world in any way.

Major elements in the game include grotesque villains with grandiose plans to rule the world, thuggish lieutenants with a brutal gimmick (razor hat brims, metal jaws, etc.), elaborate chase scenes (see the pursuit rules in the *Mastermind's Manual*), beautiful women, globetrotting between exotic locations, big set piece commando battles in secret mountain lairs, and a pounding, brassy John Barry score. Characters adopt lavish, over the top disguises, and live the lifestyles of the rich and famous.

See the Super-Spies guidelines in **Chapter 1** for this sort of game, generally power level 6 with the option of swapping out equipment between adventures and using spy-gear as normal equipment.
Prominent Archetypes: Dashing Spy, Femme Fatale, Lab Geek.
Inspiration: *James Bond, Our Man Flint, The Avengers, Alias, Get Smart* (for comedy games).

ORGANIZING MISSIONS

For the adventurous life of a costumed agent, even thrilling missions can be organized into an easily handled format. This section looks at the elements of a successful mission in detail.

STAGE ONE: THE BRIEFING

Not all missions begin with a briefing (a lot of police patrol missions begin with something as simple as a code number for the type of incident and a location, for example). Most agency-type missions should have at least a briefing handout for the players to read, so they understand what is expected of their agents. A mission briefing should include the following:

- **Mission Name:** This is the official name of the mission, usually a codename like "Operation Greengrass," "Operation Kid Gloves,"

"Operation Hocus Pocus," etc. The name should be clever and at least loosely related to an element of the mission.

- **Situation Overview:** The overview answers the basic questions: who, where, and when? It provides needed background and informs agents when a piece of intelligence is based on speculation.

- **Mission Objectives:** This is what the agency expects the characters to do, and (equally important) what *not* to do. When a mission has multiple objectives, the briefing informs the agents which ones have the highest priority. If a mission should be scrubbed when one objective is not met, they should be told here.

  A mission map is a good hand out at this point. Make a map of the location and expected challenges.

  Many missions involve "McGuffins," a term for an item everyone wants. In grittier modern games, this includes missing data disks or documents, nerve gas agents, radioactive materials, weapon prototypes, or pathogens. In more Silver Age games, this can be plans or components for a doomsday machine (weather control, melting the polar ice caps, giant magnets that pull asteroids toward earth, weapons that shut down jet engines and rockets in midair, all of which can be used to blackmail nations).

- **Expected Opposition:** The briefing identifies the expected opposition and their armament (or supervillain support). Also, places where security monitoring is going to present a particular problem should be noted; likewise, background on important NPCs (even if they do not present a direct threat) should be provided).

STAGE TWO: THE INVESTIGATION

Some missions require the characters gather more information ("intel" in agent parlance) or double check information. Investigation missions generally use three techniques to advance the story: Checking a crime scene for clues, interviewing a witness or an involved party, or stumbling on a developing plot by accident.

Crime scene investigations discover anomalies in the evidence, provide new leads to check out, or involve confrontations with witnesses or involved parties.

To organize an investigation, make a chart with the following notes:

- **The crime.** What was the crime, who committed it, who was the victim, where did it happen, and when did it happen? Were instruments like a murder weapon used and, if so, where are they now?

- **The criminals.** How did they do it, and what was their motive? When they planned the crime, was it committed in stages? (If so, include witnesses to those stages on the witness list.)

- **The crime scene.** What was its security system, and how did the criminals get around it? What trace evidence is available at the crime scene, and what skills/equipment will be needed to analyze it?

- **The witnesses.** What did they see, why were they there, are they willing to come forward, and where are they now? Would they be considered reliable in a court of law?

- **Outside obstacles.** Is someone attempting to cover up the crime, either by destroying evidence, threatening or killing witnesses, or putting political pressure on the police to close the case? Is someone being framed? Is some DA or defense attorney using a high profile case to make inroads with the press?

- **Continuing consequences.** Is this crime part of a bigger unsolved crime, like a drive-by shooting that is part of the local narcotics trade? Is it unfolding under a timetable, like a kidnapping where the victim is still being held or a diamond heist where the loot will be cut in a few weeks to cover the crime? Is this part of a serial crime spree that will be repeated, and if so, when is the next crime scheduled?

Witnesses either confirm the evidentiary record or produce contradictions that need to be investigated. Some witnesses are reluctant to talk, and either intimidation (tricking the witness into thinking one's death is imminent unless they talk) or trickery (such as pulling a con that persuades the witness to accidentally spill his guts) is necessary to get at the truth.

Accidents are the clumsiest way to drive the story, but might be necessary when the PCs become fixated on an unproductive track. They are also useful uses of hero points for inspiration when the investigation hits a dead-end.

STAGE THREE: THE PLOT TWIST

There is almost invariably a plot twist in this genre: the enemy's objective turns out to be different than expected, or the objective has properties no one knew about. This includes twists like an everyday object turning out to be an alien artifact, the target of an investigation turning out to be someone in the Witness Protection Program, or the object they are after turning out to be a fake (forcing them to track down the real object).

OPTION: THE TEASER

You might want to start off an agent adventure with a "teaser" scene, rather than going right into the briefing. This is the sort of scene that usually appears right before the credits of a television show or film and sets up the action of the story. There are three main types of teasers:

The Foreshadowing Teaser provides a look at the start of the villain's nefarious plan. Here we see the first step, the event that tips off the agency, be it a robbery, hijacking, or kidnapping. This sort of teaser is usually non-interactive; the GM just imparts information to the players. However, you can give the players the roles of supporting characters in the scene in order to put them "in the action," letting them run guards, innocent bystanders, or even the bad guys, if you want.

The In Media Res Teaser starts off with action in a later part of the adventure. Then, after the teaser, things go back to the briefing and we see how the agents got themselves into that situation. The tricky part of this kind of teaser is matching up what happens in the initial scene with how the agents get there during the game. It may require some GM Fiat to make it all blend seamlessly.

The Action Teaser runs the agents through a short, unconnected action sequence right before getting down to the mission. It might be the conclusion of their previous mission, connected with a foreshadowing teaser, an appearance by an old foe or a loose end that needs wrapping up, and so forth. Its primary purpose is to start the adventure off with a bang rather than with the agents sitting around a conference room table.

Betrayal is a common plot twist: someone who is supposed to be a friend turns out to be an enemy (either through malice or cowardice) or someone who is supposed to be an enemy is actually on the same side. The heroes may also face unexpected opposition from bureaucrats and politicians who get in their way or rival or enemy agencies that show up unexpectedly. The unexpected trap is another plot twist. The heroes arrive in an environment, and there is either a natural disaster or a pre-laid trap that pits them against the elements.

These sorts of setbacks usually qualify the players for a hero point or two, which helps to pump them up for....

STAGE FOUR: THE CLIMACTIC FIGHT

In the agent genre, everything builds toward a big confrontation. Staging is everything, and exotic locations are even more important. Don't build up to a climactic battle in a dank old warehouse in the middle of town; have people fight in hothouses, amusement parks, or on the top of huge monuments like the Statue of Liberty.

Whenever possible, don't use a static location. Two agents wrestling around in a warehouse is dull compared to a fight in a sawmill where the buzz saw is running. Stage battles in hazardous places like burning buildings or the sides of melting glaciers about to fall into the sea. So what if only a fool fights in a burning house? Whoever wrote that wasn't running an RPG!

False endings are also a genre staple, though this can be overdone. The PCs fight the villain they have been dying to fight for the last two years, and then discover he was only the henchman of the real villain. The villain had a twin brother or clone. The villain has miraculous regeneration powers no one knew about. The villain had a booby trap set to the moment of his death. Allow the heroes to catch their breath for a second, and then punch them in the solar plexus with a shocking twist.

Ironic, gruesome deaths are also a trademark of the genre. The Big Bads must die in *style*. Stage your battles so the hero is knocked down next to the spear of Alexander the Great, conveniently positioned so the villain will impale himself on it when he charges for the killing stroke. Don't just shoot your master villain—have him stagger back, fall into the piranha tank, and die screaming as some smartass agent intones: "I promise to feed the fishes while you're away." Let giant props fall and crush them. The more bad quips your PCs can make about a bad guy's death, the better!

STAGE FIVE: THE DENOUEMENT

Logically, missions should end with a debriefing. If the heroes need a bit of chewing out or backslapping, a mission debriefing is in order. Otherwise, find a good cinematic ending (the agents against the sunset or a flag, a hero kissing a freed femme fatale who helped them in the final scene) and cut the scenario there.

CAMPAIGN OPTION: CRISIS LEVEL

Unlike in most comics, on the game table, there's no guarantee of the heroes' success. Climactic moments are resolved by the players' wits and the luck of the dice (along with a few hero points). This creates a problem for the campaign narrative. What happens if the player characters are knocked cold, and no one prevents Overshadow from throwing the switch on the Transdimensional Omni-Destructo Beam? Unless the Gamemaster has preplanned for every contingency, the apocalypse can be a real hassle to adjudicate. The last thing anyone wants is a villain who isn't prepared to follow through.

The campaign's "Crisis Level" tracks the repercussions of the heroes missions, providing in-game ramifications for their successes and failures. Before play begins, the GM selects the campaign's style, establishing a Crisis Level baseline for the series. It's generally a good idea to talk over campaign style with your players, so no one's disappointed when they start fighting sentient cartoon creatures or blood-sucking vampire spawn. See **Style** in **Chapter 10** of *Mutants & Masterminds* for some discussion of campaign styles.

Campaign styles in the crisis level system range from utopian, in which the heroes have solved most of the world's problems, to terminal, in which they've probably played a role in speeding the destruction of the planet. Most campaigns are either four-color, realistic, or gritty. At the beginning of the campaign, public attitude, personal conditions, social conditions, and global conditions are dictated by the campaign style. Once play begins, however, the fate of the world is truly in the hands of the player characters.

CHANGING CONDITIONS

Every time the heroes finish a major adventure, they gain a pool of "victory points" equal to the power level of the adventure's highest-level opponent (defeating the PL 15 Overshadow, for instance, nets the heroes 15 victory points). The heroes may, as a team, spend victory points to improve personal conditions, social conditions, or global conditions by one step per 10 victory point. Surplus points are retained for later use.

CAMPAIGN CRISIS LEVEL

CRISIS LEVEL	CAMPAIGN TYPE	PUBLIC ATTITUDE	PERSONAL CONDITIONS	SOCIAL CONDITIONS	GLOBAL CONDITIONS
Green	Utopian	Helpful	Heroes revered and genrally considered the authorities.	Crime rare; Organized crime occasional.	Disasters rare.
Yellow	Four-Color	Friendly	Personal trouble rare.	Crime occasional; Organized crime rare.	Disasters occasional.
Orange	Realistic	Indifferent	Personal trouble occasional.	Crime common; Organized crime occasional	Disasters common.
Red	Gritty	Unfriendly	Personal trouble common	Crime daily; Organized crime common	Disasters daily.
Black	Against All Odds	Hostile	Heroes considered villains, though may still retain supporters.	Crime constant; Organized crime daily.	Disasters constant. End of the world scenario.
Terminal/Ultra	Hopeless	N/A	Rock bottom. Heroes considered a stain on history. Utter failure.	Complete anarchy and the breakdown of the system. Back to caveman times.	The world is destroyed with everyone on it.

THE CAPER DRAMA

Of all the adventures an agent can embark on, the caper drama ranks among the most memorable. The goal of such operations is grand larceny.

Caper dramas occur for a number of reasons. Good-guy agencies such as AEGIS may suspect a bad guy has an incriminating or dangerous item, but there's not enough evidence for a search warrant, so the agents have to go in covertly to steal the evidence. The characters might be amoral mercenaries who want to steal something, though it is often from a drug lord or corrupt businessman, which makes it less morally dubious. Sometimes the stolen item is in the possession of someone who wronged the character, in which case the operation is motivated by revenge.

The object can be anything from a valuable jewel, to a lost arcane tome, to a villain's loved one (who will be exchanged for someone they kidnapped from you), to bookkeeping records that can send a previously untouchable criminal to prison for tax fraud, to the photographs a bad guy is using to blackmail you.

The caper drama has three stages: the information gathering phase, the job, and the escape.

The information gathering stage involves learning about the existence of an object, its whereabouts, the layout of where it is being held, and the strength of the security guarding it. Knowledge of an object's existence can come from many sources, such as the dusty journals of a great-grandfather scoffed at by the world at large. This may involve tracking down and talking to witnesses (and keeping them alive when assassins show up). It may require gas-lighting a stubborn witness into revealing information, or infiltrating a party in disguise to overhear a couple of bad guys' private discussion, or breaking into a safe to take pictures of a security system.

The second phase, the job, is the actual burglary. If characters have access to the blueprints, show some sort of layout to the players (building plans are easy to find on the Internet; download some and add locations for cameras and a security office) and detail the security pitfalls accordingly. The players enter and make their checks. For added spice, include something unexpected: the vault gets an unexpected visitor, a safe was unexpectedly upgraded, someone else is trying to break in and steal the same object, and so forth.

The third stage, the getaway, involves leaving the building safely with the object and returning to an area of safety. Sometimes, something happens at the very end of the operation, and a security team will be alerted, so a chase scene begins.

If the players are thieves, they will have the added complication of fencing or dividing the loot, possibly inviting greed and treachery. In this case, a caper may be just the beginning of another adventure.

The GM is free to assign no victory points for unchallenging or irrelevant adventures (the world's greatest superheroes shouldn't net 5 victory points for beating up a lone ninja, for example). He also has the option to disallow certain condition shifts if the change doesn't seem appropriate. Breaking up a series of local jewel heists, for instance, might change social conditions, but it probably won't have any impact upon global conditions.

Major villains who defeat the PCs grant the GM victory points equal to the villain's power level (Overshadow, for instance, gains 15 victory points for defeating a group of heroes). These points may be spent to shift personal conditions, social conditions, or global conditions, causing more problems for the PCs. Try to shift the Crisis Level in a manner appropriate to the successful crime.

Public attitude represents the starting attitude of the "man on the street," which may color the heroes' interactions with those they have sworn to protect. For more about interaction checks, see page 175 of the Mutants & Masterminds rulebook. After play begins, public attitude matches the Crisis Level of personal or social conditions (whichever is lower).

Improvements to the Crisis Level exceeding the starting levels dictated by the campaign style should not last longer than one adventure. Heroes who manage to improve the Crisis Level of a non-native world by two levels gain the benefit of the Fame feat when visiting that world. Unlike changes to the Crisis Level of the heroes' native world, changes to the Crisis Level of foreign worlds last indefinitely.

In all cases, changes to a campaign's Crisis Level occur during the downtime between adventures.

CRISIS LEVEL EFFECTS

As global tension increases, the heroes may have to juggle multiple calamities. Should they save the volcanic island, or repair damaged PR? The approximate frequency of crisis level events is described as follows:

RARE

Random events happen every few months of game time, and are considered anomalous. The condition does not register on the public's mind.

OCCASIONAL

Events happens every few weeks of game time. Symptoms of the condition surface as uninteresting news stories. The public feels problems are being adequately handled by the parties involved.

COMMON

Events happen every few days of game time, and are followed constantly by an insatiable media. The public is concerned, but daily life continues as usual. Water cooler chatter and misinformation is on the rise.

DAILY

At least one event occurs daily. The heroes should begin to feel overwhelmed. The conditions are at the front of people's minds, and the population is fearful. The media provides non-stop news coverage.

CONSTANT

Critical events are happening everywhere, all the time. As soon as the heroes put out one fire, another one immediately pops up. The world is in a state of emergency, and people are afraid to leave their houses. The authorities make desperate pleas for help. Basic services are frequently interrupted.

CRISIS LEVEL AND ALERT STATUS

The Crisis Levels are comparable to AEGIS' alert status (see Alert Status in Chapter 3) and you can use each Crisis Level as a guideline to the sort of challenges characters should face or the point when AEGIS command is likely to raise (or lower) the alert status.

SUPPORTING CAST: THE ARCHETYPE FILES

No game can exist without memorable non-player character allies and villains. The agent genre has a rich cast of characters that have little overlap with superheroes (or who make great allied NPCs for a superhero game). Just give them a name, fill out or alter their personalities a little, and you'll be ready to charge into battle.

These archetypes come from a number of different types of media; some are inspired by movies, some by comic books, some may be very recognizable from animated cartoons, and a few are necessitated by the structure of the organizations in this book. They do not all mesh well together, so the Gamemaster should pick the ones that fit the tOne of their campaign and ignore the rest.

The archetypes, with a few exceptions, are designed around a standard Action-Agents campaign: PL 5, 100 Power Points. Skills with 8 ranks are Primary skills, skills at 6-7 ranks are Secondary skills, skills at 3-5 are Tertiary skills, and skills at 1-2 are Trivial skills. When adjusting characters, Primary skills are always at the maximum allowed rank for the power level, Secondary skills should be at two-thirds to three-quarters of the maximum level, Tertiary skills should be at one-quarter to half of the allowed level, and Trivial skills may be dropped altogether (if need be) or bought at 1 rank.

SUPPORTING CHARACTERS

In the agent genre, there are protagonists, and then there are bit players who form the supporting cast. The main characters in an agent series tend to fall into a few categories. In the appropriate sub-genre, some of the supporting cast members are elevated to main players: in an Air Aces campaign, the main PCs are Ace Pilots, in a semi-realistic CIA game, Defense Analysts may be the dominant archetype, and in a comedy game, the Con Artist is often the perfect fit.

ACE PILOT

You are an ace pilot, the king of the skies. Everyone in the agency has his or her own niche, and this one's yours. Your job is to ferry your superiors to important conferences (and land the plane reasonably intact when it invariably gets shot down), to provide air cover for the ground troops, and appear out of the clear blue sky when the agents need the cavalry to show up. Occasionally you get to dogfight an enemy hotshot, but it seems like you are always cast in the supporting role (even when your ego tells you that you should be the star of the game). You abide, of course, by the code of the skies (even if you are one of the bad guys).

As a hero, you are a dashing, brash egotist, the offspring of a 1950s test pilot and a female barnstormer. This archetype can also be a villain, an aging mercenary or ex-Soviet pilot (for games set in the modern era) or World War 1 or 2 pilot (for historical games) who is desperate for one last challenge in the sky (and our hero Ace Pilot is it!).

ACE PILOT					POWER LEVEL 5
Str 12	Dex 16	Con 15	Int 16	Wis 14	Cha 12

Skills: Climb 4 (+5), Computers 6 (+9), Concentration 6 (+8), Craft (mechanics) 4 (+7), Drive 2 (+5), Intimidate 2 (+3), Knowledge (physical sciences) 2 (+5), Knowledge (tactics) 6 (+9), Knowledge (technology) 6 (+9), Medicine 2 (+4), Notice 6 (+8), Pilot 10 (+13), Profession (pilot) 4 (+6), Search 6 (+9), Swim 2 (+3)

Feats: Assessment, Benefit (rank) 1, Defensive Roll 1, Equipment 4, Fearless, Improved Initiative, Luck, Skill Mastery (Computers, Knowledge [tactics], Notice, Pilot)

Combat: Attack +5, Damage +1 (unarmed), Grapple +6, Defense +5 (+3 flat-footed), Knockback –1, Initiative +7

Saving Throws: Toughness +3 (+2 flat-footed), Fortitude +5, Reflex +8, Will +6

Abilities 25 + **Skills** 17 (68 ranks) + **Feats** 11 + **Powers** 0 + **Combat** 20 + **Saves** 11 = 84

ANIMAL HANDLER

Some folks can't live without a pet. Okay, you're a big shot commando, you've received the best military training in the world, you could walk into fight and hold your own... so why do you have to go everywhere with a spider monkey hanging on your soldier? Next thing you know, you'll actually be talking to the little ape... oh nuts...

This can easily be seen as a very cheesy archetype, suitable only for quirky campaigns or if you are playing a game with a kid's cartoon in mind, or as a former agent turned naturalist NPC if the heroes are dispatched to investigate an environmentalist dispute.

ANIMAL HANDLER					POWER LEVEL 5
Str 12	Dex 16	Con 13	Int 14	Wis 12	Cha 18

Skills: Acrobatics 2 (+5), Bluff 4 (+8), Climb 2 (+3), Concentration 5 (+6), Diplomacy 2 (+6), Gather Information 2 (+6), Handle Animal 8 (+12), Intimidate 4 (+8), Knowledge (behavioral sciences) 1 (+3), Knowledge (current event) 2 (+4), Knowledge (life sciences) 1 (+3), Knowledge (tactics) 2 (+4), Medicine 1 (+2), Notice 4 (+5), Ride 4 (+7), Sense Motive 4 (+5), Stealth 2 (+5), Survival 4 (+5), Swim 2 (+3)

Feats: Animal Empathy, Assessment, Endurance, Equipment 4, Inspire, Sidekick 10 (animal companion), Speak with Animal*, Teamwork

*A limited version of the Comprehend (Animals) power as a feat; see the *Mastermind's Manual* for details.

Combat: Attack +5, Damage +1 (unarmed), Grapple +6, Defense +5 (+3 flat-footed), Knockback –0, Initiative +3

Saving Throws: Toughness +1, Fortitude +4, Reflex +8, Will +6

Abilities 25 + **Skills** 14 (56 ranks) + **Feats** 20 + **Combat** 20 + **Saves** 13 = 92

COMBAT ENGINEER

A lot of people consider agents crazy, but you are the one other agents shake their heads at. You *enjoy* going into booby-trapped buildings and disarming the most devious improvised explosives; it's not a job, it's a

ARCHETYPES AND EQUIPMENT

A number of archetypes in this book are ranks in the Equipment feat but do not have all (or sometimes even any) of their equipment points allocated. The unallocated points are intentionally left for the GM or player to assign as they see fit. The various agencies in this book have a number of equipment packages for quick assignment of equipment, or you can choose equipment as best suits the agent's current assignment and activities.

challenge and an adrenaline rush. You are well trained in other areas; you are a capable investigator and can handle yourself in a firefight, but it's when you are called upon to blow up a bridge or disarm a bomb in a toilet that you really shine.

The communications/surveillance specialist requires a lot of odd skills; you have to be unobtrusive and stealthy, and disguise skills are a definite plus. In addition, you spend a lot of time in communications vans, so being able to make a quick getaway is also a useful survival skill.

COMBAT ENGINEER — POWER LEVEL 5

Str 12	Dex 16	Con 13	Int 18	Wis 13	Cha 12

Skills: Bluff 2 (+3), Computers 4 (+8), Concentration 6 (+7), Craft (chemical) 8 (+12), Craft (mechanical) 4 (+8), Craft (structural) 8 (+12), Disable Device 6 (+10), Drive 4 (+7), Gather Information 2 (+3), Intimidate 2 (+3), Investigate 2 (+6), Knowledge (current events) 2 (+6), Knowledge (physical sciences) 6 (+10), Knowledge (popular culture) 2 (+6), Knowledge (technology) 4 (+8), Notice 2 (+3), Search 6 (+10), Sense Motive 2 (+3), Sleight of Hand 2 (+5), Stealth 2 (+5).

Feats: Beginner's Luck, Benefit (rank) 1, Diehard, Equipment 5, Improvised Tools, Luck 2, Skill Mastery (Craft (chemical), Craft (mechanical), Craft (structural), Disable Device)

Combat: Attack +5 , Damage +1 (unarmed), Grapple +6, Defense +5 (12 flat-footed), Knockback –0, Initiative +3

Saving Throws: Toughness +1, Fortitude +4, Reflex +7, Will +5

Abilities 24 + Skills 19 (76 ranks) + Feats 12 + Powers 0 + Combat 20 + Saves 11 = 86

COMMUNICATIONS SPECIALIST

You are one of the most valuable support players, as the information you gather is often the difference between success and failure on a mission. You spend many long hours spying on people and listening to their conversations. It's for your country, so it's okay.

COMMUNICATIONS SPECIALIST — POWER LEVEL 5

Str 12	Dex 12	Con 12	Int 18	Wis 14	Cha 12

Skills: Climb 4 (+5), Computers 4 (+8), Concentration 6 (+8), Craft (electronic) 4 (+8), Diplomacy 2 (+3), Disable Device 2 (+6), Disguise 4 (+5), Drive 2 (+3), Escape Artist 2 (+3), Gather Information 6 (+7), Investigate 6 (+10), Knowledge (behavioral sciences) 2 (+6), Knowledge (civics) 2 (+6), Knowledge (current events) 2 (+6), Knowledge (streetwise) 2 (+6), Knowledge (technology) 6 (+10), Medicine 2 (+4), Notice 8 (+10), Search 6 (+10), Sense Motive 4 (+6), Stealth 4 (+5).

Feats: Assessment, Beginner's Luck, Benefit (rank) 1, Connected, Contacts, Equipment 5, Improvised Tools, Luck 2, Well-Informed.

Combat: Attack +5, Damage +1 (unarmed), Grapple +6, Defense +5 (12 flat-footed), Knockback –0, Initiative +1

Saving Throws: Toughness +1, Fortitude +4, Reflex +7. Will +6

Abilities 20 + Skills 20 (80 ranks) + Feats 14 + Powers 0 + Combat 20 + Saves 13 = 87

CON ARTIST

You are part comic relief, part sidekick. You make a great comic foil for overly serious, altruistic PCs. You may be a member of the team, but you always have a scheme going on the side, and when you are about to be caught, you have a talent for deflecting blame that has to be seen to be believed. Your selfishness and shortsightedness inevitably brings misery to everyone you know yet people inevitably feel sorry for you (except the bad guys, who beat you up with distressing regularity).

CON ARTIST — POWER LEVEL 5

Str 12	Dex 12	Con 12	Int 12	Wis 12	Cha 16

Skills: Bluff 7 (+10), Climb 2 (+3), Computers 2 (+3), Concentration 2 (+3), Diplomacy 6 (+9), Disguise 2 (+5), Drive 2 (+3), Escape Artist 6 (+7), Gather Information 7 (+10), Handle Animal 1 (+4), Intimidate 2 (+5), Investigate 4 (+5), Knowledge (current events) 5 (+6), Knowledge (popular culture) 5 (+6), Knowledge (streetwise) 6 (+7), Notice 4 (+5), Search 4 (+5), Sense Motive 5 (+6), Sleight of Hand 7 (+8), Stealth 6 (+7), Survival 1 (+2), Swim 2 (+3)

Feats: Assessment, Benefit (rank) 1, Connected, Contacts, Distract (Bluff), Dodge Focus 2, Luck 2.

Combat: Attack +4, Damage +1 (unarmed), Grapple +5, Defense +4 (+1 flat-footed), Knockback –0, Initiative +1

Saving Throws: Toughness +0, Fortitude +5, Reflex +6, Will +6

Abilities 14 + Skills 22 (88 ranks) + Feats 9 + Powers 0 + Combat 12 + Saves 15 = 72

DEFENSE ANALYST

Another type of lab technician is the defense analyst. You work in think tanks and intelligence departments, analyzing data to determine the best plan of attack against a hidden enemy. While most analysts remain in their cubicles at HQ, some of the most famous defense analysts like to go into the field and investigate the evidence in person.

DEFENSE ANALYST — POWER LEVEL 5

Str 12	Dex 12	Con 12	Int 18	Wis 16	Cha 12

Skills: Bluff 4 (+5), Computers 4 (+8), Concentration 2 (+5), Diplomacy 3 (+4), Drive 2 (+3), Gather Information 6 (+7), Investigate 2 (+6), Knowledge (behavioral sciences) 2 (+6), Knowledge (civics) 8 (+12), Knowledge (current events) 4 (+8), Knowledge (streetwise) 2 (+6), Knowledge (tactics) 2 (+6), Knowledge (technology) 4 (+8). Medicine 2 (+5), Notice 6 (+9), Profession (agent) 3 (+6), Search 4 (+8), Sense Motive 3 (+6), Sleight of Hand 2 (+3), Stealth 3 (+4).

Feats: Assessment, Benefit (rank) 1, Connected, Contacts, Equipment 4, Jack-of-All-Trades, Master Plan, Taunt, Skill Mastery (Computers, Investigate, Knowledge (tactics), Sense Motive), Well-Informed

Combat: Attack +4, Damage +1 (unarmed), Grapple +5, Defense +4 (+2 flat-footed), Knockback –0, Initiative +1

Saving Throws: Toughness +1, Fortitude +5, Reflex +5, Will +8

Abilities 22 + Skills 17 (68 ranks) + Feats 13 + Powers 0 + Combat 16 + Saves 13 = 81

ENVIRONMENTAL SPECIALIST

You are the master of your domain (usually a choice between desert, alpine, and swamp). When your team's adventures take them into your element, that's when you take charge and shine—and heaven help anyone who doesn't take your advice. The bad guys may have an impregnable fortress nearby, but this is your world, not *theirs*, and you're going to have fun.

This archetype isn't one that's found in a lot of classic agent books, but it's very prevalent in agent-based cartoons, of course, and there's no reason it's not appropriate for a globetrotting *Agents of Freedom* game.

AGENCY EQUIPMENT PACKAGES

STAR SQUAD OFFICER (EQUIPMENT 8, 40 POINTS)

Sub-machine gun (+4 damage, Autofire, 12 points), riot armor (Toughness +4), tear gas, climbing harness, gas mask, flash goggles, camo-clothing, handcuffs, police radio

AEGIS AGENT (EQUIPMENT 3, 15 POINTS)

Blaster pistol (+5 damage, 10 points), body armor (Toughness +2, 2 points), handcuffs (1 point), commlink (1 point), multi-tool (1 point)

AEGIS FIELD INVESTIGATOR (EQUIPMENT 4, 20 POINTS)

Blaster pistol (10 points), body armor (Toughness +2, 2 points), handcuffs (1 point), commlink (1 point), multi-tool (1 point), investigator's kit (2 points), broom (1 point), camera (1 point), PDA (1 point)

AEGIS COMMANDO (EQUIPMENT 5, 25 POINTS)

Blast rifle (16 points), body armor (Toughness +2, 2 points), handcuffs (1 point), commlink (1 point), binoculars (1 point); flash goggles (1 point), gas mask (1 point), multi-tool (1 point), night-vision goggles (1 point)

UNISON AGENT (EQUIPMENT 2, 10 POINTS)

Pistol (6 points), cell phone (1 point), digital camera (1 point), notebook computer (2 points)

UNISON TROOPER (EQUIPMENT 4, 20 POINTS)

Assault Rifle (16 points), body armor (Toughness +2, 2 points), cell phone (1 point), night vision goggles (1 point)

UNISON SOLO (EQUIPMENT 10, 47 POINTS)

Holdout pistol (4 points), sniper rifle (13 points), sleep gas pellets (12 points), burglar's kit (2 points), disguise kit (1 point), concealed commlink (2 point), binoculars (1 point), concealed flash goggles (2 points), concealed gas mask (2 points), concealed multi-tool (2 points), night vision goggles (1 point), digital camera (1 point), notebook computer (2 points), broom (1 point), GPS (1 point), plus 3 points worth of additional equipment.

SHADOW AGENT (EQUIPMENT 3, 15 POINTS)

Blaster pistol (10 points), body armor (Toughness +4, 4 points), commlink (1 point).

SHADOW COMBAT AGENT (EQUIPMENT 4, 20 POINTS)

Blaster rifle (16 points), body armor (Toughness +3, 3 points), commlink (1 point).

SHADOW INFILTRATION AGENT (EQUIPMENT 5, 24 POINTS)

Blaster pistol (10 points), body armor (Toughness +2, 2 points), commlink (1 point), multi-tool (1 point), cleaner's kit (1 point), investigator's kit (1 points), video camera (2 point), PDA (1 point), camouflage field (4 points), burglar's kit (1 points).

OVERTHROW TERRORIST (EQUIPMENT 7, 30 POINTS)

Hold-out pistol (5 points), holo-disguise (8 points), radio scrambler (3 points), commlink (1 point), burglar's kit (1 points), gas mask (1 point), sleep gas grenades (11 points).

ENVIRONMENTAL SPECIALIST				POWER LEVEL 5	
Str 15	Dex 14	Con 17	Int 12	Wis 13	Cha 12

Skills: Bluff 4 (+5), Climb 8 (+10), Computers 3 (+4), Diplomacy 4 (+5), Disable Device 4 (+5), Drive 6 (+8), Gather Information 4 (+5), Handle Animal 2 (+3), Intimidate 4 (+5), Investigate 6 (+7), Knowledge (behavioral sciences) 2 (+3), Knowledge (civics) 4 (+5), Knowledge (current event) 4 (+5), Knowledge (tactics) 3 (+4), Knowledge (technology) 2 (+3), Medicine 2 (+3), Notice 6 (+7), Pilot 2 (+4), Search 2 (+3), Sense Motive 6 (+7), Sleight of Hand 6 (+8), Stealth 6 (+8), Survival 10 (+11), Swim 4 (+6)

Feats: Attack Focus (ranged) 1, Benefit (rank) 1, Defensive Roll 1, Diehard, Environmental Adaptation (pick one), Endurance 1, Equipment 4, Improvised Tools, Inspire 1, Luck 3, Move-by Action, Precise Shot 1, Track.

Combat: Attack +4 (melee), +5 (ranged), Damage +2 (unarmed), Grapple +7, Defense +5 (+3 flat-footed), Knockback –2, Initiative +2

Saving Throws: Toughness +4 (+3 flat-footed), Fortitude +8, Reflex +7, Will +6

Abilities 23 + Skills 26 (104 ranks) + Feats 18 + Powers 0 + Combat 18 + Saves 15 = 100

FIELD MEDIC

You are a sawbones, a field medic. Commandos may think you are crazy when it comes to the Hippocratic Oath—who would have moral qualms over not saving the life of the enemy, even a clone or a demon? —but you live by your principles, because that is the only way to live. It does not mean you won't defend yourself or your friends, you just have to remember to fix whatever damage you caused. It does mean that you have to be a man or woman of unimpeachable character, the sort of person that you would trust with your life, because that is your daily responsibility.

FIELD MEDIC				POWER LEVEL 5	
Str 10	Dex 15	Con 13	Int 14	Wis 18	Cha 14

Skills: Computers 4 (+6), Concentration 5 (+9), Diplomacy 2 (+4), Gather Information 2 (+4), Intimidate 2 (+4), Investigate 2 (+4), Knowledge (behavioral sciences) 2 (+4), Knowledge (life sciences) 5 (+7), Medicine 8 (+10), Notice 4 (+6), Profession (doctor) 4 (+6), Search 2 (+6), Sense Motive 2 (+4)

Feats: Assessment, Benefit (rank) 1, Connected, Equipment 8, Improvised Tools, Luck 2, Ultimate Effort (Medicine skill checks), Well-Informed.

Combat: Attack +4, Damage +0 (unarmed), Grapple +5, Defense +4 (+3 flat-footed), Knockback –0, Initiative +2

Saving Throws: Toughness +3, Fortitude +5, Reflex +6, Will +5

Abilities 24 + Skills 11 (44 ranks) + Feats 15 + Powers 0 + Combat 16 + Saves 11 = 74

GREASE MONKEY

You are a grease monkey, wrench monkey, gear-head, whatever; you carry a toolbox and, unlike these strutting clowns who are playing soldiers, you actually work for a living. They take terrible care of their stuff, and then are prone to blame you whenever their craft has the slightest hiccup. You may be an in-your-face smartass, but you are still a valued and respected member of the team, even if people often treat you like something they scraped off their shoe.

Note: There are villainous grease monkeys, too: sneaky chain-smoking thugs who like to hit people over the head with a wrench.

GREASE MONKEY				POWER LEVEL 5	
Str 14	Dex 12	Con 13	Int 18	Wis 12	Cha 12

Skills: Computers 5 (+9), Craft (mechanical) 8 (+12), Disable Device 6 (+10), Drive 4 (+5), Escape Artist (+1), Knowledge (physical sciences) 1 (+5), Knowledge (streetwise) 1 (+5), Knowledge (technology) 5 (+9), Notice 5 (+6), Sleight of Hand 5 (+6)

Feats: Assessment, Benefit (rank) 1, Improvised Tools, Inventor, Luck 2, Skill Mastery (Craft (electronic), Craft (mechanical), Disable Device, Repair)

Combat: Attack +5, Damage +2 (unarmed), Grapple +7, Defense +5 (12 flat-footed), Knockback –0, Initiative +1

Saving Throws: Toughness +1, Fortitude +4, Reflex +3, Will +5

Abilities 21 + **Skills** 10 (40 ranks) + **Feats** 7 + **Powers** 0 + **Combat** 20 + **Saves** 9 = 67

LAB GEEK

You're not a mad scientist; you're that nerdy guy over in R&D. You are brilliant and you develop cool gadgets and devices in the war against evil, although nobody really wants to talk with you for more than thirty seconds at a time. People are strange to you. After all, you don't even mention your *Dungeons & Dragons* game! Perhaps they are confusing you with one of those mad scientist types whose inventions you keep stumbling over.

This is primarily an NPC archetype. However, because your agency sometimes needs someone more specialized than a field investigator at a crime scene, you sometimes get to go out of the office into places where it's dangerous. However, you're a patriot (and you can talk about your cool adventures in the secret agency chat room), so you'll take the risk.

Customization: The player should choose an area of specialization in one of the following skills: Computers, Knowledge (earth sciences), Knowledge (life sciences), or Knowledge (physical sciences) and add 4 ranks to it.

LAB GEEK				POWER LEVEL 5	
Str 10	Dex 12	Con 12	Int 18	Wis 11	Cha 10

Skills: Computers 4 (+8), Concentration 7 (+7), Craft (chemical) 6 (+10), Craft (mechanical) 6 (+10), Disable Device 6 (+10), Gather Information 8 (+8), Investigate 6 (+10), Knowledge (earth sciences) 4 (+8), Knowledge (life sciences) 4 (+8), Knowledge (physical sciences) 4 (+8), Knowledge (popular culture) 5 (+9), Knowledge (technology) 8 (+12), Medicine 4 (+4), Notice 4 (+4), Search 4 (+8), Sense Motive 4 (+4)

Feats: Benefit (rank) 1, Eidetic Memory, Improvised Tools, Inventor, Well-Informed

Combat: Attack +1, Damage +0 (unarmed), Grapple +5, Defense +2 (+1 flat-footed), Knockback –0, Initiative +1

Saving Throws: Toughness +1, Fortitude +2, Reflex +2, Will +5

Abilities 13 + **Skills** 22 (88 ranks) + **Feats** 5 + **Powers** 0 + **Combat** 9 + **Saves** 7 = 56

MASTER OF DISGUISE

You are the ultimate undercover agent. You are a role-player who lives for the look on your enemy's face when they realize that they have been had. You might have the most dangerous job in the world—going into the heart of the enemy's territory, eating their food, looking them in the eye without stopping to blink, and learning their darkest secrets—and returning to tell the tale.

You are used to working alone, or with a partner to provide a distraction. But, you are still good enough in a firefight that you can pull out your weapon and fight alongside the hard-charging commandos. Of course, the enemy has its own Masters of Disguise, so you have to watch out, or in the great agency game of cat and mouse, you might end up being the rodent.

MASTER OF DISGUISE				POWER LEVEL 5	
Str 12	Dex 16	Con 12	Int 16	Wis 14	Cha 16

Skills: Bluff 6 (+7), Climb 6 (+7), Computers 3 (+6), Demolitions 4 (+7), Diplomacy 4 (+5), Disable Device 6 (+9), Disguise 8 (+9), Drive 3 (+6), Gather Information 6 (+7), Intimidate 2 (+3), Investigate 6 (+9), Knowledge (behavioral sciences) 2 (+5), Knowledge (civics) 4 (+7), Knowledge (current events) 4 (+7), Knowledge (history) 1 (+4), Knowledge (technology) 2 (+5), Medicine 1 (+3), Notice 6 (+8), Perform (Acting) 6 (+7), Pilot 2 (+5), Search 2 (+5), Sense Motive 6 (+8), Sleight of Hand 6 (+9), Stealth 6 (+9), Survival 2 (+4), Swim 4 (+5)

Feats: Attractive, Benefit 1 (rank), Equipment 4, Evasion, Improved Aim, Improved Disarm, Improved Grab, Improved Trip, Luck 3

Combat: Attack +5, Damage +1 (unarmed), Grapple +7, Defense +5 (+3 flat-footed), Initiative +3

Saving Throws: Toughness +1, Fortitude +6, Reflex +7, Will +8

Abilities 26 + **Skills** 27 (108 ranks) + **Feats** 14 + **Powers** 0 + **Combat** 20 + **Saves** 15 = 102

NAVY SEAL

You are the naval equivalent of the Roughneck Commando, the elite badass of the sea, and their big rival in the special-forces world. As agencies like AEGIS often perform sea salvage and other maritime missions, having a Navy SEAL as an officer or advisor is commonplace.

Like other specialists, you never get enough missions in your favored environment to keep you truly happy. However, you are proud to serve your country even in your limited capacity, although all those jarheads *really* get on your nerves.

NAVY SEAL				POWER LEVEL 5	
Str 16	Dex 18	Con 16	Int 12	Wis 12	Cha 12

Skills: Acrobatics 4 (+8), Climb 2 (+5), Concentration 6 (+7), Demolitions 3 (+4), Disable Device 4 (+5), Escape Artist 3 (+7), Intimidate 6 (+7), Investigate 2 (+3), Knowledge (current events) 1 (+2), Knowledge (popular culture) 1 (+2), Knowledge (streetwise) 1 (+2), Knowledge (tactics) 6 (+7), Knowledge (technology) 2 (+3), Medicine 2 (+3), Notice 6 (+7), Pilot 2 (+6), Profession (soldier) 2 (+3), Search 2 (+3), Stealth 7 (+11), Survival 6 (+7), Swim 8 (+11)

Feats: All-out Attack, Attack Focus (ranged) 2, Attack Specialization (rifle) 1, Benefit 1, Die-Hard, Equipment 5, Improved Aim, Improved Critical (rifle, punch), Improved Sunder, Inspire 2, Leadership, Precise Shot 1, Quick Draw, Startle

Combat: Attack +5 (melee), +7 (ranged), +9 (rifle), Damage +3 (unarmed), Grapple +8, Defense +5 (+3 flat-footed), Knockback –1, Initiative +4

Saving Throws: Toughness +3, Fortitude +8, Reflex +9, Will +5

Abilities 26 + **Skills** 19 (76 ranks) + **Feats** 21 + **Powers** 0 + **Combat** 20 + **Saves** 14 = 100

SHARPSHOOTER

You are the best shot in your state, except for that mutant marksman (who doesn't count). This archetype is often a Boy Scout with a hint of mischief, who is happy to serve his country and even happier to get the keys to his nation's arsenal. You may not be on the front lines with the machine gunners and the commandos, but they are all a little safer because of the cover fire you provide.

You are trained as a generalist; you are often going to be standing in the rear where you are vulnerable to unexpected enemy flank attacks, so you should be able to defend yourself in every contingency.

SHARPSHOOTER				POWER LEVEL 5	
Str 14	Dex 18	Con 14	Int 12	Wis 12	Cha 10

Skills: Climb 2 (+4), Computers 2 (+3), Concentration 6 (+7), Diplomacy 2 (+2), Disable Device 2 (+3), Drive 2 (+6), Gather Information 2 (+2), Intimidate 6 (+6), Investigate 2 (+3), Knowledge (current events) 2 (+3), Knowledge (popular culture) 2 (+3), Knowledge (streetwise) 2 (+3), Knowledge (tactics) 6 (+7), Knowledge (technology) 2 (+3), Medicine 2 (+3), Notice 6 (+7), Pilot 2 (+6), Profession (rifle instructor) 2 (+3), Repair 2 (+3), Search 2 (+3), Sleight of Hand 2 (+6), Stealth 2 (+6), Survival 6 (+7), Swim 2 (+4).

Feats: All-out Attack, Attack Focus (ranged) 3, Benefit (rank) 1, Equipment 4, Improved Critical (rifles), Improved Aim, Improved Sunder, Leadership, Precise Shot 2, Quick Draw 2, Sneak Attack, Startle, Teamwork

Combat: Attack +5 (melee), +8 (ranged), Damage +2 (unarmed), Grapple +7, Defense +5 (+3 flat-footed), Knockback –1, Initiative +4

Saving Throws: Toughness +2, Fortitude +6, Reflex +9, Will +6

Abilities 20 + **Skills** 17 (68 ranks) + **Feats** 20 + **Powers** 0 + **Combat** 20 + **Saves** 14 = **89**

THE STRONG GUY

You are a modern day Little John, the burly sidekick who constantly amazes your teammates with your feats of physical strength. You are not the smartest member of the team, and you are always the butt of a few jokes, but there is not a shadow of a doubt that everyone respects you, and no one wants you to get *too* angry at them, because a week in the infirmary's not much fun. You are like everyone's kid brother, and people lean on you like the proverbial Rock of Gibraltar. It gets old sometime, but you are a team player, and you like to help out.

Your big rival on the bad guy's side is the Brute Lieutenant, and the two of you always seem to get into some sort of wrestling contest whenever you collide.

THE STRONG GUY				POWER LEVEL 5	
Str 20	Dex 12	Con 18	Int 12	Wis 12	Cha 12

Skills: Bluff 4 (+5), Climb 6 (+11), Computers 2 (+3), Concentration 6 (+7), Diplomacy 2 (+3), Disable Device 2 (+3), Escape Artist 4 (+5), Gather Information 2 (+3), Intimidate 8 (+9), Investigate 2 (+3), Knowledge (current events) 4 (+5), Knowledge (tactics) 2 (+3), Medicine 2 (+3), Notice 6 (+7), Pilot 2 (+3), Search 6 (+7), Sense Motive 2 (+3), Sleight of Hand 2 (+3), Stealth 4 (+5), Survival 4 (+5), Swim 6 (+11)

Feats: All-out Attack, Attack Focus (melee) 1, Benefit (rank) 2, Diehard, Endurance 1, Equipment 4, Improved Grab, Improved Grapple, Improved Overrun, Improved Pin, Power Attack, Teamwork 1, Move-by Action, Set-Up.

Combat: Attack +5 (melee), +4 (ranged), Damage +5 (unarmed), Grapple +10, Defense +5 (+3 flat-footed), Knockback –2, Initiative +1

Saving Throws: Toughness +4, Fortitude +9, Reflex +6, Will +6

Abilities 26 + **Skills** 20 (80 ranks) + **Feats** 19 + **Powers** 0 + **Combat** 18 + **Saves** 15 = **97**

BAD GUYS: ARCHETYPES OF MASS DESTRUCTION

Of course, the bad guys also have their crew. Many of the professional types (such as combat engineers, field investigators, and the master of disguise) can be ported to the bad guys' side without significant changes. Furthermore, some heroic archetypes need only a name change to become villains (a Grease Monkey becomes a "Sneaky Guy With A Wrench," a Modern Day Amazon becomes an "Out of Control Hellcat," and a Hot-Headed Lieutenant becomes "Incompetent Whiner").

However, there are a few villainous archetypes that can give the bad guys more of a distinctive flavor, including the following.

BUREAUCRAT FROM HELL

"WESTERN CIVILIZATION WILL COLLAPSE UNLESS YOU FILL OUT THOSE FORMS IN TRIPLICATE."

Unlike other bad guy archetypes, this one doesn't have to actively ally with the heroes' enemies to make their lives miserable.

You can take anything that is lively and good and strangle it with enough red tape. You are annoyed by anything that is not thoroughly crammed into the bureaucracy, and cowboys like secret agents, commandos, and mercenaries like nothing better than to break the rules. When you are allied with the bad guys, however, you become an unholy terror, blocking government support, grounding their air fleet to check that they meet emissions standards, and demanding they meet minority and gender quotas before being allowed to operate in the city limits.

For the most part, bureaucrats like you are officious nerds who would not come within three miles of an honest firefight; you are more comfortable behind the scenes. However, you will grab a gun and a hostage when you are finally exposed for the criminal you are.

BUREAUCRAT FROM HELL				POWER LEVEL 3	
Str 10	Dex 10	Con 11	Int 14	Wis 12	Cha 14

Skills: Bluff 8 (+10), Computers 2 (+4), Concentration 4 (+5), Diplomacy 4 (+6), Gather Information 6 (+8), Intimidate 8 (+10), Investigate 2 (+4), Knowledge (behavioral sciences) 2 (+4), Knowledge (civics) 8 (+10), Knowledge (current events) 2 (+4), Notice 4 (+5), Profession (bureaucrat) 6 (+7), Sense Motive 8 (+9)

Feats: Connected, Contacts, Distract (Bluff, Intimidate), Eidetic Memory, Luck 2, Master Plan, Well-Informed

Combat: Attack +0, Damage +0 (unarmed), Grapple +5, Defense +0, Knockback –0, Initiative +0

Saving Throws: Toughness +0, Fortitude +3, Reflex +2, Will +6

Abilities 11 + **Skills** 16 (64 ranks) + **Feats** 9 + **Powers** 0 + **Combat** 0 + **Saves** 10 = **46**

BRUTE LIEUTENANT

"SUNAMI CRUSH YOU!"

When one has the brains, one usually recruits henchmen for brawn, and that is where you come in. You are a Man Mountain who practically makes the earth shake just by taking a quiet stroll down the street, and that's without superpowers. With your knowledge of sumo wrestling, you are a feared combatant—and you are an enforcer who sits on the right hand of a monster.

There are other types of Brute Lieutenants—the burly Russian wrestler, the Thai giant who mastered Muay Thai, the huge escaped convict who has had his nerve endings dulled through surgery, the convicted heavyweight boxer whose knockout punch killed five people– but the sumo wrestler is one of the oldest examples of the archetype, and your boss has a taste for the classics.

BRUTE LIEUTENANT				POWER LEVEL 5	
Str 20	Dex 10	Con 20	Int 10	Wis 12	Cha 10

Skills: Concentration 4 (+5), Handle Animal 4 (+4), Intimidate 8 (+8), Knowledge (tactics) 4 (+4), Notice 4 (+5), Perform (acting) 4 (+4), Sense Motive 4 (+5).

Feats: Assessment, Benefit (rank) 3, Chokehold, Diehard, Endurance 2, Fearsome Presence 3, Improved Grab, Improved Grapple, Improved Pin, Improved Overrun, Improved Throw, Improved Trip, Power Attack, Stunning Attack, Takedown Attack.

Combat: Attack +5, Damage +5, Grapple +10, Defense +5 (+3 flat-footed), Knockback −2, Initiative +0

Saving Throws: Toughness +5, Fortitude +5, Reflex +0, Will +1

Abilities 22 + **Skills** 8 (32 ranks) + **Feats** 20 + **Powers** 0 + **Combat** 20 + **Saves** 0 = 70

CHAMPAGNE VILLAIN

"WE'RE ALL GENTLEMEN HERE, AREN'T WE?"
HE WHISPERS, "WHEN HE TURNS HIS BACK, SHOOT HIM."

A term taken from Raiders of the Lost Ark (Steven Spielberg described Belloq as a "champagne villain" who contrasted with Indiana Jones' "beer hero"), the Champagne Villain is a variant on the Dashing Spy. Utterly charming and a gentleman on the surface, as soon as someone becomes inconvenient, this sociopath's true colors emerge, and he behaves with all the dignity of a street thug.

CHAMPAGNE VILLAIN				POWER LEVEL 5	
Str 12	Dex 16	Con 12	Int 16	Wis 14	Cha 18

Skills: Bluff 4 (+8), Climb 2 (+3), Computers 2 (+5), Concentration 2 (+4), Diplomacy 8 (+12), Disable Device (+3), Disguise (+4), Drive 2 (+5), Escape Artist (+3), Gather Info 4 (+8), Handle Animal (+4), Intimidate 4 (+8), Investigate 2 (+5), Knowledge (art) 4 (+7), Knowledge (current events) 4 (+7), Knowledge (popular culture) 2 (+5), Knowledge (tactics) 2 (+5), Knowledge (technology) 2 (+5), Notice 4 (+6), Ride 2 (+5), Search 2 (+5), Sense Motive 6 (+8), Sleight of Hand 4 (+7), Stealth 2 (+5), Survival 2 (+4), Swim 2 (+3)

Feats: Attractive (1), Connected, Contacts, Diehard, Eidetic Memory, Equipment (4), Evasion (1), Fascinate (1), Improved Disarm, Luck (2), Uncanny Dodge, Well-Informed

Combat: Attack +5, Damage +1 (unarmed), Defense 15 (12 flat-footed), Initiative +3

Saving Throws: Toughness +5 (+5 flat-footed), Fortitude +6, Reflex +8, Will +7

Abilities 28 + **Skills** 17 (68 ranks) + **Feats** 16 + **Powers** 0 + **Combat** 20 + **Saves** 15 − **Drawbacks** 0 = 96

CLEANER

"DO YOU IDIOTS HAVE TO MAKE SUCH A MESS? IT'S GONNA TAKE HOURS TO COVER IT UP."

You know that television series where those guys find a sliver of evidence, make the most absurd leap of logic, and still manage to be right about the crime? Well those guys are the ones you are supposed to fool.

You remove dead bodies from crime scenes and make sure that no one realizes they died. You dispose of murder weapons. Without them, the bad guys would have a lot higher lawyer fees.

Investigate is this archetype's big skill, but Disguise is also useful for entering a place undetected, and Bluff helps in looking inconspicuous when you are walking away from a job. The good guys can have cleaners too, but this is a skill most often associated with the other side of the fence.

CLEANER				POWER LEVEL 5	
Str 12	Dex 12	Con 15	Int 18	Wis 16	Cha 13

Skills: Bluff 3 (+4), Climb 2 (+3), Computers 4 (+8), Concentration 4 (+7), Craft (chemical) 4 (+8), Craft (structural) 4 (+8), Diplomacy 3 (+4), Disable Device 4 (+8), Disguise 8 (+9), Drive 2 (+3), Gather Information 6 (+7), Intimidate 2 (+3), Investigate 8 (+12), Knowledge (behavioral sciences) 4 (+8), Knowledge (life sciences) 2 (+6), Knowledge (physical sciences) 2 (+6), Knowledge (popular culture) 2 (+6), Knowledge (streetwise) 4 (+8), Medicine 2 (+5), Notice 8 (+11), Profession (forensics) 4 (+7), Search 8 (+12), Sense Motive 4 (+7), Sleight of Hand 2 (+3), Stealth 4 (+5),

Feats: Assessment, Equipment 5, Improvised Tools, Inventor, Skill Mastery (Investigate, Search, Sense Motive, Sleight of Hand), Well-Informed

Combat: Attack +4, Damage +1 (unarmed), Grapple +5, Defense +5 (12 flat-footed), Initiative +1

Saving Throws: Toughness +2, Fortitude +7, Reflex +5, Will +8

Abilities 26 + **Skills** 25 (100 ranks) + **Feats** 10 + **Powers** 0 + **Combat** 18 + **Saves** 14 = 93

CRIME LORD

"I'M JUST A SIMPLE BUSINESSMAN. KILL HIM."

You sit in the center of a criminal web, eating the flies that get caught in your trap. You are a capable fighter when your back is against the wall, but you would rather play a game of human chess than get your hands dirty. Agents may feel you are just local rabble who should do what you are told for the good of your country. But the Crime Lord's no patriot, though you revere dead presidents more than anything else in the world.

The Crime Lord is rarely a major player in the grand schemes of an *Agents of Freedom* campaign. Rather, your involvement in the criminal scene makes you a player who tries to manipulate complex situations for your benefit, whose favor both the heroes and their enemies try to woo, even though both sides understand that you make the most loathsome of allies.

CRIME LORD — POWER LEVEL 5

Str 12	Dex 10	Con 15	Int 18	Wis 14	Cha 14

Skills: Bluff 8 (+10), Computers 6 (+10), Concentration 6 (+8), Diplomacy 8 (+10), Gather Information 8 (+10), Intimidate 8 (+10), Investigate 4 (+8), Knowledge (behavioral sciences) 6 (+10), Knowledge (business) 6 (+10), Knowledge (civics) 2 (+6), Knowledge (current events) 6 (+10), Knowledge (history) 2 (+6), Knowledge (streetwise) 8 (+12), Notice 6 (+8), Profession (criminal) 6 (+8), Search 6 (+10), Sense Motive 8 (+10), Sleight of Hand 4 (+4), Stealth 4 (+4)

Feats: Assessment, Contacts, Connected, Luck 2, Equipment 3, Minions 5, Precise Shot, Well-Informed

Combat: Attack +5, Damage +1, Grapple +6, Defense +5 (+3 flat-footed), Knockback –1, Initiative +0

Saving Throws: Toughness +2, Fortitude +7, Reflex +5, Will +8

Abilities 23 + **Skills** 28 (112 ranks) + **Feats** 15 + **Powers** 0 + **Combat** 20 + **Saves** 16 = 102

EVIL LAWYER

"YOUR HONOR, I HAD NOTHING TO DO WITH THE WITNESS' EVISCERATION. WHAT DO YOU MEAN THEY HAVEN'T RELEASED THE FACT THAT HE WAS EVISCERATED? LET'S JUST CALL IT A LUCKY GUESS, YOUR HONOR."

They make jokes about your profession, and the reason you eat shark fins is to make some of them true. You mock the laws and use the scales of justice as a spittoon. You consider lawyer-client privilege to be 90% of the fun in the profession, with the other 10% coming when you see the broken-down shells of the District Attorneys you've destroyed, shaking in their seats in an alcoholic stupor and still unable to forget what you did to them in the courtroom.

Of course, you do have to worry about government investigations, the bar, and killer vigilantes who have put your name on the top of a hit list. That is one reason why you turn to the evil agency for protection. It's a mutually beneficial relationship. There are also evil lawyers who run terror cells on the side, but not many of your kind mix business and pleasure. Some of you are indolent old men, but there are a few young attorneys who are combat trained and quite capable of pulling out a weapon and getting into a firefight. It sure beats the firm's quarterly paintball game!

EVIL LAWYER — POWER LEVEL 3

Str 10	Dex 10	Con 11	Int 16	Wis 12	Cha 18

Skills: Bluff 8 (+12), Computers 2 (+5), Concentration 4 (+5), Diplomacy 8 (+12), Gather Information 4 (+8), Intimidate 6 (+10), Knowledge (behavioral sciences) 3 (+6), Knowledge (business) 3 (+6), Knowledge (civics) 8 (+11), Knowledge (history) 2 (+5), Knowledge (popular culture) 2 (+5), Notice 4 (+5), Perform (oratory) 8 (+12), Profession (lawyer) 10 (+11), Sense Motive 8 (+9)

Feats: Benefit (Law License), Connected, Distract (Bluff), Eidetic Memory, Leadership, Luck 2, Master Plan, Well-Informed

Combat: Attack +1, Damage +0, Grapple +0, Defense +4 (+2 flat-footed), Initiative +0

Saving Throws: Toughness +0, Fortitude +2, Reflex +0, Will +4

Abilities 17 + **Skills** 20 (80 ranks) + **Feats** 9 + **Powers** 0 + **Combat** 10 + **Saves** 5 = 61

HIGH-TECH SPY

"THE DATA DISK IS MINE, MR. REED. SUCH A PITY ABOUT YOUR EYE. UNTIL NEXT TIME..."

Everyone needs an adversary, even dashing spies. You are one of the most capable members of a rival spy agency, and the PC's opposite number. Often you are a ruthless sadist who tortures and murders your way to the PC's objectives, and does so for fun. Some adversaries are fanatics for their organization; others are slippery weasels who betray their employers at the drop of a hat.

HIGH-TECH SPY — POWER LEVEL 5

Str 12	Dex 14	Con 12	Int 14	Wis 12	Cha 14

Skills: Bluff 4 (+6), Climb 2 (+3), Computers 4 (+6), Concentration 4 (+5), Craft (electronic) 1 (+3), Craft (mechanical) 1 (+3), Diplomacy 2 (+4), Disable Device 8 (+10), Disguise 2 (+4), Drive 2 (+4), Escape Artist 4 (+6), Gather Information 4 (+6), Intimidate 4 (+6), Investigate 4 (+6), Knowledge (Art) 1 (+3), Knowledge (current events) 1 (+3), Knowledge (tactics) 4 (+6), Knowledge (technology) 2 (+4), Languages (pick 2), Notice 4 (+5), Pilot 2 (+4), Ride 2 (+4), Search 6 (+8), Sense Motive 4 (+5), Sleight of Hand 2 (+4), Stealth 2 (+4), Survival 4 (+5), Swim 2 (+3)

Feats: Blind-Fight, Connected, Critical Strike, Defensive Roll 3, Diehard, Eidetic Memory, Equipment 8, Improved Critical (pistols), Improved Disarm, Luck 2, Quick Draw, Ultimate Effort (Reflex saves), Uncanny Dodge (auditory), Well-Informed

Combat: Attack +5, Damage +1, Grapple +6, Defense +5, Knockback –2, Initiative +2

Saving Throws: Toughness +4 (+1 flat-footed), Fortitude +6, Reflex +9, Will +6

Abilities 18 + **Skills** 21 (84 ranks) + **Feats** 24 + **Powers** 0 + **Combat** 20 + **Saves** 17 = 100

THE IRON DUKE

"WE'RE GOING TO PARTY LIKE IT'S 1939..."

You are a warrior of the Third Reich, born decades too late. You lead a group of agents bent on establishing a Fourth Reich over the entire globe. At your disposal is a force of ragtag agents who dare to call themselves soldiers; you treat them like dogs, for that is what they are. Yet these are the only tools that you have to rebuild a fallen empire (that and the natural willingness of the weak to admire and follow the strong, regardless of what moralists say), so you make do with them as you can.

As the Iron Duke, you wield the Agony Gauntlet, an artifact of torture that may be (aside from your collection of memorabilia) the only thing you truly love.

THE IRON DUKE — POWER LEVEL 8

Str 16	Dex 16	Con 18	Int 13	Wis 15	Cha 16

Skills: Acrobatics 2 (+5), Bluff 8 (+11), Climb 4 (+7), Computers 6 (+7), Concentration 2 (+4), Craft (mechanical) 4 (+5), Craft (structural) 4 (+5), Diplomacy 6 (+9), Disable Device 4 (+5), Gather Information 5 (+8), Intimidate 10 (+13), Knowledge (art) 2 (+3), Knowledge (behavioral sciences) 6 (+7), Knowledge (current events) 8 (+9), Knowledge (history) 8 (+9), Knowledge (tactics) 8 (+9), Notice 8 (+10), Perform (oratory) 8 (+11), Pilot 2 (+5), Search 5 (+6), Sense Motive 10 (+12), Sleight of Hand 5 (+8), Stealth 8 (+11), Survival 5 (+7), Swim 2 (+5)

Feats: All-out Attack, Assessment, Connected, Contacts, Defensive Roll 1, Equipment 10, Fast Overrun, Fearless, Improved Aim, Improved Critical (Agony Gauntlet), Inspire 2, Leadership, Move-by Action, Precise Shot, Prone Fighting

Equipment: Armored uniform (+3 Toughness), plus 47 points in additional equipment.

Powers: Device 6 (Agony Gauntlet, hard to lose)
Agony Gauntlet: Nauseate 8 (Ranged)

Combat: Attack +8, Damage +3 (unarmed), Grapple +11, Defense +8 (+4 flat-footed), Knockback –4, Initiative +3

Saving Throws: Toughness +8 (+7 flat-footed, +5 without armor), Fortitude +10, Reflex +10, Will +8

Abilities 34 + Skills 35 (140 ranks) + Feats 24 + Powers 24 + Combat 32 + Saves 19 = 168

LUNATIC DEMO GUY

"BOOM BABY, BOOM!"

Evil is not, despite what some of its advocates might claim, emotionally stable. You are a sociopath/borderline psychotic whose only joy in life is watching earth-shattering kabooms. You are not one of the world's great tacticians, and everyone knows that and holds you in contempt for it. But you don't care, as long as you get to ply your trade.

You are also not as stupid as everyone thinks. Demolition is a very technically challenging skill, and you do a very good job when you are given a chance—much to your enemy's dismay. Your enemy also has Lunatic Demo Guys, but they tend to be a little more controlled.

LUNATIC DEMO GUY — POWER LEVEL 5

Str 11	Dex 13	Con 16	Int 14	Wis 8	Cha 9

Skills: Bluff 4 (+3), Climb 4 (+4), Computers 2 (+4), Concentration 8 (+7), Craft (chemical) 8 (+10), Craft (mechanical) 8 (+10), Craft (structural) 8 (+10), Disable Device 8 (+10), Disguise 2 (+1), Escape Artist 2 (+3), Intimidate 8 (+7), Investigate 4 (+6), Knowledge (physical sciences) 1 (+3), Knowledge (tactics) 3 (+5), Knowledge (technology) 3 (+5), Notice 6 (+5), Profession (demolitions) 3 (+2), Search 2 (+4), Sense Motive 2 (+1), Sleight of Hand 4 (+5), Stealth 6 (+7)

Feats: Assessment, Luck 2, Equipment 6, Improvised Tools, Inventor

Combat: Attack +5, Damage +0 (unarmed), Grapple +5, Defense +5 (+3 flat-footed), Knockback –1, Initiative +1

Saving Throws: Toughness +3, Fortitude +7 Reflex +4, Will +3

Abilities 11 + Skills 25 (100 ranks) + Feats 11 + Powers 0 + Combat 20 + Saves 11 = 77

MAD SCIENTIST

YOU CALL IT MADNESS. I CALL IT.... GENIUS!"

You are a Mad Scientist. You live in your laboratory, test tubes are your closest friend, and the warm hum of the portable nuclear accelerator is as cozy as a fireplace on a winter's day. With your faithful sidekick (robot, beautiful daughter, cloned replica of a beautiful daughter, or hunchback) at your side, you wake up every day wondering what new scientific frontiers you will cross.

Beyond your few loved ones, you have no ethical concerns at all—it was the boundaries set by self-righteous fools that wrecked your life and steered you towards the path of evil in the first place! It's *their* fault! It's everyone's fault but yours... and they're going to pay!

MAD SCIENTIST   POWER LEVEL 5

Str 10	Dex 10	Con 10	Int 20	Wis 13	Cha 12

Skills: Computers 5 (+10), Concentration 5 (+6), Craft (chemical) 5 (+10), Craft (electronics) 5 (+10), Diplomacy 2 (+3), Disable Device 6 (+11), Escape Artist 4 (+4), Gather Information 6 (+7), Handle Animal 6 (+7), Intimidate 2 (+3), Investigate 4 (+9), Knowledge (behavioral sciences) 2 (+7), Knowledge (earth sciences) 4 (+9), Knowledge (life sciences) 4 (+9), Knowledge (physical sciences) 4 (+9), Knowledge (technology) 6 (+11), Medicine 4 (+5), Notice 4 (+5), Sense Motive 4 (+5), Sleight of Hand 6 (+6)

Feats: Diehard, Eidetic Memory, Equipment 10, Improvised Tools, Inventor, Master Plan, Minions 10, Sidekick 10, Well-Informed

Combat: Attack +5, Damage +0 (unarmed), Grapple +5 Defense +5 (+3 flat-footed), Knockback –0, Initiative +0

Saving Throws: Toughness +0, Fortitude +1, Reflex +1, Will +6

Abilities 15 + **Skills** 22 (88 ranks) + **Feats** 36 + **Powers** 0 + **Combat** 20 + **Saves** 7 = 100

ROGUE NINJA

"YOU FIGHT WITH HONOR. BUT I FIGHT WITH EFFECTIVENESS!"

Somehow, the bad guys always seem to have a rogue ninja on their side. You may be an agent of a villain from the sinister Orient (although it's not particularly sinister to you), planted inside the bad guys' operation. You may simply be an agent for hire. You may be drawn to the cause of tearing down the annoying chaos of modern society and replacing it with a New World Order. Whatever your background, you are on the outs with your ninja clan, and in with a whole new set of bad guys. Whatever they are paying you, they are getting their money's worth.

ROGUE NINJA   POWER LEVEL 5

Str 12	Dex 18	Con 14	Int 12	Wis 14	Cha 10

Skills: Acrobatics 8 (+12), Climb 4 (+5), Computers 2 (+3), Concentration 8 (+10), Craft (mechanical) 2 (+3), Disable Device 6 (+7), Disguise 4 (+4), Drive 2 (+6), Escape Artist 8 (+12), Gather Information 4 (+4), Handle Animal 2 (+2), Intimidate 6 (+6), Knowledge (current events) 2 (+3), Knowledge (streetwise) 2 (+3), Knowledge (tactics) 4 (+5), Medicine 4 (+6), Notice 6 (+8), Profession (assassin) 4 (+6), Search 4 (+5), Sense Motive 2 (+4), Sleight of Hand 4 (+8), Stealth 10 (+14), Swim 2 (+3)

Feats: Defensive Attack, Defensive Roll 3, Equipment 10, Improved Block 2, Improved Disarm, Improved Sunder, Improved Trip, Instant Up, Skill Mastery (Acrobatics, Climb, Escape Artist, Stealth), Startle, Track, Trance

Combat: Attack +5, Damage +1 (unarmed), Grapple +6, Defense +5 (+3 flat-footed), Knockback –2, Initiative +4

Saving Throws: Toughness +5 (+3 flat-footed), Fortitude +5, Reflex +8, Will +6

Abilities 20 + **Skills** 25 (100 ranks) + **Feats** 24 + **Powers** 0 + **Combat** 20 + **Saves** 11 = 100

RUTHLESS EXECUTIVE

"I CAN'T WAIT TO EXPLOIT AMERICAN CHILDREN."

They say that crime doesn't pay... but suppose one decided not to call it crime? That's your answer to the crime problem; as far as you are concerned, your involvement in a nefarious criminal organization is just another business deal. While you are a driven young man who is also capable of handling himself in a fight, business ventures are where you shine, and that is where you provide the most services for your host organization.

Clearly, you serve two masters: your agency and money. Some consider you opportunistic and untrustworthy, but your understanding of the world doesn't just come from a gun, and your talents might be quite useful as your organization struggles to become financially solvent without taking on high-risk jobs.

RUTHLESS EXECUTIVE   POWER LEVEL 5

Str 12	Dex 12	Con 13	Int 18	Wis 15	Cha 16

Skills: Bluff 6 (+9), Computers 2 (+6), Concentration 4 (+6), Diplomacy 6 (+9), Disable Device 2 (+6), Drive 2 (+3), Gather Information 4 (+7), Intimidate 4 (+7), Investigate 4 (+8), Knowledge (behavioral sciences) 2 (+6), Knowledge (business) 8 (+12), Knowledge (civics) 4 (+8), Knowledge (current events) 4 (+8), Knowledge (technology) 2 (+6), Notice 4 (+6), Profession (business) 6 (+8), Search 2 (+6), Sense Motive 6 (+8), Sleight of Hand 2 (+3), Stealth 2 (+3)

Feats: Assessment, Beginner's Luck, Equipment 3, Improvised Tools, Inspire 1, Leadership, Luck 2, Skill Mastery (Bluff, Diplomacy, Gather Information, Intimidate), Ultimate Effort (Skill: Bluff, Save: Will), Well-Informed

Combat: Attack +2, Damage +1 (unarmed), Grapple +3, Defense +2 (+1 flat-footed), Knockback –0, Initiative +1

Saving Throws: Toughness +1, Fortitude +3, Reflex +5, Will +5

Abilities 26 + **Skills** 19 (76 ranks) + **Feats** 14 + **Powers** 0 + **Combat** 8 + **Saves** 9 = 76

TOUGH-AS-NAILS MERCENARY

'FINE, WE'LL STOP THAT PLATOON. BUT IT'LL COST YOU EXTRA!'

You work for money, and lots of it. This gang of agents may not be the most professional bunch you've ever worked with, but let's face it, the rest of the world is full of misfits too, and this bunch pays well and sees a lot of action. People call you a bad guy, but those sorts of allegiances—goodness, truth, justice, and country—belong to the boy scouts. And the only time you ever came close to a Boy Scout was when you were a kid, when you beat them up and took their merit badges.

You tend to be loyal to your employer, so people who try to bribe you into abandoning them are gonna be disappointed—you know the "other side" would use any excuse to throw you in a prison cell for the rest of your life, so you really don't have a good reason to work with them. But, it still irks you when your employer fails to treat you like a pro.

TOUGH-AS-NAILS MERCENARY   POWER LEVEL 5

Str 16	Dex 15	Con 16	Int 12	Wis 10	Cha 13

Skills: Bluff 4 (+5), Climb 6 (+9), Computers 2 (+3), Diplomacy 4 (+5), Disable Device 4 (+5), Disguise 2 (+3), Drive 4 (+6), Escape Artist 2 (+4), Gather Information 2 (+3), Intimidate 8 (+9), Investigate 2 (+3), Knowledge (business) 2 (+3), Knowledge (current events) 4 (+5), Knowledge (history) 6 (+7), Knowledge (tactics) 4 (+5), Knowledge (technology) 2 (+3), Medicine 2 (+2), Notice 6 (+6), Pilot 2 (+4), Ride 2 (+4), Search 6 (+7), Sense Motive 2 (+2), Sleight of Hand 4 (+6), Stealth 6 (+8), Survival 6 (+6), Swim 2 (+5), Demolitions 4 (+5)

Feats: All-out Attack, Assessment, Connected, Contacts, Defensive Attack, Defensive Roll 1, Equipment 4, Evasion, Improved Aim, Improved Critical (rifle), Move-by Action, Precise Shot, Set-Up, Sneak Attack, Stunning Attack, Teamwork

Combat: Attack +5, Damage +3 (unarmed), Defense +5 (+3 flat-footed), Knockback –2, Initiative +2

Saving Throws: Toughness +4 (+3 flat-footed), Fortitude +8, Reflex +6, Will +5

Abilities 22 + **Skills** 25 (100 ranks) + **Feats** 19 + **Powers** 0 + **Combat** 20 + **Saves** 14 – **Drawbacks** = 100

CALLSIGNS/CODENAMES

In cartoons and comics, characters have codenames, similar to aviation callsigns, which are engraved on nametags, sewn on one's clothes, and/or used in broadcasts to hide the caller's identity. Callsigns tend to fall into two categories: puns on the character's real name, and comments on the character's physical abilities, achievements, or role.

A tall, red headed English agent named Robert Costello works as a UNISON combat engineer. He might receive a callsign like "The Abbot" (a reference to the classic comedy team Abbott and Costello), "Carrotstick" (a reference to his slim physique and red hair), or "London Bridge" (a reference to his job and his country of origin).

Agents do *not* get to choose their own codenames. They are chosen by their squad-mates or their commanding officer; it's considered bad luck to pick your own callsign. Callsigns are often not very complimentary (particularly those given by mean-spirited commanders at the start of one's career). It is always possible, however, after a particularly special achievement, for one's fellow agents to get together and give you a new, more honoring name, after an outstanding performance in the field.

In an *Agents of Freedom* campaign where the PCs are a tight band of agents, get the team together and have them select callsigns for each other by the end of the third or fourth session. If you are looking for quick code-names, here are some suggested code-names for the archetypes in **Chapter 1** and **Chapter 6**.

HERO ARCHETYPES

- **Dashing Spy:** Card Shark, Caviar, Crown Jewel, Dapper Dan, Double Nought, Easy Street, Inside Man, Man of the Hour, Party Boy, Russian Roulette, Roll of the Dice, Wolf in Sheep's Clothing.
- **Field Investigator:** CSI, Eyesight, Oracle, Patience, Post-Mortem, Quincy, Séance, Science Hero, Scopes, Sherlock, Spyglass, Voodoo.
- **Hard-Nosed Commander:** Bad Day, Big Bad Wolf, The Boss, Captain Sir, Grim Reaper, Hardcore, Howler, Mister Respect, Nightmare, No Mercy, The Terror, Zeus.
- **Heroic Everyman:** Baby Face, Blue Eyes, Broken Record, Caltrops, Fresh Meat, Latrine, Lucky Charms, New Kid, Piñata, Stumbling Block, Target Practice, Washout, Wedgie, Wide Eyes.
- **Femme Fatale:** Dame Doom, Devil Woman, Femme Fatana, Hell's Belle, Hellina, Hornet, Lady Vixen, Mata Harriet, Natalia, Nefaria, Pretty Poison, Shadow Rose, She-Devil, Witchcraft.
- **Martial Arts Expert:** Bruce Chi, Combat King, Hong Kung Fuey, Jet Chi, Karate, Kiai, Psycho, Sick Kick, Ultimate, Whirling Dervish.
- **Roughneck Commando (Hot-Headed Lieutenant):** Baby Boss, Hard Charger, Junior, Loose Cannon, Maverick, Overrun, Renegade, Trample, Wildfire, Wolf Cub, Wonder Boy.
- **Roughneck Commando (Modern Day Amazon):** Artemis, Beauty, Cookie, Crazy Legs, Distressing Damsel, Flame, Glamor Girl, Hotcakes, Lady Luck, Magnolia, Rose's Thorn, Ruby Red, Snow White Knight, Wiccan.
- **Roughneck Commando (in general):** Alamo, The Axe, Beachcomber, Clockstopper, Dog of War, Full Auto, Hamburger Hillclimber, Hammerhead, Hard Charger, Hot Dog, Howler, Killzone, Kong, Long-Arm, Normandy, Nukes, Pump Action, Screwball, SMG, Tiger.

SUPPORTING CAST ARCHETYPES

- **Ace Pilot:** Air Enforcer, Airlift, Altitude, Bluesky, Blue Max, Highspot, Hot Dog, Jet, Plane Truth, Skydog, Sky High, Snake on a Plane, Twelve O'Clock, Winger.
- **Animal Handler:** *Birds:* Birdman, Chickadee, Eagle, Eyrie, Raptor, Rooster; *Cats:* Catnip, Leo, Nocturnal, Stray Cat, Tiger Tail; *Dogs/Wolves:* Bad Dog, Doggerel, Hellhound, Kennel Club, Loup Garoux, Mad Dog, Mongrel, Rabies, Rex, Tricks, Wild Hunt, Wolfhead.
- **Combat Engineer:** Booby Trap, Boom, Breach, Bricklayer, Bridge Builder, Cobbler, Constructs, Demo, Scotty, Scrap Pile, Traps, Wreckage.
- **Communications/Surveillance Specialist:** Airwave, Antenna, Big Broadcast, Chatroom, Fast Talk, Hot Mike, Network, Rabbit Ears, Radar, Sonar, Stereo, Watchman.
- **Con Artist:** None. Con artists in an agent unit generally have codenames of other types of characters (to conceal their true nature).
- **Defense Analyst:** Birdwatcher, Clancy, Cut-Out, Dangler, Data Cruncher, Eye Spy, Intelligent Designer, Shoeshine.
- **Environmental Specialist:** *Desert:* Bedouin, Camel Clutch, Dune, Heatstroke, Nomad, Oasis, Sahara, Sandy, Sirocco, Vulture. *Arctic:* Arctic, Chilly, Frostbite, Icicle, North Pole, Permafrost, Santa, Snowblind, Snowline, Whiteout.
- **Field Medic:** Blue Cross, Bloodbank, Bones, Code Blue, Doc, Heartbeat, M*A*S*H, Medicine Man, Red Cross, Sawbones, Trauma Unit, Vaccine.
- **Grease Monkey:** Crowbar, Gearshift, Grease Monkey, Lugnut, Machine Shop, Monkey Wrench, Motormouth, Pit Stop, Six Cylinders, Warranty.
- **Lab Geek:** Beaker, Chain Reaction, Equation, Geek, Lab Kit, Log In, Math Mage, O.S., The Professor, Scrambled Egghead, Super Collider, Telescope, Test Tube.
- **Master of Disguise:** Cavalier, Deep Cover, Diablo, Good Shadow, Highwayman, In Deep, Masked Man, Mirror Image, Most Wanted, Partisan, Solitary.
- **Sharpshooter:** Clint, Crosshairs, Dead Aim, Eagle Eye, Hard Target, Longarm, Mohican, New Paladin, Pistol, Remington, Rifleman.
- **The Strong Guy:** Ahnold, Biceps, Big Rig, Buick, Brick, Dead Lift, Grizzly Bear, Hercules, Little John, Musclehead, Muscles, Rock, Samson, Tank, Troll, Truck.

VILLAIN ARCHETYPES

- **Brute Lieutenant:** Attila, Barbarossa, Brute, Bruticus, Crusher, Drakus, Firbolg, Lothar, Ogri, Overkill, Pulvar, Reichhammer, Trollo.
- **Bureaucrat from Hell:** Red Tape, Speed Bump, Tapeworm.
- **Cleaner:** Bloodsucker, CS Eye, Custodian, Janitor, Mr. Clean, Passkey, Window Polish.
- **Crime Lord:** Big Man, Boss, Corruptor, Hoodlum, Kingfish, Spider.
- **Evil Lawyer:** Mouthpiece, Public Offender, Samuel Jones, Scam and Sham, Scary Mason, Shyster, Solicitor, Trial and Error, Valeyard, Wolfram.
- **Iron Duke:** Agonisto, Baron Blitzen, Count Fear, Dr. Cerberus, The Duke, Eisenpanzer, Hammermueller, Hellmeister, Iron Gauntlet, Lord Pain, Satan Smith, Reichdrakken, Rottensturm.
- **Lunatic Demo Guys:** Anarko, Billy Boom, Blast Radius, Bombshell, Boomtown, C-Forcer, Cinders, Courier, Destructor, Firebomb, Infernox, Nitro Knight, Plastic, WMD.
- **Mad Scientist:** Cagliostro, Dr. Damocles, Dr. Lucifer, Dr. Sturmundrang, Elector, Factor Phobos, The Hyper-Technologist, Largo, Master Technician, Maxmillian Mayhem, Professor Fehr, Professor Perdition, Vincent Frankenstein.
- **Rogue Ninja:** Black Shiro, Hellshade, Kami, Roninja, Shadowkiller, Shonen, Shurikenja, Swift Shadow, Twilight Death, Umbran.
- **Ruthless Executive:** CEO, Das Capitalist, Fifty-One Percent, Hostile Takeover, The Investor, Kingfish, The Senior Partner, Stockholder, Titan of Industry, Venture.
- **Tough-as-Nails Mercenary:** Black Bart, Blood, Dollar Sign, Foreigner, Mad Dog, Newcomer, Omega-2, Paycheck, Silencer, Tourist.

ADVENTURE: RETURN OF SHADOW

Intended as a starting adventure for an Action-Agents *Agents of Freedom* campaign, *Return of SHADOW* establishes the player characters as a new AEGIS squad in Freedom City. It does not require the *Freedom City* sourcebook, but it is recommended for this adventure (and any game in that setting).

Return of SHADOW is intended for a team of four to six agents, power level 5, built on 100 power points. Advice is offered for running the adventure with superheroes of power level 10 (see the sidebar on page 1119), but *Return of SHADOW* is primarily meant for agent-level play.

GETTING STARTED

If you are playing in this adventure, please do not read any further. You will only be spoiling your enjoyment and possibly other people's fun.

If you are the Gamemaster, read over the adventure carefully. Always feel free to add, subtract, and change the plot elements to best suit your campaign. Wherever possible, tie the backgrounds of the villains to those of the player characters. It will make for a more intense and memorable game experience.

Before the adventure begins, make sure the characters are acquainted with each other. There should be one player character designated as team leader who is willing to take charge of the squad. Make sure the team includes one character with an investigator's background, and at least two characters with good (commando level) combat skills. If you are looking to get started quickly, have the players choose from agent archetypes in **Chapter 1**.

ADVENTURE SYNOPSIS

The heroes are assigned bodyguard duty to local businessman and city councilor Ray Gaglardi, whose proposed redevelopment of the slum area of *Freedom City* known as the Fens has provided a ray of

hope for long-suffering residents of the area, but has also raised concern about the impact of the development on transients, the homeless, street gangs, and the area's less than savory trades.

Gaglardi has received several death threats. None of them would have attracted the attention of AEGIS, except that several of the death threats have been written on paper that has burst into flames a few seconds after it was opened. AEGIS believes it is the work of Pyrestorm, a mercenary arsonist super-criminal.

The agents have to investigate the death threats and serve as bodyguards for Gaglardi. During the course of the investigation, they discover Gaglardi has a shady past from the days of crooked mayor Franklin Moore, and Gaglardi's former business partner was Moore's aide Bobby Bennett. Unknown to everyone, Bennett plans to use the controversy to get back at Gaglardi for putting him in prison, by sending SHADOW agents to plant evidence of corruption in his personal files, under AEGIS' very eyes, and kidnapping his son to provide leverage.

SHADOW hasn't been seen in Freedom City in years. Once

they appear in the adventure, the player characters will be ordered to track them to their source, so AEGIS can determine the level of threat that they pose to the city. Tracking down Bennett's holdings, they find a small SHADOW base under an abandoned building in the Fens. They will have a chance to shut down Bennett's operation and uncover other clues that can be spun into a long-term campaign.

CASTING CALL

Aside from our heroes, the adventure involves the following characters:

RAY GAGLARDI

A member of a mob family that had some power in Freedom City until the death of family patriarch "Rugged Rich" Gaglardi in 1972, Ray Gaglardi began his career as a crooked used car salesman who made his fortune in real estate scams in the 1980s. Despite his past, he always had a conscience, and when superheroes saved his daughter's life from a rival mobster, Gaglardi experienced a change of heart. He turned on Franklin Moore's corrupt regime and supported Michael O'Connor's mayoral bid. O'Connor's election won him popular respectability. Gaglardi testified against his former business partners, which won him a suspended sentence and allowed him to launch a successful political career.

Gaglardi is (perhaps understandably) extremely reluctant to talk about his family's old mob connections and his shady business days, though most of his enemies hail from that period in his life. His two biggest enemies are "Muscle" Mark Marcelli (the son of a deceased mob boss Gaglardi sent to jail) and Bobby Bennett (a former business partner and Moore ally who spent only six months in prison because he turned state's evidence.)

Gaglardi has two grown daughters, both living outside Freedom City. He lives in a comfortable upper middle class home with his wife Patricia and his 17-year-old son Ian.

Ian's best friend, Tony Duke, is a Bystander. Use the stats from *Mutants & Masterminds*, **Chapter 11**.

"D-STONE" AND THE FENS C

This is a street gang that is a little more vicious than the norm. They've had lousy lives in a lousy place, and most of them are addicted to bad drugs. Use the stats for Thugs and Gang Leaders from *Mutants & Masterminds*, **Chapter 11**.

D-Stone and his gang serve as a red herring and an excuse to fight street gang members.

"MUSCLE" MARK MARCELLI

The Marcellis were enforcers for mob boss August Roman during the 1980s. The Marcellis were also heavily tied to corrupt mayor Franklin Moore, and when he fell from power, the police uncovered files that resulted in the conviction of many family members. Rumors say Ray Gaglardi was responsible for the files falling into the hands of the police, and Marcelli's son Mark vowed revenge.

Mark, following a turn as a professional bodybuilder, is rumored to have gone back into the family business. He owns a gym in the Riverside district, and the (heavily 'roided) patrons ("the Gym Rats") serve as his unofficial gang as he starts testing the waters of crime with drug trafficking and a protection racket. He is a huge guy with an ego to match, and just enough fighting skill to get in serious trouble when he challenges a real hand-to-hand fighter (like a PC).

Mark's purpose in the scenario is to provide a red herring for the agents' investigation.

SHADOW

For SHADOW forces involved in the scenario, see the game stats from **Chapter 5**. For SHADOW leader Bobby Bennett, use the Ruthless Executive archetype from **Chapter 6**.

SHADOW's appearance may not come as a major surprise to players familiar with the Freedom City setting, but unless they have been active in the campaign prior to this session, it should come as something of a surprise to agents that SHADOW is active again in Freedom City after an absence of close to fifteen years.

INTRODUCTION

The characters are an AEGIS team stationed at Freedom City's AEGIS base. Have the PCs in the middle of some action when they are called to a briefing. Actions appropriate to the genre include: practicing martial arts, on the firing range, playing a practical joke on another squad who pranked them, or being caught in the middle of a routine (and very dull) intelligence briefing.

In any case, there will be a call over the loudspeaker for the PC's squad to report to a conference room *immediately* for a mission briefing. Those who are late will get a chewing out.

THE BRIEFING

"Hello team. Welcome to Operation: Safety Pin. During the last week, city counselor Ray Gaglardi has received three death threats. What makes this AEGIS business and not routine police work is the paper on which the death threats were written. The paper ignited a few seconds after they were opened, the calling card of a supervillain named Pyrestorm.

"Pyrestorm is a mercenary who first showed up five years ago. He is credited with over twenty major cases of arson across the

country, including the River Arms fire right here in Freedom City. People have only seen him from a distance, and no superhero has ever fought him: eyewitnesses describe him as an eight-foot, man-shaped bonfire. He leaves these sealed messages at places he plans to destroy—or to sign his handiwork when he has done the job. The lab boys figure he must have a superpower that allows him to create combustible chemicals out of thin air. Forensic evidence suggests he also has demolitions training. We would love to know more about this guy, especially who's funding him.

"However, your number one priority is protecting Gaglardi. Rolling Ray has a bit of a shady past, and thirty years ago, his father was an enforcer for the local mob. However, Ray has been clean for years. He supported Mayor O'Connor back in the days when it was unhealthy to do so, and helped blow the whistle on former mayor Moore and his cronies. Today, Gaglardi is a land developer with big plans for a Fens redevelopment. It's a controversial project, but there is no evidence that he is corrupt.

"Gaglardi is aware of the death threats. He has agreed to allow AEGIS to station a team in his home—that's you. Your squad has two goals: one is to investigate the death threats

RAY GAGLARDI — POWER LEVEL 3

Str 12	Dex 10	Con 12	Int 17	Wis 14	Cha 13

Skills: Bluff 6 (+7), Computers 2 (+5), Concentration 4 (+6), Diplomacy 8 (+9), Disguise (+1), Drive 2 (+2), Gather Information 4 (+5), Intimidate 6 (+7), Knowledge (behavioral sciences) 2 (+5), Knowledge (business) 8 (+11), Knowledge (civics) 6 (+9), Knowledge (history) 2 (+5), Knowledge (streetwise) 2 (+5), Notice 4 (+6), Profession (businessman) 6 (+8), Search 2 (+5), Sense Motive 6 (+8), Sleight of Hand 2 (+2), Stealth 2 (+2)

Feats: Benefit (city councilman) 1, Connected, Contacts, Eidetic Memory, Luck 2, Well-Informed

Combat: Attack +4, Damage +1 (unarmed), Defense +4, Knockback -0, Initiative +0

Saving Throws: Toughness +1, Fortitude +4, Reflex +1, Will +6

Abilities 18 + Skills 20 (77 ranks) + Feats 7 + Powers 0 + Combat 16 + Saves 8 = 69

PATRICIA GAGLARDI — POWER LEVEL 1

Str 8	Dex 10	Con 10	Int 14	Wis 14	Cha 14

Skills: Bluff 5 (+7), Concentration 4 (+6), Diplomacy 5 (+7), Drive 1 (+1), Gather Information 2 (+4), Intimidate 2 (+4), Knowledge (business) 1 (+3), Knowledge (civics) 1 (+3), Knowledge (current events) 2 (+4), Knowledge (history) 1 (+3), Notice 2 (+4), Sleight of Hand 1 (+1), Stealth 1 (+1)

Feats: Connected, Well-Informed

Combat: Attack +0, Damage -1 (unarmed), Defense +1, Knockback -0, Initiative +0

Saving Throws: Toughness +0, Fortitude +1, Reflex +1, Will +5

Abilities 10 + Skills 7 (28 ranks) + Feats 2 + Powers 0 + Combat 2 + Saves 5 = 26

IAN GAGLARDI — POWER LEVEL 2

Str 12	Dex 12	Con 10	Int 11	Wis 8	Cha 12

Skills: Bluff 1 (+2), Climb 2 (+3), Computers 2 (+2), Drive 1 (+2), Escape Artist 1 (+2), Gather Information 1 (+2), Intimidate 1 (+2), Knowledge (current events) 1 (+1), Knowledge (popular culture) 2 (+2), Knowledge (streetwise) 1 (+1), Sleight of Hand 2 (+3), Stealth 4 (+5), Swim 1 (+2)

Feats: Chokehold, Luck

Combat: Attack +2, Damage +1 (unarmed), Defense +1, Knockback -0, Initiative +1

Saving Throws: Toughness +0, Fortitude +3, Reflex +4, Will +0

Abilities 5 + Skills 5 (20 ranks) + Feats 2 + Powers 0 + Combat 6 + Saves 7 = 25

and determine who is behind them, the other is bodyguarding—don't say babysitting, respect the mission—Mr. Gaglardi, his wife Patricia, and their seventeen year-old son, Ian.

"Patricia Gaglardi is a former school teacher who is a prominent social activist. It's not inconceivable that she is the target.

"Ian is a problem kid, just smart enough to get into trouble. He has had discipline problems at school, and some of his friends are known drug-users. In all likelihood, the kid is a casual user who keeps his nose clean at home, but uses at parties.

"Gaglardi is a key backer of the campaign to reclaim the Fens, so I don't have to tell you how important it is that nothing happens to him or his family. That's a project with the potential to help change a lot of lives for the better."

MISSION SUMMARY

Mission Title: Operation Safety Pin
Chief priority: Protect Gaglardi and his family from death threats.
Secondary priority: Discover who is issuing the death threats and stop them.
Tertiary priority: Gather more data on a mercenary supervillain named Pyrestorm.
Target: Ray Gaglardi, Caucasian male, 49; Patricia Gaglardi, Caucasian female 47; Ian Gaglardi, Caucasian male, 17.
Known Operatives: None
Suspected Operatives: Pyrestorm, gangs in the Fens.
Possibility for complications: High.

MEET THE GAGLARDIS

The agents' first task is to descend on the Gaglardi home and familiarize themselves with the family and their location.

THE HOUSE

The house is a two story, four-bedroom home in the Bayview Heights district of Freedom City. It's a modern home built in the early 1990s. The décor is modern, but still homey with traditional touches.

FRONT YARD

The property is situated at the crest of a moderately steep hill, facing the street. It has a small front yard with a well-manicured lawn and small rose garden. There's a small Japanese cherry tree on one edge of the property.

BACK YARD

The back yard slopes down to a fenced area that backs onto another property. Two big (60 ft. tall) pine trees, a 40 ft. tall cherry tree, and a smaller (15 ft. tall) apple tree are spread across the property.

BOTTOM FLOOR

This is the living area. There is a living room, study, kitchen, dining room, bathroom, a master bedroom, and a home office (Gaglardi does much of his work from his home). Entrances: *Front door, back door, garage entrance.* There are also large windows in the living room and dining room.

TOP FLOOR

This is the sleeping area. There are three bedrooms, two empty and kept for when Gaglardi's daughters visit from college and Ian's bedroom, Ian's study/computer room, a bathroom, and a storage room (with boxes full of campaign records). The roof is sloped so the bedroom windows open onto it; it would be easy to enter and exit the house from a bedroom window.

FAMILY BUSINESS

Ray views AEGIS' arrival as an intrusion, but takes the supervillain threat seriously. He is respectful to agents, but guarded about his privacy and won't talk much about his past unless it's clear it's a matter of life and death to his family. He is hot-tempered, but devoted to his family, even though he yells at them a lot.

Patricia Gaglardi is playing hostess. She is also guarded, and like her husband, she is very strong-willed. It becomes clear her relationship with her husband is a bit strained, and she privately admits the Fens redevelopment project is a bad idea that will disrupt too many lives. She may also take a shine to a handsome male agent and do some mild flirting to make her husband jealous (flirting with her will give a +2 bonus to any Gather Information check involving Patricia).

Ian is a handful. At the best of times, he is a sneaky, self-important whiner. He is a bit panicked by AEGIS' initial presence in his home, but after his first impression, he will settle into a manic frenzy. He will want to see everyone's guns, ask which agent is the best in a fight (and he'll want to see them), and ask which combat drugs people are taking. Eventually, Ian will challenge the toughest looking agent to a mock sparring session where he has to let Ian pretend to beat him up (this is a necessary part of any Gather Information check with Ian; Ian's a big fan of mixed martial arts competitions and the UWL).

Ian also has an annoying talent for breaking off conversations to have long phone calls (with his best friend, Tony Duke, mostly about the very sad state of their dating lives), sneaking behind people's backs, and leaving the house without supervision in order to run off with his friends.

THE INVESTIGATION

After a few days of examining Gaglardi's background, the investigators should be able to compile a list of enemies. This can be done with a Gather Information check conducted over several days of interviewing Gaglardi's family. Three names top the list: the Fens C street gang, "Muscle" Mark Marcelli, and Bobby Bennett.

THE FENS C

The Fens Cs is an offshoot of the Southside Cs, a street gang led by a charismatic and brutal gang leader who calls himself "D-Stone." They hang around in the area near the north end of the Pennsylvania St. Bridge in some rundown tenements known to locals as "Destruction Junction." They will defend their turf from anyone, even AEGIS.

Any attempt to gather info on D-Stone will reveal that his headquarters is at the Rubicon, an abandoned film theater in the Fens. In the 1940s, this was one of the great movie houses of Freedom City, but it became rundown in the 1970s when the city started building multiplexes. Now, it is a broken down hovel. D-Stone is something of a movie buff, particularly of violent gang-related films like "Scarface" and "the Warriors," or war films like *Apocalypse Now*. He will always have a gang of 8–12 gang members (two per PC) surrounding him at all times. D-Stone has converted the green room into his bedroom and conducts his business in the theater. He usually eats delivered meals; local restaurants and pizza joints cook for him and his boys in exchange for protection. The place is filled with litter and more than a few rats' nests. ("Just the way we like it in the Fens.")

If the PCs begin to muscle around his turf, D-Stone will invite them to his theater to talk. It's an ambush; he'll have 3 gang members per PC waiting to gun them down, armed with submachine guns (Blast 4 (ballistic) Autofire). The theater will be lit only in the front row (where D-Stone and a pair of bodyguards will be waiting), and the other half will be lying down in the aisles, waiting for a signal to ambush.

When the gang members are subdued, D-Stone will admit that they made a few phone calls (several weeks ago) but they don't "hang with people who can torch them with a stare." They weren't involved in the crime, although three days ago, he did receive a phone call from someone with a voice like gravel asking if they were willing to pull a snatch and grab on Gaglardi's kid, Ian. They gave D-Stone a phone number to get back to them, but he lost it almost immediately. If they search the (garbage ridden) theater, a Search check (Dc 20) will find it on the back of a pizza box. If someone calls the number, a (muffled) recorded voice will say, "I'm sorry, Mr. Stone. AEGIS has become involved. There's no longer any room for amateurs."

The recording can be traced to a telephone exchange, and then the trail hits a dead end.

"MUSCLE" MARK MARCELLI

Mark is the last member of a family of hit men turned in to the police in the 1990s. He owns a gym in Southside and has been charged twice (but never convicted) for selling steroids; he is guilty of that and more: he's trafficking in Max, the superpowers drug, and has started a small protection rack.

If cornered in his gym, he will have a gang of muscle-heads (1 per PC) grab hand weights and attack. He wasn't involved in the death threat, but he is up to something; if the PCs break into his office and crack his safe to get into his personal files, they will find (along with illegal anabolic steroids, Max, and nearly a hundred thousand dollars in cash) photos of the Gaglardi house and schedules for each of the family members, particularly Ian. Marcelli's been planning a kidnapping. He claims the PCs planted them, though under sustained intimidation, he

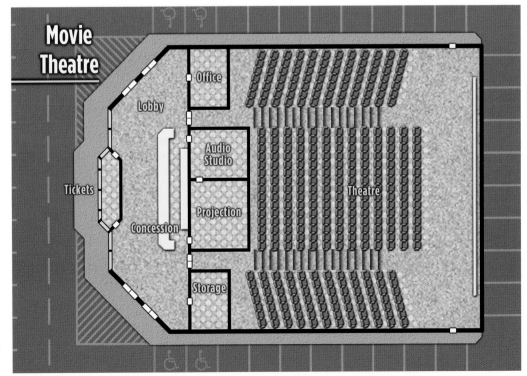

Movie Theatre

Office
Lobby
Audio Studio
Tickets
Concession
Projection
Theatre
Storage

Gymnasium

1. Front Entrance
2. Foyer
3. Office
4. Men's Locker Room and Showers
5. Women's Locker Room and Showers

will admit that he hired a private detective named Victor Walsh to check on the kid, and thought about kidnapping him, but never went through with it.

If the PCs try to track down Walsh, they will find him dead in his office, a victim of recreational drug use. If our heroes check on Walsh's background, they will discover that Walsh was a low-life, but not a drug user, and not stupid. Someone wants to shut him up and make it look like an accident.

If you need a dramatic scene after all this investigation, when the PCs are in Walsh's office, lock the doors behind them and set off incendiary devices in the trash-can and other corners of the office.

BOBBY BENNETT

Bobby Bennett was influential during the tenure of Franklin Moore, and was Gaglardi's business partner in several development projects. Bennett was involved in corruption with members of the Franklin Moore administration and spent six months in prison on corruption charges, thanks to Gaglardi's testimony. He has managed to get his licenses restored and is still in the real estate game; he has bought many properties in the Fens. He works out of a real estate office in the downtown core, a 12-story office tower that he has built through the careful use of city reconstruction funds; each time a supervillain destroys it, he finds the money from FEMA reparations funds to build it a little higher.

He also owns property in other cities. Coincidentally, some of these were also destroyed and rebuilt after a Pyrestorm attack.

Bennett can be encountered in the penthouse of his tower. Before SHADOW becomes active in the scenario, he will pretend to be glad to answer questions and allow AEGIS to come up and visit him. He won't willingly leave the office under any circumstances, and will push a panic button on his belt if the PCs try to take him by force, summoning a security team (and calling a top lawyer; it will also transmit security camera footage of the abduction). Those who make a Notice Check DC 20 will note that the security guards share similar features: they are all about the same age, same height and build, and have very similar facial features. Those who track Bennett's movements will find that he never leaves the office by any publicly accessible exit. For more on Bennett's surroundings, refer to **Bennett's Office** in the SHADOW base section.

Bennett says that he supports the Fens redevelopment project, and would lose a fortune if anything happened to "his old pal." He says that everything is water under the bridge, and he is looking to the future, not the past.

Despite his smooth talk, it should be obvious that he still hates Gaglardi's guts. Furthermore, there are some unusual security devices in Bennett's office; his walls and windows give off a faint vibration that foils listening devices, he never uses cell phones, and he has a phone line out of his office that can't be accessed through normal channels.

"MUSCLE" MARK MARCELLI				POWER LEVEL 4	
Str 18	Dex 10	Con 14	Int 10	Wis 10	Cha 13

Skills: Acrobatics 2 (+2), Bluff 2 (+3) Climb 2 (+6), Concentration 4 (+4), Diplomacy 2 (+3), Gather Information 2 (+3), Intimidate 5 (+6), Knowledge (business) 1 (+1), Knowledge (civics) 1 (+1), Knowledge (popular culture) 1 (+1), Knowledge (streetwise) 3 (+3), Notice 2 (+2), Profession (bodybuilder) 2 (+2), Survival 2 (+2), Swim 1 (+5)

Feats: Chokehold, Connected, Endurance, Improved Grab, Improved Grapple, Improved Pin, Improved Trip, Power Attack, Stunning Attack, Takedown Attack

Combat: Attack +3, Damage +4 (unarmed), Grapple +7, Defense +3 (+2 flat-footed), Knockback -1, Initiative +0

Saving Throws: Toughness +2, Fortitude +4, Reflex +1, Will +1

Abilities 15 + **Skills** 8 (32 ranks) + **Feats** 10 + **Powers** 0 + **Combat** 12 + **Saves** 4 = 49

GYM RATS				POWER LEVEL 3	
Str 16	Dex 10	Con 12	Int 10	Wis 10	Cha 12

Skills: Acrobatics 1 (+1), Climb 1 (+4), Concentration 1 (+1), Gather Information 1 (+2), Intimidate 4 (+5), Knowledge (popular culture) 1 (+1), Knowledge (streetwise) 2 (+2), Notice 1 (+1), Profession (bodybuilder) 1 (+1), Stealth 1 (+1), Swim 2 (+5)

Feats: Chokehold, Endurance, Power Attack

Combat: Attack +3, Grapple +6, Damage +3 (unarmed), Defense +3 (+2 flat-footed), Knockback -0, Initiative +0

Saving Throws: Toughness +1, Fortitude +3, Reflex +0, Will +0

Abilities 10 + **Skills** 4 (16 ranks) + **Feats** 3 + **Powers** 0 + **Combat** 12 + **Saves** 2 = 31

He also has one of the most expensive and successful lawyers in the country on retainer. If the player characters decide to investigate his base, refer to the **Shadow Base** section of this adventure.

If the PCs came in an AEGIS vehicle, and the vehicle was unguarded during their visit, then a SHADOW grease monkey will cut the brake lines. At some point on the way back to AEGIS HQ or the Gaglardi home, the PCs will discover this fact while in the middle of heavy traffic. They will need to make a Drive check DC 20 to safely bring the vehicle to a stop. A failed check results in damage from a crash: have the agents make Toughness saving throws against a DC of 10, plus the amount by which the Drive check failed; so a result of 10 on the Drive check indicates a DC of 20 on the Toughness save against crash damage.

Award a hero point to each player after the potential crash for the complication of the cut brake lines.

PYRESTORM

The sources for the mercenary villain scene are unusually quiet. No one has heard anything about a villain named Pyrestorm coming to town. Anyone who is using streetwise skills to comb the city's underbelly may attempt a Knowledge (streetwise) check DC 13; if successful, this will turn up a witness to one of the arsons, a drug dealer named Stan Walker who was near the River Arms building when Pyrestorm allegedly torched it. For a price ($25,000), he will tell what he knows.

He says he never saw a supervillain, but he did see a pair of men scoping out the building and entering with a pack of gear. He's not 100% sure, but they looked like SHADOW agents!

Stan Walker is a low-life, but local police can confirm that when he's not in prison, he deals drugs in the area of the River Arms, so he *might* be a credible witness.

BACK AT THE HOUSE

As the investigation progresses, a number of things will start to happen at the Gaglardi house.

JEALOUSY

Ray Gaglardi will start getting *really* jealous. Even if the player characters haven't done anything worth getting jealous over, he'll get angry about his wife's longing looks toward handsome agents. If there are any good-looking female agents in the squad, then he will start flirting with them, which will bring down the wrath of Patricia Gaglardi.

IAN

Ian uses his cell phone to take pictures of agents and send them to his friend Tony Duke. He will take pictures of agents eating, arguing, sleeping, and even showering if he can get away with it. He will display an almost admirable ingenuity in making himself a complete pest. He also has cell phones stashed in various hiding places around the house, in case the agents confiscate them.

Things should eventually come to a head with Ian; he will get tired of being picked on (even when he starts the trouble), and will try to run away. After several attempts, he will take advantage of a diversion to make his escape so he can get to his friends (see the section **Hostage Drama**).

THE SHADOW OPERATION

On the third day of the stakeout, a mail carrier will come to the door to deliver mail. Unbeknownst to him, in his mail sack is a package that, when

GATHER INFORMATION CHECKS

Further information can be obtained through a Gather Information check:

DC	Information
10	Gaglardi has many enemies and a shady past, but changed his tune sometime before O'Connor became the mayor, and is now almost a model citizen. His three biggest enemies are the Fens C, "Muscle" Mark Marcelli, and Bobby Bennett. The Fens Cs are mostly talk, but one or two of them might be crazy enough to try something. Marcelli is a little more serious. He is in the early stages of putting together a drug ring and protection racket and probably isn't doing anything – yet. Bennett has always been out for revenge, and he has acquired a lot of cash lately. Some of his profits came from insurance money and FEMA grants from buildings torched by Pyrestorm.
15	Gaglardi was once involved with Franklin Moore, but changed his ways when Bowman saved his daughter's life. He's legit. The Fens Cs are too busy fighting turf wars to mess with Gaglardi; they're not involved. Marcelli's preoccupied putting together his gang, but he hired a private eye to keep tabs on Gaglardi and his family. Some people in the villain community doubt that Pyrestorm really exists; he's too much of a ghost. Bennett's latest office tower went way over budget, and some of the contractors are suspected of having ties to the underworld. There are discrepancies between his submitted plans and what was supposedly built.
20	There are rumors that SHADOW agents were seen in the area supposedly torched by Pyrestorm. Bennett has been bribing people at the local power company to look the other way regarding the power requirements of his office building. It uses 300% of the power that is normally needed for a building of that size. The private eye who spied for Marcelli was later hired by Bobby Bennett to pass along the information he found out. Bennett also hired him to find out where Marcelli had that information hidden. He is probably setting him up for a frame.
25	Bennett was an assistant to Ralph Bernard, a SHADOW Penumbra member who was murdered by Overshadow in the SHADOW Wars of the late 1980s. It is rumored he never severed his ties to the organization, even after Overshadow's death. Someone has invented a number of fake supervillains to commit crimes to swindle the government out of FEMA money, and Pyrestorm's one of them. Commit a crime, use a hologram so witnesses see a supposed supervillain, and voila! Big government payoff in reconstruction funds, thanks to regulations that were enacted after the Terminus Invasion. No one is sure who is behind the fake villains, but one former SHADOW Penumbra member thinks it has the fingerprints of Franklin Folkes, the only known member of the Penumbra who is not in custody. AEGIS has long feared that Folkes is allying with Nacht-Krieger to bring SHADOW back to life. Getting the federal government to fund it would appeal to Folkes' sense of irony.

triggered, will overload every circuit in the house and start an electrical fire. The mailman will be incinerated. Suddenly, sparks will fly out of every electrical appliance and outlet in the house, and the home will burst into flames.

This is SHADOW's Plan A. If the PCs monitor the mail and keep the mailman away from the house, then the attempted sabotage will fail. Then SHADOW goes to Plan B. They will send a truck that's loaded with explosives into the driveway, and blow it up by remote control. As AEGIS is drawn out by the diversion, a SHADOW intrusion team (two Infiltrator agents, with four Standard agents as backup, see **Chapter 6**) will make their way into Gaglardi's study, open his safe, plant some incriminating documents, and start a fire by hand before making their escape.

That is stage one of the operation. Stage two is kidnapping Ian. A second SHADOW team will capture some of Ian's friends, and then force them to call the young Gaglardi on their cell phones. This will allow a SHADOW communications van, parked down the street, to pinpoint Ian's location via cell phone. If a SHADOW intrusion team can capture him, they will.

A few minutes after the firebomb is detonated, the police will arrive with a warrant. They received a report from a reliable source that Gaglardi was attempting to destroy documents that would incriminate him of fraud. The documents indicate that Gaglardi's redevelopment is a scheme to swindle the city, insurers, and the federal government of hundreds of millions of dollars. The police will want to search the house as soon as the fire department says it is safe. They will have a warrant, which they claim gives them jurisdiction. They will not accept "no" for an answer, and if the agency is called, they will back the local authorities' right to search.

- *If both phases of SHADOW's operation are successful* (they planted the documents and kidnapped Ian), then Gaglardi will receive a phone call. Bennett will be on the line, informing him that he has his son, and if he wants to see him alive again, Gaglardi needs to confess to the authorities that the documents are genuine and accept his punishment Gaglardi immediately agrees to the demand, and surrenders to the police. It will be up to the PCs to clear his name.

- *If the PCs intercepted the documents before SHADOW could plant them,* the police open the safe and find nothing. Realizing they have no grounds for an arrest, they make a lukewarm apology and give the PCs a funny look while they are leaving the house.

- *If the PCs intercept the SHADOW team that's after Ian*, then the panicked Ian will still try to escape. If he gets away, it then becomes

a race against SHADOW to track Ian down—but SHADOW has already tracked down Ian's closest friends and taken them hostage (see **Hostage Drama**), and they are waiting for Ian to show, because that is precisely where he's going. If he doesn't get away, he will receive a phone call from Tony Duke revealing that he is being held prisoner, and unless he surrenders in the next half hour, Duke and his family will be killed. At this point, Ian will want his "good AEGIS buddies" to lock and load and rescue them. Annoyingly, he wants to be used as bait. (He thinks it'll be cool).

- *If the scenario's stalled at this point* (the documents were intercepted, and the PCs either took the Dukes into protective custody, or Ian's being kept under wraps with no ability to talk to anyone), then the GM may need to resort to more radical methods to keep the scenario moving. If the PCs keep investigating Bennett, then let them drive the scenario. If the PCs are floundering, then Bennett loses all patience. Later that night, two SHADOW combat squads will be sent to the Gaglardi home with orders to kill everyone in the house.

In general, though, let the PCs be the driving force of the scenario unless it is going absolutely nowhere.

HOSTAGE DRAMA

Ian's friend Tony Duke will be held hostage at his home in the Bayview Heights section of Freedom City. It's a small older home, a single-story bungalow that dates back to the 1920s. Tony lives with his grandmother, and both are being held hostage in the living room by a team of three SHADOW (standard) agents.

If Ian was captured, he will be there too. He will be expecting our heroes to show up, and if they make eye contact with him, he will wait a few minutes for them to get into position, then nod and make a signal to distract the hostage-takers.

If they are successfully rescued, SHADOW's involvement in the operation should be apparent. The rescued hostages can testify that the SHADOW agents reported back via phone to some boss in "the tower" and promised, "We will hand you your revenge." This should, if they haven't figured it out, lead the player characters back to Bennett.

If the rescue fails, however, AEGIS will have a problem, particularly if Ian is badly hurt or killed. It was the rescue of his daughter that brought Gaglardi into the light, but the death of his son could send him hurtling back into the darkness.

THE SHADOW BASE

The SHADOW base is a large area in a hidden sub-basement buried under the Bennett Tower in downtown Freedom City. There are two ways to access it: a private elevator that is located in Bennett's penthouse suite, and a teleportal link from Nifelheim, the prime SHADOW base. At some point, the heroes should put two and two together, connect Bennett with the SHADOW attacks, and return to Bennett's for a big showdown.

The SHADOW base is not the biggest SHADOW base in the city, but Bobby Bennett is a member of the Penumbra and an important figure in SHADOW. Taking him down will definitely make a mark.

BENNETT'S OFFICE

Bobby Bennett's office is a large corner window office with an east facing view of Freedom City. He sits at a dark oak desk, with a desktop computer terminal seated on a small desk behind him. There is a matching oak circular conference table in front of the desk. There's a wet bar in the far corner of the room, and a large out of scale model of the city (with Bennett's proposed real estate developments shown as red buildings) occupying most of the rest of the room.

The key to finding the SHADOW base is hiding right in plain sight. If someone knocks over the Centurian statue in Riverside Park on the city model (anyone who makes an Investigate Check DC 10 will find this object has been frequently handled), a secret panel on the far wall opens to reveal a small elevator.

After SHADOW has been exposed, Bennett will retreat to the SHADOW base to prepare the defenses. He expects that AEGIS might take a run at him, so he will wait in the base and let them come down to him.

ELEVATOR

The elevator comfortably fits six people, and can support up to 2800 lbs. This private elevator has only two buttons, "U" and "D." The "D" button will take the elevator to a sub-basement where the main SHADOW base is located. There are two cameras in the ceiling on opposite corners; these cameras watch the elevator from the base's security system. The PCs have one round to deal with them before they trigger the security systems. If they set up a feedback loop to make the elevator look empty (Disable Device DC 15 and an Electronics or Burglar Kit required), then they can proceed unscathed. Otherwise, the base goes on alert and various traps are set. If the alert is set in the elevator, then the elevator trap will be triggered: Sleeping Gas. Anyone without protection must make a saving throw against Sleep 6 every round until the elevator reaches the bottom.

It takes 60 seconds (10 rounds) for the elevator to reach the landing. The shaft (should the PCs open the door and climb down) is 300 ft. deep; it requires a Climb check DC10 to safely navigate. There are no cameras or internal security within the shaft.

The PCs might go down the shaft, find the base, say "Aha, a SHADOW base!", and call in the troops. In this case, SHADOW will detect the intrusion and abandon the base before a strike team can be assembled. (If the GM wants to be particularly dirty, they will set up booby traps before they leave or trigger the autodestruct when AEGIS has one of their best investigation teams crawling in the lower level.)

THE LOWER LEVEL

This is the lower level of the complex, a small to medium-sized SHADOW base.

ALERT AND SECURITY

There are cameras at the top corner of every wall that are viewed in the Security room (#3). If the alert has not been sounded, then every round the AEGIS team is in the complex, the security team will have a chance to make a Notice Check (+5 skill bonus to their check) against a DC equal to a d20 plus the lowest Stealth Skill among the PCs. If the security team succeeds, the complex goes on alert. The cameras may be disabled by the same method as the elevators, though a new check will need to be made every time the PCs get within 30 ft. of the end of a corridor.

Shadow agents use blasters and the most basic equipment. When they go unconscious, they die, regardless of the weapon's damage type. Each agent is tattooed with a bar code, FC1993, followed by a six digit alphanumeric, and there is a small chip implanted in their brainstem; when the agent dies, he is marked "deceased" in the SHADOW database and all records of him are expunged.

POWER

The base runs on power from the city, but it has an emergency generator below the complex in case the PCs knock the power out. It is accessible through a small hatch in the clone tank room.

COMMUNICATIONS

Because the base is radio shielded, it will be impossible for agents to communicate with the outside world via conventional means while down in the complex. However, there are communications terminals in the Security Room (#3) and the central headquarters (#12) that can be accessed to reach AEGIS HQ.

If the PCs call for backup, the agency says they will send a surveillance team to monitor the situation and try to put together a strike team. However, their other forces are committed to other operations,

If you are running this adventure for superheroes and not agents, make the following changes.

- Increase the PL of all traps to PL12.
- Double the number of agents. Include one Flame-in-SHADOW, Fist-in-SHADOW, or Shadow-in-SHADOW mutate with all agent defenders.
- Include a radar sensor by the elevator to help detect invisible heroes.
- Increase the toughness of all walls to 15.
- In the headquarters room, increase the defenders to one mutate per PC, plus 2 squads of six. If this is still insufficient to challenge the superheroes, add a mercenary supervillain of the same PL as the superheroes.

and the PCs should scout out the complex as thoroughly as soon as possible, retreating only if they face heavy opposition.

1. ELEVATOR

This is where the elevator opens up into the main base.

If the base is on alert, two SHADOW Troopers (See **Chapter 5**) will be set up at position 2. These are pawns intended to lure people down to the trap at #2.

2. SECURITY TRAP

If the base is on alert, and someone comes to engage the two agents at hand-to-hand range—or if two people enter the zone and the base is on alert—then steel doors will come down on each side and trap the intruders. A Reflex save DC 16 is required to avoid the trap. Those caught in the trap will be subject to a Blast 10 (electrical) field every round until they are released from the trap. The walls are composed of a titanium alloy (Toughness 13). Disabling one of the walls will terminate the trap. There is also a panel on each side of the trap where someone can disable the trap by inputting the correct code (which can be done in a full round with an electronics kit and a Disable Device check (DC 16). If the check is failed, then the panel becomes electrified (Blast 10 to whoever is making the check).

If there is no security alert, then a single trooper will be stationed here. Unless he is rendered unconscious before his Initiative, an alert will be called.

3. SECURITY OFFICE

This room is a nest of monitors and computer controls. Two SHADOW agents are stationed here, sitting in large leather chairs and watching the monitors. Behind the monitors are three small cells with glowing force field doors—SHADOW's prison cells.

If the place is on alert, then a security door will slam shut (again, a Toughness 13 alloy door). One trooper and one SHADOW advanced trooper (See **Chapter 5**) will be stationed here. As soon as they see a PC, they will cry, "Into the SHADOWS!" and attack with their blasters. If the base is on alert, the security protocols will be transferred to the Headquarters (room 12).

On a Computer check DC 12, the heroes can bring up a schematic on the complex (which, among other things, will show the false wall (at #7).

There are three holding cells (Toughness 17). The force fields can be

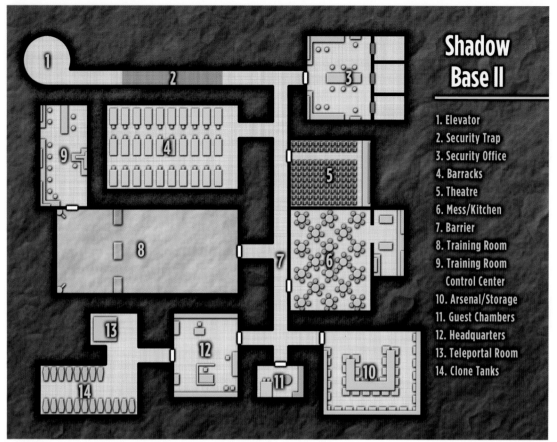

Shadow Base II

1. Elevator
2. Security Trap
3. Security Office
4. Barracks
5. Theatre
6. Mess/Kitchen
7. Barrier
8. Training Room
9. Training Room
   Control Center
10. Arsenal/Storage
11. Guest Chambers
12. Headquarters
13. Teleportal Room
14. Clone Tanks

7. BARRIER

When the security alert is signaled, a fake wall comes down over this section, making it look like a corner that leads intruders into the training room. A Notice DC 18 (use the check of the first hero who shows up here, or anyone who does an active search in the area) will discover the fake wall. For purposes of breaking through to the other side, the wall is Toughness 10.

8. TRAINING ROOM

This training room is a stone floor surrounded by metal walls. This is where agents hone their fighting skills. Large stone blocks have been set in the middle of the room. As soon as the heroes enter, the door (Toughness 13) will slam shut behind them, and agents will pop up from where they are hiding and fire.

turned off by a button on the security controls or by a manual override on the side of the cells. They will be empty, although if the Gamemaster feels like putting a prisoner in the base to further a future plot, this is a perfect place for it.

4. BARRACKS

This is the barracks for the agents. Thirty bunk beds are lined up in three rows of ten, with a footlocker at the base of each bed. The room is unoccupied (unless the PCs come late at night and the base is not on alert).

An examination of the room indicates that only 25 beds have been recently occupied; either the base is being prepped for more agents, or it was once a bigger base, but agents have been assigned elsewhere.

Each agent has a footlocker where they keep their personal gear. There is some basic agent gear, one change of civilian clothes, and some uniforms for security duty in the tower.

5. THEATRE

This is a 120-seat theatre that looks on a stage/screen area. Films include such gems as "Overshadow, Overlord," "Why Light Cannot Exist Without SHADOW," "My Special Brotherhood," (how clones can rely on each other but no one else) and "Fight Club" (the actual movie, which is presented as confirmation of society's decadence).

6. MESS/KITCHEN

This is where the agents eat their food. About 20 tables with 5 chairs each are spread around the room. There is a kitchen area in the back where meals are prepared, with a freezer to store meat.

There are five basic troopers and one advanced trooper stationed in the room; the stone blocks provide them with cover (+4 Defense). Worse, there are two heavy defense cannons (Attack +5, Blast 10) stationed on opposite corners of the room, fired by remote control by the defenders in the control center. The controlling agents can either fire a cannon every phase, or generate an Illusion 10 holographic image of a SHADOW agent somewhere in the room, to confuse the PCs. Alternatively, they can use a holographic image of a flaming villain who matches Pyrestorm's description. This is the hologram of Pyrestorm that was seen in the arson attacks.

9. TRAINING ROOM CONTROL CENTER

This is another high-tech looking control center. Two basic SHADOW agents are controlling the machines in the control center. If the PCs enter, they draw pistols and attack.

10. ARSENAL/STORAGE

This is the storeroom for the headquarters. If there is an alert, this door is magnetically sealed (Toughness 13, Disable Device DC 13). Along one wall is a rack of SHADOW weapons and body armor, on the other side, foodstuffs and other gear.

11. GUEST CHAMBER

This is a lavish bedchamber for very special guests (such as Overshadow on his inspection tour). Unless the GM wishes SHADOW to have a very special guest, it is currently unoccupied.

12. HEADQUARTERS

This is a room with numerous computer monitors and a large central area that Bennett uses as his real office. Consoles line the walls, as well as a bulletin board that is littered with photos of SHADOW's local enemies (including Gaglardi). There is also a holographic map display of the United States, with Freedom City and a few other prominent SHADOW targets marked with a pulsing red glow.

This is the nexus of the entire headquarters, and where the defenders are set to make their stand. A Flame-In-SHADOW and a Fist-In-SHADOW mutate lead the attack, along with one advanced trooper per PC.

On one end of the room is a large mainframe computer; a data terminal that links to the main SHADOW network. When the base goes on alert, its access channels are severed, though Nifelheim will monitor its security as soon as the base goes on alert and take direct control if it looks like SHADOW is threatened. Two private areas are cordoned off for Bennett: a small office where he keeps his personal records (including evidence of both his plotting against Gaglardi, as well as his schemes to create phony super-villains like Pyrestorm to perpetuate insurance fraud) and his bedroom.

The personal records also contain a memo: "To Junior PENUMBRA Member Bennett: You are authorized to use whatever force is needed to complete your proposed task. Complete secrecy is no longer essential to our operations in Freedom City. Make an example of this council-man. Plant him in the SHADOWs." – signed, Hilda Reinholdt, senior Penumbra Officer, head of Freedom City Operations. (This will fore-shadow Reinholdt's direct involvement in future adventures, and tell the PCs they didn't hit the main SHADOW base. If you have another leader in mind, replace Reinholdt's name).

13. TELEPORTAL ROOM

This room has a control console and an enormous pyramid shaped force field (10 ft. high and 14 ft. wide at the base) on a raised dais.

The console triggers a portal to the SHADOW base at Nifelheim. Bennett is in this chamber. When the heroes arrive, he'll shout, "It's too late! SHADOW is forever!" If the PCs attack him, he'll be knocked down. Half of his body will land in the teleportal, the other half will land outside the field, just as the teleportal activates—half of him teleports and he'll die. A similar result awaits him if the controls are shot (and the teleportal misfires). Otherwise, he escapes one round after the encounter. If the PCs manage to prevent him from entering the teleportal, the portal blows, blood starts to trickle out of Bennett, and he has time to gasp, "No, not me!" before the poison that's flooding his system kills him.

In any event, the controls short out, and the target location becomes untraceable.

14. CLONE TANKS

This section is filled with twenty sarcophagus-like metal tanks. If the PCs enter this section, the tanks open and sixteen of the clones emerge, staggering from their tanks, and attacking the nearest intruder. The agents are naked, except for patches of goo conveniently covering body parts that can't be shown by the Comics Code. They have no weapons; they'll try to grapple the heroes and pummel them as a group. They are still somewhat in shock from the birthing process. Use SHADOW trooper stats, but reduce their Defense to 10 and their movement rate to 20.

IF THE HEROES FAIL

At some point in the adventure, the heroes may fall victim to superior firepower. In this case, the heroes are bound in a thick metal mesh that wraps around their bodies like a shroud, from the neck down. They are thrown into the training room (#8), where they are tied to the tops of the

stone blocks. Regardless of how badly they were hurt, everyone wakes up at the same time. Bennett appears via hologram and addresses them.

"I could have executed you. I probably should have, but where's the fun? A job well done can only take you so far. I want you to experience the fear of SHADOW before you die, so I've triggered the autodestruct of this base. In five minutes, the entire tower will be destroyed, and you will be less than a stain, or even a memory. SHADOW will move its activities to another base, and we won't miss a step for your efforts."

At this point, a countdown timer appears, and the heroes have five minutes (50 rounds) to either escape or deactivate the Self-Destruct. The bonds can be escaped by an Escape Artist check DC 18. The self-destruct is found in the Headquarters (Room 12) (Computers check, DC 20, to deactivate). Otherwise, the SHADOW base has been emptied.

If the building is destroyed (whether the PCs escape or not), it will be a big deal, as it may, depending on the time of the assault, kill hundreds of people who were occupying offices on the other floors and who had nothing to do with SHADOW.

When the PCs escape his death trap, Bennett will be disgraced, but not destroyed. However, his efforts to destroy Gaglardi will be put on a backburner as he contemplates his losses and how he's going to recover his empire (and get back at AEGIS, of course).

BACK AT HQ...

With the Bennett threat to Gaglardi's life ended, life can return to relative normalcy. Provided there was no loss of life or significant property damage, things will go back to normal. SHADOW isn't done with him, and the Fens redevelopment is going to be a continuing controversy for AEGIS and the city's Star Squad.

FURTHER ADVENTURES

The big twist of the adventure is that SHADOW is back, openly working in Freedom City, and they have a big base somewhere in the city, commanded by Hilda Reinholdt. An investigation of her background will show that she is a former AEGIS agent (see **Chapter 5** for details).

Beyond that:

- Ian may come snooping around AEGIS HQ looking for his buddies, and hook himself into the team as a form of mascot.

- If a PC has started an affair with Patricia Gaglardi, she may want to continue it even after the mission, depending on the PC's personal charm.

- A PC who has shown himself to be particularly competent may get an offer from Gaglardi to leave AEGIS and take a six-figure salary working for the city.

- If Bennett escaped alive, he puts a bounty of $10,000 on the head of every AEGIS agent in the city.

- The Fens C (or the Southside Cs who sponsored them) begin to go after AEGIS, attacking monuments, the homes of suspected agents, and such in an effort to show them who's boss.

- Mark Marcelli's records give the PCs a chance to go undercover and investigate the local Max trade.

AWARDS

The PCs get one power point if they solved the case without getting any of the Gaglardi family killed or causing significant property damage. They get a second power point if they made it to the headquarters section of the base and confronted Bennett (and didn't back away from the fight).

INDEX

A

Ace Pilot...101
AEGIS...44–58
 History...44
 in Freedom City.................................51–54
 Operations...55–58
 Personnel...50
 Resources...48–50
 Structure...47
AEGIS Agent, Basic.................................51
AEGIS Battle Cries..................................58
AEGIS Code...57
AEGIS Code Phrases................................58
AEGIS Headquarters............................49–50
 Large Base...50
 Military Base..50
 Satellite HQ...49
 Secret Base..50
 Small Base...50
AEGIS Psi-Agent.....................................53
AEGIS Vehicles.......................................48
Al-Assad, Dr. Ibn....................................81
Alert Status..58
Alternate Movement (Flight).....................23
Alternate Movement (Swimming).............23
Animal Handler.....................................101
Armored Hovercraft.................................25
Ashe, Dominic...................................75, 78
Assembly Required (flaw).........................12

B

Baker, Dr. Winston..................................81
Benefit (rank) (feat).................................11
Bonham, Stewart.....................................51
Boot Jets..22
Brainwashing Machine.............................85
Broom..22
Brotherhood of the Yellow Sign.................92
Brute Lieutenant....................................106
Bureaucrat From Hell.............................106

C

Callsigns/Codenames.............................111
Camouflage Field.....................................22
Champagne Villain.................................107
Character Niche.......................................26
Character Niches.....................................35
Chemical Weapons..................................20
Cleaner..107
Cloaked Gunship.....................................24
Cloaking Truck..24
Clones...75
Collapsing..23
Collapsing Attack Helicopter....................24
Combat Engineer...................................101

Combat Motorcycle.................................24
Combat Speedboat..................................25
Combat Van..24
Comic Book Firearms...............................18
Communications......................................23
Communications Specialist......................102
Computer...23
Con Artist...102
Connected (feat)......................................11
Corona, the..81
Costume Changer....................................23
Crew Required (flaw)...............................12
Crime League..92
Crime Lord...108
Crimson Mask...................................75, 80
Crisis Level......................................99–100

D

Dashing Spy...27
Decombustion Cannon.............................40
Defense Analyst....................................103
Delacourt, "Black" Jacques......................74
DeMaurier, Damantha..............................52
Directorate, the..................................73–74
Disguise..23
Disguised (power feat).............................12
Disguising Car..24
Dowd, Dominic.......................................73
Dr. Sin...74, 92
Drawbacks...13
Drone Helicopter.....................................24

E

Eclipse Guard...81
Ejector Seats..23
Environmental Specialist........................103
Equipment.....................................15–26, 48
Evil Lawyer..108
Exotic Weapons......................................18
Explosives..16
Eye-In-SHADOW.....................................89

F

Factor Four..92
Femme Fatale...28
Field Investigator....................................29
Field Medic..104
Fist-In-SHADOW.....................................89
Flame-In-SHADOW..................................90
Flight Suit..22
Flying APC...24
Flying Motorcycle....................................24
Flying Platform..24
Folkes, Franklin......................................75
Footwear Phone......................................22

G

Gaglardi, Ian..114
Gaglardi, Patricia..................................114
Gaglardi, Ray..114
Gate-In-SHADOW....................................90
Geiger Counter.......................................22
Gemini..46
Grease Monkey.....................................104
Grenades...16
Gym Rats...116

H

Hades..92
Hard-Nosed Commander..........................30
HAZMAT Suit..22
Headquarters..25
Heavy Weapons......................................18
Heinz, Rudolph.......................................81
Hellman, Holtz..71
Heroic Everyman.....................................31
High-Tech Spy.......................................108
HISTORY...59–61
Holo-Disguise...22
Hologram Cube.......................................22
Hostage Drama.......................................95

I

I-Bots..83
Iceberg, the..53–55
Iron Duke...108
Ironjaw..42

J

Johnson, Chalcedony...........................64–65
Jones, Dr. Gemini....................................81
Jumping Jacks..24

L

Lab Geek..105
Lady Lunar...92
Liberty league Mansion....26, 50, 53, 63, 86
Listening Drone.......................................22
Longarms...16
Luck (feat)...11
Lunatic Demo Guy.................................109

M

Machine Guns...16
Mad Scientist..109
Malador...92
Marcelli, "Muscle" Mark.........................116
Martial Arts Expert..................................32
Mastermind..92
Master of Disguise.................................105

MAX Armor 49
Midnight Invective 82
Mikos
    West 65
Military Transport Plane 24
Mission Check 95
Missions 97–99
MOLLE Vest 22
Mr. Infamy 93

N

Nacht-Krieger 75
Navy SEAL 105
Nitro Injectors 24

O

Off Road Movement 24
Origami Escape Glider 85
Overshadow 72–73
Overthrow 77–78
Overthrow Equipment 85

P

Parachute 22
Patriot, the 53
Penumbra, the 74–75
Personal Cloak 22
Pistols 15
Police Show Archetypes 42–43
Power Armor 49
Power Overload Box 85
Power Level 94
Prince Vultorr the Cruel 75
Project Eyespy 52
Project Gorgon 53
Project Ironmonger 53
Project Mimir 83
Psi-Detector 22
Psions 92

R

Radio Scrambler 22
Ragnarok 75, 91
Rank
    AEGIS 47
    UNISON 61
Recall Device 22
Reinforced Van 24
Reinholdt, Hilda 73, 75

Reputation 14
Rogue Ninja 110
Roughneck Commando 33
Ruthless Executive 110

S

Scions of Sobek 81
Scions of Sobek Flying Pyramid 26
Scourge Emperor 74
SHADOW 66–93
    History 66–72
    in Freedom City 92–93
    Operations 82–84
    Organization 72–75
    Personnel 88–91
    Resources 84–87
Shadow-In-SHADOW 90
SHADOW Advanced Trooper 88
SHADOW Headquarters 85–87
    Deathtrap 86
    Large Cell 86
    Medium Cell 86
    Small Cell 86
SHADOW Infiltrator 88
SHADOW Sleeper Agent 83
SHADOW Trooper 88
SHADOW Umbra Guard 89
SHADOW Vehicles 84
SHADOW Weapons 84
Sharpshooter 105
Signal Flare Gun 22
Skill Kits 20–21
Skills 8–10
Sleep Gas Launcher 41
Snowmobile 25
Snow Movement 24
Soldier 83
Special Training 10
Speedy Racing Car 25
Spy Jet Ski 25
Spymaster 34
Spy Motorcycle 25
Spy Sports Car 25
Spy Surveillance Van 25
STAR Squad
    History 37–38
    Personnel 41–42
    Structure 39–40
STAR Squad Headquarters 41
STAR Squad Officer 41

STAR Squad 37–43
Stealth Attack Helicopter 24
Stress Check 95
Strong Guy 106
Super-MAX Armor 49

T

Talos 92
Taser Cannon 40
Taurus 74, 92
Team Crusher 41
Team Mad Dog 41
Team Ripper 41
Tenth Man, the 75
Terra-King 93
Thinktank Machine 85
Thule Society 78–80
Thule Society Sorcerer 79
Tire Inflators 24
Tough-as-Nails Mercenary 110
Tyranny Syndicate 92

U

Una 93
UNCOT 63
UNICORN 63
UNIQUE 63
UNISON 59–65
    Personnel 64–65
    Resources 62–63
    Structure 61
Unison Agent 64
UNISON Headquarters 63
    Central Headquarters 63
    Mobile Military Command 63
    Secret Base 63
Unison Solo 64

V

Vehicles, Air 24
Vehicles, Features 23
Vehicles, Ground 24
Vehicles, Other 25
Volk, Dr. Doris 52
VSTOL Folding Fighter Jets 24

W

Wheel-In-SHADOW 90

CONTRIBUTORS

SCOTT BENNIE, DESIGN

Whie the rest of the world thinks of him as just another cranky middle aged game writer, Scott Bennie fighs a never ending battle in pursuit of truth, justice and the timely payment of utility bills. Laboring in a secret stronghold nestled in the heart of Canada's Fraser Valley, this stalwart paragon of the word processor has been battling the forces of darkness for twenty-five years. His other contributions to the battle against evil include: *Testament* for Green Ronin, numerous supplements for Hero Games (including the award-winning *Villainy Amok*), *Old Empires* for TSR, and design for such classic computer games such as *Castles, Lord of the Rings, Starfleet Academy*, and the upcoming *Gestalt: The Hero Within.*

BEN ROBBINS, ADDDITIONAL DESIGN

Many moons ago, Ben's parents encouraged him to revise a gaming article for publication rather than work on getting his degree. Now he spends all his time writing adventures for Lame Mage Productions (www.lamemage.com) or crafting pithy advice for aspiring GMs. What were they thinking?

STEVE KENSON, DEVELOPMENT

Steve is the author of the award-winning *Mutants & Masterminds Roleplaying Game* and the *Freedom City* campaign setting, as well as a lifetime fan of comic books. Steve has been an RPG author and designer since 1995, having worked on dozens of products. He maintains a website at members.aol.com/talonmail. Steve lives in Merrimack, New Hampshire with his partner, Christopher Penczak.

JOANNA G. HURLEY, EDITING

Joanna G. Hurley is a freelance editor from New Jersey. Although she now works for companies such as Green Ronin and Dark Quest Games, she got her start editing her aunt's dissertation while still in high school. Later, while working as an engineer, she was frequently called upon to write documentation for projects. Since 2004, she has combined her experience with her love of gaming and taken on the role of a freelance editor. She is owned by her cats, Othello and Puck, who occasionally assist her as ergonomic wrist rests.

HAL MANGOLD, GRAPHIC DESIGN

Hal has been involved with roleplaying games since he was 9 years old, and shows no sign of stopping now. His graphic design skills have been applied to over well over si gaming products, and he's written material for Pinnacle Entertainment Group, White Wolf Publishing, Atlas Games, Twilight Creations, and Green Ronin Publishing. Hal resides in Alexandria, VA.

JIM PINTO, ART DIRECTION

jim pinto was born without capital letters. Several attempts were made to transplant them, but his body rejected the donors. Doctor's say he can live without them, like an appendix. He lives in Long Beach, California, which ironically has three capital letters.

ATTILA ADORJANY, ART

Comicbook creator and sci-fi/fantasy artist Attila Adórjány was born in Canada. He spent many years in Australia before returning to Canada to attend OCAD. Since 1995 He has worked as an illustrator, conceptual artist, graphic designer and sculptor. He has worked in all areas of the print and entertainment industries from magazines, gaming and comic-books to film, TV and Video Games. His credits include work for Dungeon Magazine, Wizards of the Coast, Image Comics, Udon Entertainment, White Wolf, Warner Bros, Mirimax, Sony Entertainment, EA Games, and BBDO. His upcoming comic projects include *Breathe*, and the *Night*. Attila collaborates regularly with his friends Tom Fowler, Eric Kim and Ramon Perez in a group called the Hive. They can be reached at www.enterthe-hive.com. Attila's website can be found at www.600poundgorilla.com.

STORN A. COOK, ARTIST

Freelanced through art school, Columbus College of Art and Design, due to an insane love of Role Playing Games, which I've been involved in since 1978. I strive to be a little bit better every day. I continue to freelance, wishing to get my artwork in every superhero (or villain) RPG possible.

JEFF CARLISLE, ART

Jeff Carlisle has designed and illustrated for magazines, roleplaying games, collectable card games, video games, and entertainment environments for clients such as Alderac Entertainment Group, COSI Studios, Green Ronin Publishing, Lucasfilm, Ltd., Paizo Publishing, Presto Studios, The Scarefactory, Inc. and Wizards of the Coast. His work has appeared in *Dragon, Dungeon/Polyhedron*, and *Star Wars Gamer* magazines as well as the *Warlord* CCG, *Legend of the Five Rings* CCG and the *Star Wars: New Jedi Order, Star Wars: Power of the Jedi*, and *Mutants & Masterminds Annual* sourcebooks. He lives in Columbus, Ohio with his wife and cat.

ANTHONY GRABSKI, ART

Anthony Grabski is a self taught artist who has worked professionally as an illustrator for the last 10 years. He has done work for Alderac Entertainment, Z-man Games, Sabertooth Games and Fleer.

JONATHAN HUNT, ART

Jonathan Hunt was born on July 30, 1966 in New Haven, CT. He likes to draw stuff and he tends to stay up really late. No one is quite sure what he does when left alone in the studio all night, but everyone is afraid to ask. When he grows up he would like to be an artist so he can play with his crayons all the time. Jon has published 11 children's books with publishers such as Houghton Mifflin and Simon & Schuster. In addition to his gaming assignments, he is currently publishing prints, books and comics through red•eye•studio. Visit him on the web at www.huntillustration.com.

SCOTT JAMES, COVER/ART

Scott graduated from Northern Illinois University in 1995, and hasn't looked back since. He began freelancing right out of collage. He began working for Fasa's *Battletech, Shadowrun*, and *Earthdawn*. At this time he began to do work for White Wolf and Pinnacle Entertainment Group as well. He then began doing work for AEG, which he parlayed into a part time staff position for a year working on all their game lines. After that, he did conceptual design for Hasbro on the movie *Small Solders* doing character designs, and creating the look for the toy and computer animated cartoon *Action Man*. He continues to freelance for a multitude of companies, along with teaching college art classes.

JAKE PARKER, ART

Jake Parker dropped out of school to pursue a career in the animation industry, and he now works as an art director for Reel FX Creative Studios. He lives in Dallas with his wife Alison and two children, Tate and Lucy. His freetime is spent working on projects like FLIGHT (www. flightcomics.com) and his website (www.agent44.com)

TONY PARKER, ART

Tony Parker is an Arizona-based artist who has worked in the fields of RPG illustration, graphic novels, card art and book cover art. He still enjoys giving hugs.

CRAIG TAILLIFER, ART

Born November 29, 1968 in Ottawa Canada, Craig was raised on a diet of crayons, play-doh, and comic books. An early exposure to Uncle Scrooge, Asterix, Turok Son Of Stone, and the works of Edgar Rice Burroughs left an indelible impression on the budding young artist's psyche. Stumbling into professional work at a very young age, Craig has made a living of sorts at drawing for the better part of the past two decades. His work has spanned the black and white boom at Aircel and Malibu to a long residency at WaRP Graphics working on the *ElfQuest* titles. Craig currently works in TV Animation, RPG Illustration, and selfpublishes *Wahoo Morris* through his company Too Hip Gotta Go Graphics. He splits his time between work with an unhealthy obsession for comic books, old records, and hammocks.

OPEN GAME LICENSE

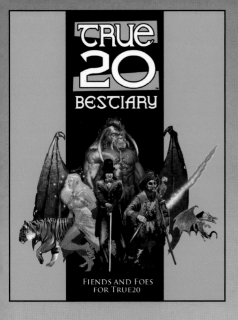

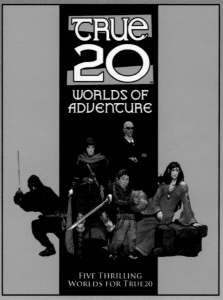

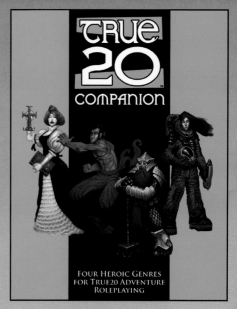

True 20 Bestiary
A True20 System Sourcebook
Author: Matthew E. Kaiser
Cover Artist: Christophe Swal
Format: 192 pages, B&W, softback
MSRP: $29.95 **Product Code:** GRR1706
ISBN: 1-932442-68-5

True 20 Worlds of Adventure
A True20 System Sourcebook
Authors: Robert J. Schwalb, et al
Cover Artist: Vincent Dutrait
Format: 128 pages, B&W, softback
MSRP: $22.95 **Product Code:** GRR1705
ISBN: 1-932442-65-0

True20 Companion
A True20 System Sourcebook
Authors: Erica Balsley, Dave Jarvis, et al
Cover Artist: Mike Franchina
Format: 128 pages, B&W, softback
MSRP: $23.95 **Product Code:** GRR1708
ISBN: 1-932442-83-9

They say a hero is measured by the quality of his enemies, and the *True20 Bestiary* is chock full of fearsome foes to test your hero's mettle! In the pages of this book, you'll find hundreds of ready-to-use adversaries for your *True20 Adventure Roleplaying* games, ranging from goblins and zombies to undead, dragons, constructs, and more!

Monsters! The *True20 Bestiary* offers more monsters than you can shake a sword at: from classic favorites to new creatures like the angel of death, moon dragons, and the corpse-stitched abomination. With the creatures in this book, it's easy to use almost any classic fantasy adventure in conjunction with the *True20* game.

Creature Creation! With expanded creature creation and conversion guidelines, the *True20 Bestiary* is your complete resource for formidable foes in your game. Create your own mythic monsters and strange alien beings and use the creature types as easily as heroic roles to whip up any monster you need at a moment's notice!

Are your heroes up to the challenge? Pit them against the most fearsome foes, with the *True20 Bestiary*.

Fantastic worlds of adventure await you! The *True20 Adventure Roleplaying* game introduced players to four unique campaign settings, and now *True 20 Worlds of Adventure* opens up whole new vistas with new heroes to play, new battles to fight, and new stories to tell.

The book features four more winners from the **True20 Setting Search**, plus a new setting from Green Ronin's own Robert J. Schwalb.

- Fight against the horrifying forces of the unknown in Agents of Oblivion

- Struggle to save a fantasy world drowning in the Age of Blood in Blood Throne

- Earn glory and honor for your clan in the Asian fantasy of Land of the Crane

- Explore the depths of dreams—and nightmares—in Nevermore

- Save your neighborhood from the wolf-man, the monster under the bed, and the creature in the closet as a kid in The Razor in the Apple.

That's five new fantastic worlds for your *True20* adventures. True fun, true excitement, true inspiration... *True 20 Worlds of Adventure*!

The *True20 Adventure Roleplaying* rulebook provides everything you need to explore worlds of adventure. Now the True20 Companion helps you create some of those worlds, with advice and expanded information on adapting the True20 game system to various genres from adventure fiction, from fantasy to science fiction and beyond. The *True20 Companion* also offers ways of customizing heroic roles and even creating your own!

Role Creation: Build your own heroic roles for True20, or just modify the roles of adept, expert, and warrior to suit the style of game you want to run. With the easy to use system you can create any heroic role you want, or even eliminate roles altogether, making each character's progression unique!

Genre Development: This book also presents information on four popular genres of roleplaying: fantasy, science fiction, horror, and modern action, with guidelines, suggestions, and optional rules for using *True20 Adventure Roleplaying* to create heroes and tell stories in those genres.

The *True20 Companion* gives you the tools you need to make the True20 System your own and create the games you want to play.

AVAILABLE NOW

AVAILABLE NOW

FEBRUARY 2007

THEY'RE THE BEST THERE IS AT WHAT THEY DO...

...AND WHAT THEY DO ISN'T VERY PRETTY. GO BACK TO THE GRIM DAYS OF THE '80S AND '90S, WHEN SUPER-
VIGILANTES IN LEATHER AND CHAINS DISPENSED HARSH JUSTICE. IRON AGE LOOKS AT THE DARKEST ERA OF
COMIC BOOK HISTORY AND HOW YOU CAN BRING IT TO LIFE IN YOUR **MUTANTS & MASTERMINDS** GAME. IT
INCLUDES AN OVERVIEW OF THE PERIOD, HOW TO CREATE AND RUN IRON AGE CHARACTERS AND GAMES, AND
DETAILS ON THE IRON AGE OF GREEN RONIN'S AWARD-WINNING **FREEDOM CITY** CAMPAIGN SETTING. **IRON
AGE** IS A SHOTGUN BLAST OF SUPER-POWERED CRIME, BETRAYAL, AND VENGEANCE. IT AIN'T PRETTY, BUT
SOMEONE HAS TO CLEAN UP THE STREETS.

IRON AGE - A MUTANTS & MASTERMINDS SOURCEBOOK
AUTHORS: SETH JOHNSON AND JON LEITHEUSSER • **FORMAT:** 128 PAGES, FULL COLOR, SOFTBACK